006226

D1558154

MAY 8 '92

The Hispanic
Experience
in the
United States

The Hispanic Experience in the United States

CONTEMPORARY ISSUES AND PERSPECTIVES

Edited by

Edna Acosta-Belén

and

Barbara R. Sjostrom

PRAEGER

New York
Westport, Connecticut
London

Copyright Acknowledgment

The editors and publisher are grateful to Tato Laviera for allowing the use of verses from his poem, "The salsa of bethesda fountain."

Library of Congress Cataloging-in-Publication Data

The Hispanic experience in the United States : contemporary issues and
  perspectives / edited by Edna Acosta-Belén and Barbara R. Sjostrom.

    p.   cm.
  "Most of the papers included in the volume are drawn from the
conference 'The Hispanic Community in the United States,' held at
SUNY-Albany in the spring of 1985"—Pref.
    Bibliography: p.
    Includes index.
    ISBN 0-275-92740-7 (alk. paper)
    1. Hispanic Americans—Congresses.   I. Acosta-Belén, Edna.
II. Sjostrom, Barbara R.
E184.S75H568   1988
973'.0468—dc 19   87-37690

Library of Congress Catalog Card Number: 87-37690

ISBN: 0-275-92740-7

First published in 1988

Praeger Publishers, One Madison Avenue, New York, NY 10010
An imprint of Greenwood Publishing Group, Inc.

Printed in the United States of America

The paper used in this book complies with the
Permanent Paper Standard issued by the National
Information Standards Organization (Z39.48-1984).

10 9 8 7 6 5 4 3 2

This book is dedicated to our parents,
Marcolina Belén, David Acosta,
Dorothy Burke, Lew Burke (in memoriam),
Bill Goodfellow, and Anna Goodfellow

Contents

Preface

Most of the chapters in this volume are drawn from the conference "The Hispanic Community in the United States" held at SUNY-Albany in the spring of 1985. The conference brought together a diverse group of leading scholars who study the Hispanic experience in the United States from theoretical, empirical, and policy-oriented viewpoints. This collection of essays deals with the history and development of the diverse Hispanic communities, and the cultural, social, and economic implications of Hispanic immigration and population growth. Hispanic contributions to a redefinition of ethnicity in the United States and group efforts to maintain a distinctive cultural identity are also a major focus, as are problems such as racism and discrimination. A final objective of this book is to gather the most recent data on U.S. Hispanics and provide readers not only with current information on demographic and socioeconomic indicators, but also to interpret this information and analyze its implications for the present and future of the community.

The various chapters reflect individual group issues and comparative approaches. Chapter 1 has been reprinted from another source because it complements and supplements the original conference papers (Chapters 2, 5, 6, 9, 10). Four others were specifically written for the book (Chapters 3, 4, 7, 8). The chapters are organized under three major categories: (1) demographic profiles; (2) immigration, assimilation, and cultural identity; and (3) socioeconomic profiles.

The 1980s has been a significant decade for U.S. Hispanics. Based on the last population census, it has been projected that Hispanics could well become the largest minority group in the United States by the early part of the twenty-first century. The implications of such a projection are manifold, and the editors have attempted to include in this volume a wide

selection of writings dealing with them. Some of the central questions
addressed in this volume are the following: Who are the Hispanics and
where have they come from? How does Hispanic immigration or migration
differ from that of previous groups? What are the cultural, social, and
economic implications of the Hispanic population growth for U.S. society?
What are the factors that affect the status of Hispanics? What has been the
particular cultural and social experience of the major Hispanic groups?
What have been their contributions to American life? Why haven't
Hispanics assimilated?

   The SUNY-Albany campus has distinguished itself for its support of and
interest in minority issues and activities. The Department of Latin
American and Caribbean Studies has played a crucial role promoting the
kind of scholarly exchange that leads to volumes such as this, in which
current knowledge and information are disseminated to the academic
community. We would like to acknowledge the support of the individuals
and organizations that provided encouragement, financial support, or time
and effort in putting the 1985 conference together or in the preparation of
this volume:

   The Affirmative Action Office at SUNY-Albany and its director, Gloria DeSole

   The Bilingual Education Bureau of the New York State Education Department
and its chief, Carmen A. Pérez

   The Center for the Caribbean and Latin America at SUNY-Albany and its
director, James W. Wessman

   The College of Social and Behavioral Sciences and its dean, John W. Webb

   The Department of Hispanic and Italian Studies and its former chair, Frank G.
Carrino

   Fuerza Latina, the Hispanic student organization at SUNY-Albany

   The New York Council for the Humanities for its mini-grant

   The New York State Writers' Institute at SUNY; its director, William Kennedy; its
associate director, Tom Smith; and the assistant to the director, Jean Finley

   The former executive vice-president for academic affairs, Judith Ramaley

   The former vice-president for research and educational development, John
Shumaker

   The former vice-president for student affairs, Frank G. Pogue.

Our appreciation also goes to the following students and staff: Blanca
Ramos, Josie Soto, Vicki Horwitz, Philippe Abraham, Carlos Laboy,
Nicky Pión, and Martín Sánchez; and to Christine E. Bose for her valuable
insights, encouragement, and personal support. Finally, and as many times
before, Susan P. Liberis Hill deserves most of the credit for the preparation
of the index.

   With this volume the editors reaffirm their professional and personal commitment to the study of cultural diversity, and to promoting cultural pluralism. The United States is a nation that was built and still runs with the energy, imagination, and perseverance of many ethnic groups. Nonetheless, ethnocentric misconceptions and a false sense of homogeneity about what it means to be an American have, more often than not, clouded the recognition of and respect for cultural differences. As has been the case in the past, waves of newcomers continuously reach this land in order to fulfill their dreams of prosperity and freedom. We hope that this volume provides a better understanding and enhances the increasing body of research on one of those many groups.

Until recently, Hispanics have been relegated to the status of an invisible minority. It is only since the 1960s that Chicanos, Puerto Ricans, Cubans, and other Latinos have begun to articulate their needs more effectively and to develop institutions and programs to advocate on their behalf for equal opportunity and recognition of their contributions to American life. Hispanics currently constitute the largest minority group in most of the western United States and have significant concentrations in at least nine states (Arizona, California, Colorado, Florida, Illinois, Michigan, New Jersey, New York, and Texas). It is their increasing population growth, and their interaction with the host society and other immigrant groups, that will mold their future. It is up to the academy to analyze and explore these dynamics.

This book is dedicated to all of our natural and adoptive parents and families for their love and support throughout the years. It is also an intellectual gift to all the children who enrich our lives: Carlitos David, Erin, Allison, Meliza, Boris, and Yara.

As a final word, we would like to thank each other for contributing equally in work and enthusiasm to this project, and for the way we have shared our respective cultures, families, and dreams for almost two decades.

I

DEMOGRAPHIC PROFILES

1

U.S. Hispanics: Changing the Face of America

Cary Davis, Carl Haub, and JoAnne L. Willette

The 1980 census counted 14.6 million persons of Spanish origin in the United States, 6.4 percent of the total population of 226.5 million. Hispanics are the second largest U.S. minority after blacks (11.7 percent in 1980) and the fastest growing. Fueled by the relatively high fertility of most Hispanic groups and increasing immigration, both legal and illegal, their numbers grew by about 265 percent from 1950 to 1980, compared with just under 50 percent for the total U.S. population. If immigration to the United States were to continue at the recent estimated total of about 1 million a year (legal and illegal Hispanics, Asians, and all others), Hispanics could number some 47 million and comprise 15 percent of the population by the year 2020, displacing blacks as the country's largest minority.

In the late 1950s, Spanish Americans consisted primarily of a few million Mexican-Americans living in the Southwest, some of whom traced their ancestry back to the original Spanish colonists and Indian inhabitants of that area. Today the umbrella term "Hispanic" covers a diverse population, still concentrated in a few states but found throughout the nation: Mexican-Americans, now beginning to move from their traditional base in the Southwest; Puerto Ricans, mainly concentrated in New York and New Jersey; Cubans, headquartered in Florida; and recent arrivals from at least 16 other Spanish-speaking countries of Latin America and Spain itself.

Like other immigrant groups before them, Hispanics are beginning to change the face of America, making their distinctive contributions to the neighborhoods in which they live. But with their growing numbers, they are

---

This is an abridged version of the essay that appeared in *Population Bulletin* 38, no. 3 (June 1983). Reprinted with the publisher's permission.

encountering the hostility historically accorded almost all newly arrived ethnic groups. Some predict that Hispanics will eventually assimilate into the American "melting pot" as the Irish, Italians, and Polish did before them. Others feel their very numbers and common language could delay assimilation and create a "Hispanic Quebec" within the United States. Hispanics also face a special problem in gaining acceptance—the presence among them of a large and growing number of illegal immigrants from Mexico and other Central and South American countries. And as America's latest great wave of immigrants, they are learning that newcomers start out at the bottom. U.S. Hispanics as a group are much less educated and much poorer, occupy lower rungs on the occupational ladder, and are much more likely to be unemployed than the non-Hispanic population. But some Hispanics, particularly Cubans, are beginning to catch up, and the evidence suggests that future generations of U.S. Hispanics will, too.

This chapter looks at where U.S. Hispanics are today, demographically and socioeconomically, and what their numbers are likely to be over the next few decades. We begin with outlining the problems of defining who is included in this increasingly visible and influential segment of the U.S. population.

WHO ARE THE HISPANICS?

While "Hispanic" has become a convenient way to refer to Americans of Spanish heritage, the catchall term masks a variety of ethnic, racial, national, and cultural backgrounds. And within the United States, the various "Hispanic" groups tend to be separated geographically and in their way of life. The four categories used by the U.S. Census Bureau are now most frequently taken to encompass the "Spanish-origin" or Hispanic population. These are, first, Mexican-Americans, or "Chicanos," the largest group, living mostly in the Southwest. Many of these are not immigrants but "Hispanos" who trace their ancestry back to the Spanish colonists and Indians who were the original inhabitants of the American Southwest. Next are Puerto Ricans, an intermixture of Spanish, Indian, and black who, as U.S. citizens at birth, are not subject to immigration restrictions. Cubans, the smallest group, assumed numerical importance as an ethnic group in the United States after the 1959 Cuban Revolution. The "Other Hispanic" category, now the second largest of the four groups, covers people from other Spanish-speaking countries of Latin America and from Spain. Many Hispanos place themselves in this category on Census Bureau questionnaires. Not included among Hispanics are immigrants from non-Spanish-language Latin America, such as French-speaking Haitians and Portuguese-speaking Brazilians.

Contrary to popular opinion, Hispanics do not all speak Spanish (11.1 million people reported speaking Spanish at home in the 1980 census, while the Hispanic count was 14.6 million) and not all are Roman Catholic, though 85 percent are estimated to be. The one thing shared by the four Hispanic groups is that all trace their heritage to Spanish-speaking nations. Using language heritage to sort out Hispanics, however, can present problems. For example, an immigrant from Argentina and one from Uruguay may clearly seem to be Hispanic, but what if the first is of Italian birth or descent and the second a German?

Defining the Hispanic Population

Defining any racial or ethnic group is a thorny problem. What characteristic determines race or ethnicity? Surname? Birthplace of parents or grandparents? Language usage? Cultural affiliation? Any of these may help classify some persons as "Irish," "Chinese," "black," or "Hispanic," but none can delimit mutually exclusive categories for any population. Racial groups, such as white or black, are often easier to identify, since racial intermarriage is still relatively rare in the United States. But classifying ethnic groups is confused by intermarriage, which is common in the countries from which immigrants come and practically a national tradition in the United States. Despite such problems, the Census Bureau has made a great effort to come up with an acceptable definition of the Hispanic population, which is needed for statistical measurements to back up such statements as "Hispanic mothers have more children than non-Hispanics," or to measure changes in the demographic and social characteristics of their population over time.[1]

Prior to the 1970 census, the concept of Hispanics as a group barely existed. Information on some components of the population, such as Mexicans, could be obtained from the usual census questions on a person's country of birth or that of his or her parents, use of a language other than English at home, and ancestry. Some earlier census reports featured data on persons of Spanish surname and on Puerto Ricans. But none of the identifiers used prior to 1970 could satisfy the need for a definition that could be applied nationwide and with reasonable consistency over time. The Census Bureau's painstakingly compiled list of 8000 Spanish surnames, for example, is only usable in five southwestern states where Spanish surnames are common (Arizona, California, Colorado, New Mexico, and Texas). Also, many of these surnames have close twins in Italian and Portuguese. And, of course, Spanish surnames can be lost or gained by marriage. A census question on birthplace or birthplace of parents obviously can account only for first- and second-generation Hispanics. A question on language usage in the home (either as a child, as was asked in 1970, or currently, as asked in 1980) misses Hispanics who do not use Spanish.

Thus we could expect that the different identifiers would produce different results, and they do, as seen in Table 1.1. These results are from

Table 1.1
Hispanic Population Counted in 1970 Census According to Six Identifiers: Total U.S. and Selected Areas

Identifier	United States	Southwestern states[a]	Middle Atlantic states[b]	Florida	Remaining states
Spanish origin	9,072,602	5,008,556	1,749,363	405,036	1,909,647
Spanish surname	—	4,667,975	—	—	—
Spanish language[c]	9,589,216	5,662,700	1,873,051	451,382	1,602,083
Spanish heritage[d]	9,294,509	6,188,362	1,052,682	451,382	1,602,083
Spanish language or surname	10,114,878	6,188,362	1,873,051	451,382	1,602,083
Spanish birth or parentage	5,241,892	2,321,642	1,738,802	336,961	844,487

Source: Jacob S. Siegel and Jeffrey S. Passel, "Coverage of the Hispanic Population of the United States in the 1970 Census." *Current Population Reports*, Special Studies, Series P-23, No. 82, 1979.

[a]Southwestern states are Arizona, California, Colorado, New Mexico, Texas.
[b]Middle Atlantic states are New Jersey, New York, Pennsylvania.
[c]Spanish language covers all persons of Spanish mother tongue and all other persons in families in which the head or wife reported Spanish mother tongue.
[d]Spanish heritage combines the following: persons of Spanish language or surname in the five southwestern states; persons of Puerto Rican birth or parentage in the three Middle Atlantic states; and persons of Spanish language in the remaining states and the District of Columbia.

Note: Different identifiers produce the same counts in states or regions where there is actually no difference in their definition. For example, in the Middle Atlantic states, "Spanish language" and "Spanish language or surname" counts are the same because the Spanish surname identifier was not used there, but only in the five southwestern states.

the 1970 census, but they illustrate the point. We can see the limitation of birthplace or parentage data, which identified only 5.2 million Hispanics nationwide. This question did perform well in the Middle Atlantic states in 1970, because of the predominance of recently arrived Puerto Ricans in the New York area, but it did poorly in the five southwestern states.

Although none of these methods may be adequate for a consistent count of Hispanics from census to census, they do have real analytic value and should certainly be used. Knowing how many people speak Spanish at home helps track cultural assimilation and birthplace or parentage separates first-generation Hispanics from second-generation Hispanics born in the United States. But for counting the population, a more consistent method was needed.

The Spanish-Origin Question

Enter the Spanish-origin census question. All of the above methods are based on objective characteristics, some of which, such as surname, can change during a person's lifetime. The Spanish-origin question is subjective in that it simply asks persons whether they identify themselves as Hispanic. It first appeared in the 1970 census as question 13b on the "long form" used with a 5 percent sample of households across the country, and did not actually ask about Spanish origin but went directly to categories, such as Mexican or Puerto Rican (see Figure 1.1). In 1980, the question appeared as item 7 on the "short form" received by all households. This was done to produce data on Hispanics in small geographic areas, thereby eliminating the effects of sampling error.

The question has some advantages over objective methods. It can easily be repeated from census to census and will consistently count those persons who consider themselves to be of Spanish origin. But it also has some built-in disadvantages. Its performance depends on the tendency of individuals to identify themselves as Hispanics at any given time. This can be influenced by such factors as the wording of the question, the language (Spanish-language questionnaires were available in 1980), the categories given as responses, and even the position of the question on the census form. The version used in 1980, honed in extensive pretests, was an improvement over 1970 (Figure 1.1). It placed the negative response ("No, not Spanish/Hispanic"), first to make it easier for non-Hispanics to respond. It added the popular term "Chicano" to potential responses and eliminated "Central or South American," which in 1970 had picked up many non-Hispanics who interpreted it to mean "Central or Southern United States" and Brazilians who are technically not Hispanic.[2] However, it kept the category "Other Spanish/Hispanic," which is often checked by Hispanos whose families have long been in the United States who properly belong in the Mexican category. Also, it is possible that many people were still

Figure 1.1
The Spanish-Origin Question in the 1970 and 1980 Censuses

1970

b. **Is this person's origin or descent—** *(Fill one circle)*

○ Mexican   ○ Central or South American
○ Puerto Rican   ○ Other Spanish
○ Cuban   ○ No, none of these

1980

7. **Is this person of Spanish/Hispanic origin or descent?**

Fill one circle.

○ No (not Spanish/Hispanic)
○ Yes, Mexican, Mexican-Amer., Chicano
○ Yes, Puerto Rican
○ Yes, Cuban
○ Yes, other Spanish/Hispanic

Instructions to the respondent for 1980 Spanish-origin question.

7. A person is of Spanish/Hispanic origin or descent if the person *identifies* his or her ancestry with one of the listed groups, that is, Mexican, Puerto Rican, etc. Origin or descent (ancestry) may be viewed as the nationality group, the lineage, or country in which the person or the person's parents or ancestors were born.

confused, even though the 1980 census form included guidelines for answering the question, as seen in Figure 1.1.

Despite imperfections, however, the Spanish-origin question does offer the possibility of a relatively consistent enumeration of Hispanics. The census figures derived from this question—9.1 million in 1970 and 14.6 million in 1980—are most often used as estimates of the U.S. Hispanic population as of those dates. And it has been adopted as the Hispanic identifier in the Census Bureau's monthly *Current Population Survey*, the primary source of information on the population between census years.

POPULATION GROWTH AND ETHNIC MIX

The Hispanic population of the United States numbered at least 15 million as of 1983, plus an uncounted number of illegal immigrants. The growth of this population began with the 1848 Treaty of Guadalupe Hidalgo, in which Mexico ceded to the United States the territory that is now Texas, New Mexico, Arizona, California, Nevada, Utah, and part of Colorado. Many Hispanics in the U.S. Southwest thus trace their ancestry to Mexico in a very direct way. But the vast majority of today's Mexican-origin population is the result of immigration in the twentieth century, beginning in the 1900s with immigrants lured north to work the farmlands of California and to build the railroads of the Southwest. This first immigration wave ended during the depression of the 1930s with the deportation of over 400,000 Mexicans, but picked up again during the 1940s with the bracero program. Designed to bring temporary workers north to alleviate U.S. labor shortages during World War II, the bracero program brought in 4.8 million Mexicans before its demise in 1964.[3] Fueled by legal and illegal immigration plus relatively high fertility, the Mexican-American population has continued to grow, but its share of the total U.S. Hispanic population has been reduced to 60 percent from 70 percent in 1950 with influx of Puerto Ricans, Cubans, and "other Hispanics" since then.

Puerto Ricans have had free access to the U.S. mainland as U.S. citizens since the Jones Act of 1917, long before the island became a commonwealth with a unique relationship to the United States in 1952, after being a U.S. territory since the Spanish-American War of 1898. Fewer than 70,000 Puerto Ricans had settled on the mainland by the time of the 1940 census, however. But in the 1950s alone, job opportunities and the advent of regular and cheap plane service between San Juan and New York City attracted a net influx of 500,000 Puerto Ricans to the mainland, primarily to New York City—a tremendous flow for a country with a 1950 population of 2.2 million.[4]

Fewer than 50,000 Cubans lived in the United States before Castro overthrew the regime of Fulgencio Batista in 1959, many of them making cigars in Florida or New York City.[5] The first postrevolution wave of exiles brought about 260,000 largely affluent, professional Cubans to the United States before air traffic between the two countries was ended, following the 1962 missile crisis. A refugee airlift agreed upon by Castro and the Johnson administration in 1965 brought in 344,000 more Cubans before Castro cut off emigration in 1973. Thousands more arrived clandestinely by small boat or through Mexico or Spain in the following years, climaxed by the mass influx of 125,000 Cubans in the Mariel boatlift that Castro permitted from April to September 1980.

Stimulated by changes in U.S. immigration law, numbers of immigrants from all other Spanish-speaking countries have increased dramatically from about 33,000 arriving in 1950-54 to nearly 300,000 in 1975-79, according to the Immigration and Naturalization Service (INS).[6] These countries taken together have now replaced Mexico as the largest supplier of legal immigrants to the United States.

Growth Since 1950

With heavy immigration added to relatively high fertility, the U.S. Hispanic population has soared since 1950. While the total U.S. population grew by just under 50 percent from 1950 to 1980, the increase for Hispanics was about 265 percent, as seen in Table 1.2. The black population—the country's other significant minority—accounted for 9.9 percent of the U.S. population in 1950 and increased its share to 11.7 percent by 1980. In the same period, the Hispanic population went from about 2.7 to 6.4 percent of the U.S. total, making it without question the country's fastest-growing minority.

The 1950, 1960, and 1970 figures for Hispanics shown in Table 1.2 are estimates that attempt to make up for some of the deficiencies in the data for this population. Collection of data on all Hispanics began only with the 1970 census. The census count for Hispanics in 1970, based on the Spanish-origin question, was 9.1 million.[7] Using this as a base, the Census Bureau projected that in 1980 the count would be 13.2 million.[8] The actual count (based on the 1980 Spanish-origin question) turned out to be 14.6 million.[9] The difference was probably due to better reporting by Hispanics in 1980.[10] The census was preceded by a well-orchestrated campaign to improve minority cooperation and coverage, the Spanish-origin question was much improved and appeared early in the questionnaires sent to every household in the country, and the very awareness of Hispanics as a population had probably increased since 1970. Another part of the story may be the increased number of illegal immigrants during the 1970s, some of whom—reassured of anonymity—were willing to answer the questionnaire. It has now been estimated that the 1980 census count of 226.5 million for the total U.S. population included at least 2 million illegal immigrants, with about 1.3 million from Latin American countries.

Table 1.2
Total U.S. and Hispanic Population: 1950-80
(Numbers in millions)

Year	Total U.S. population	Hispanics	Hispanic population increase in preceding decade	Hispanic percent of U.S. population
1950	151.3	4.0	—	2.7
1960	179.3	6.9	2.9	3.9
1970	203.2	10.5	3.6	5.2
1980	226.5	14.6	4.1	6.4

Sources: U.S. population: Bureau of the Census, various census reports; Hispanic population: JoAnne Willette, et al, *The Demographic and Socioeconomic Characteristics of the Hispanic Population in the United States: 1950-1980*, report to the Department of Health and Human Services by Development Associates, Inc., and Population Reference Bureau, Inc., January 18, 1982.

Starting from the 1980 Spanish-origin count of 14.6 million, the Hispanic population estimates shown in Table 1.2, prepared by the Population Reference Bureau for the U.S. Department of Health and Human Services, were derived by projecting the population back to 1950, using INS data on legal immigrants by country of birth and assumptions about Hispanic mortality based on available estimates. This procedure increases the 1970 figure from the original Spanish-origin census count of 9.1 million to 10.5 million. The estimates for the three decades indicate that the U.S. Hispanic population grew from about 4 million in 1950 to 14.6 million in 1980 and that the numbers added rose from about 2.9 million during the 1950s to about 4.1 million in the 1970s.

The ethnic mix of Hispanics has changed. Mexican-Americans, the overwhelming majority before 1950, accounted for only 60 percent by 1980, with 8.7 million persons (see Table 1.3). Persons of Spanish origin from countries other than Mexico, Cuba, or Puerto Rico now number 3 million and account for one of every five Hispanics, a factor that lends even more diversity to this growing minority. Puerto Ricans rank third with a count of 2 million and 14 percent of the 1980 Hispanic population, and the 803,000 Cubans are in fourth place with 6 percent.

Table 1.3
U.S. Hispanic Population, by Type: 1980

Type	Number (in thousands)	Percent	States with largest concentrations
Total Hispanic	14,609	100.0	California, Texas, New York
Mexican American	8,740	59.8	California, Texas, Illinois
Puerto Rican	2,014	13.8	New York, New Jersey, Illinois
Cuban	803	5.5	Florida, New Jersey, New York
Other Hispanic	3,052	20.9	California, New York, New Mexico

Source: Bureau of the Census, "Persons of Spanish Origin by State: 1980," *1980 Census of Population,* Supplementary Report, PC80-S1-7, August 1982.

AGE AND SEX COMPOSITION

Hispanics as a whole are younger, on average, than both the general U.S. population and blacks. In 1980, the median age of the Hispanic population was 23, compared with 30 for the total U.S. population and 25 for the black population. (The median marks the point at which half the population is younger and half is older.) Nearly one-third (32 percent) of Hispanics were younger than 15 and only 5 percent were 65 or older. By contrast, only 23 percent of all Americans were under 15 and 11 percent were age 65 or older.[11]

The youthfulness of the Hispanic population is due to relatively high fertility and to heavy immigration of young adults. These effects can be seen in the shape of the age-sex structure of the Hispanic population as of the 1980 census, contrasted with the pyramid for the total U.S. population (Figure 1.2). The relatively large proportion of children in the Hispanic

Figure 1.2
Age-Sex Composition of the Hispanic and Total U.S. Population: 1980

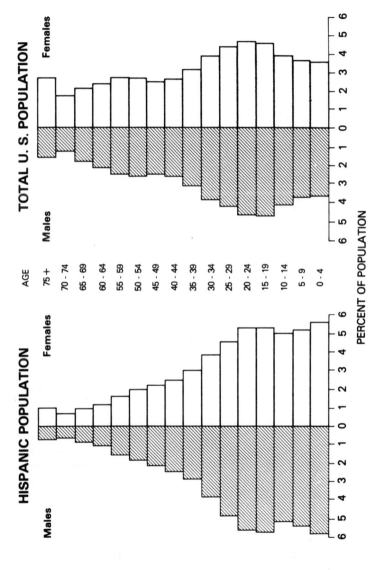

Source: Bureau of the Census, "Age, Sex, Race, and Spanish Origin of the Population by Regions, Divisions, and States: 1980," *1980 Census of Population*, Supplementary Report, PC80-S1-1, 1981.

pyramid reflects both the larger-than-average family sizes of Hispanics and the fact that a substantial proportion of immigrants is in the prime childbearing ages; in the last half of the 1970s, more than one-third of legal immigrants from Spanish-speaking countries were aged 20-34,[12] and this is undoubtedly also true of illegal immigrants. In the U.S. pyramid, the waxing and waning of the baby boom, which peaked from 1955 to 1964, is evident in the bulge at ages 15-24 and the constriction at younger ages.

As the baby boom generation passes out of the childbearing ages, succeeding U.S. birth cohorts will become smaller and smaller, if the U.S rate of childbearing remains near the current low level of 1.8 children per woman. Among Hispanics, by contrast, continuing replenishment of the childbearing population through immigration, plus a fertility rate of about 2.5 children per woman—well above "replacement" level—guarantees larger cohorts of children for some time to come.

The Hispanic population is also somewhat more "male" than the U.S. average. The 1980 census counted 99 Hispanic men for every 100 women, while there were 94 males for every 100 females in the total population. Though men slightly outnumber women among Hispanic immigrants, the main reason for this is the youthfulness of the Hispanic population; there are more Hispanics in the younger ages, where males still outnumber females (about 195 males are born for every 100 females) and fewer in the older ages, where women's longer life expectancy gives them the edge.

Relative youthfulness and large proportions of children are also evident in the 1980 age-sex pyramids for the Mexican-American, Puerto Rican, and "Other Hispanic" populations shown in Figure 1.3. Mexican-Americans have the highest fertility of all Hispanic groups, as is apparent in the broader base of their pyramid, and are the youngest, with a median age of just 22 in 1980. Their pyramid also has a slightly more pronounced bulge and excess of males in the main migration ages of 14-19 than those of Puerto Ricans and other Hispanics.

The pyramid for Cubans is radically different. The bulges at ages 40-54 and 15-24 reflect the young and middle-aged Cubans who arrived in the 1960s and early 1970s and their children; the narrow base demonstrates Cubans' very low current fertility. Not shown in this pyramid are the further distortions in the age-sex composition of the Cuban population caused by the 125,000 Cubans, mostly young males, who arrived in the Mariel boatlift too late to be counted in the April 1, 1980, census. Because Cubans are just 6 percent of all U.S. Hispanics, their low fertility (even lower than the national average) and much older age (a median of 41 years in 1980) are outweighed in statistics on all Hispanics.

WHERE HISPANICS LIVE

Today there are Hispanics in every state of the United States, including Vermont (which had the fewest in 1980, 3,304), Alaska (9,507), and Hawaii

Figure 1.3
Age-Sex Composition of the Four Hispanic Groups: 1980

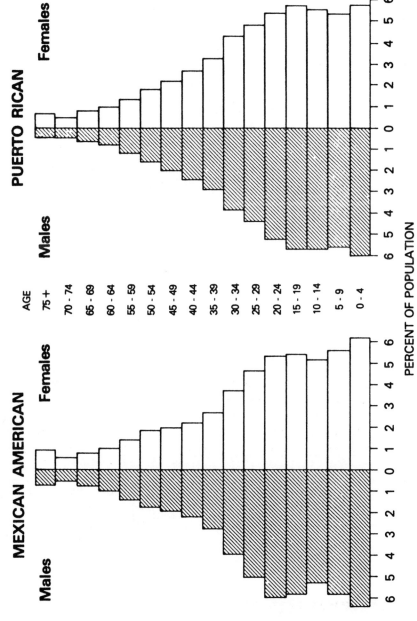

Figure 1.3 (continued)

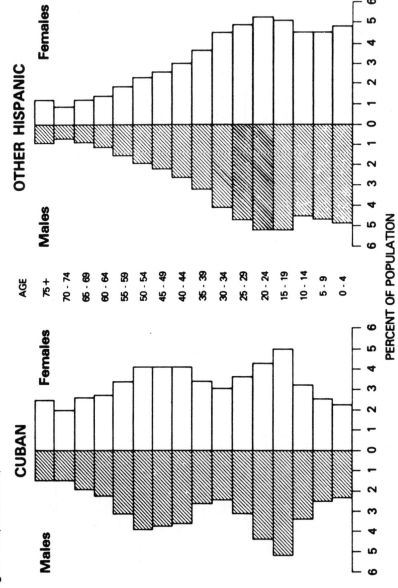

Sources: Bureau of the Census, *1980 Census of Population, General Population Characteristics*, PC80-1B, various state issues.

(71,263). But Hispanics still cluster in certain states and metropolitan areas, where they have become a powerful—even dominating—influence. California, with 4.5 million Hispanics, was home to almost one of every three Spanish-origin residents counted in the 1980 census. Add in Texas, with nearly 3 million Hispanics, and New York State, with 1.7 million, and 63 percent of the Hispanic population in 1980 has been accounted for. Florida, with 858,000 Hispanics, ranked fourth in number of Hispanics. Only five other states had more than 250,000 Hispanics each in 1980: Illinois, New Jersey, New Mexico, Arizona, and Colorado. Together, these nine states contained 85 percent of the U.S. Hispanic population—12.4 million (see Table 1.4).

Hispanics made up 19 percent of the population in California, the nation's most populous state, and 21 percent in Texas, the third most populous state. New Mexico's population has the highest proportion of Hispanics—37 percent—and Hispanics make up 16 percent of Arizona's population and 12 percent of Colorado's.

Hispanics of different origins are even more geographically concentrated. In 1980, 73 percent of the 8.7 million Mexican-Americans lived in California and Texas alone, and another 10 percent in Arizona, Colorado, and New Mexico. Illinois, with more than 400,000, was the only state outside the Southwest with a sizable number of Mexican-Americans. Fully 61 percent of the 2 million Puerto Ricans lived in New York and New Jersey, and another 6 percent in Illinois. Florida was home to nearly 59

Table 1.4
Top Nine States in Hispanic Population: 1970 and 1980
(States with 250,000 or more Hispanics in 1980)

		1970			1980	
State	Rank	Number of Hispanics	Percent distribution	Rank	Number of Hispanics	Percent distribution
United States, total	—	9,072,602	100.00	—	14,608,673	100.0
California	1	2,369,292	26.1	1	4,544,331	31.1
Texas	2	1,840,648	20.3	2	2,985,824	20.4
New York	3	1,351,982	14.9	3	1,659,300	11.4
Florida	4	405,036	4.5	4	858,158	5.9
Illinois	5	393,204	4.3	5	635,602	4.4
New Jersey	7	288,488	3.2	6	491,883	3.4
New Mexico	6	308,340	3.4	7	477,222	3.3
Arizona	8	264,770	2.9	8	440,701	3.0
Colorado	9	225,506	2.5	9	339,717	2.3
Total in nine top states		7,447,266	82.1		12,432,738	85.1

Source: Bureau of the Census. "Persons of Spanish Origin by State." *1980 Census of Population.* Supplementary Report. PC80-S1-7. August 1982.

percent of the 803,000 Cubans counted in the 1980 census, and it became even more the Cuban center when an estimated 120,000 of the "Marielitos" later chose to settle there.

The 3 million "other Hispanics" were more scattered but still only seven states had more than 100,000 each of this group. In California, with the largest number (753,000), there were sizable communities of Salvadorans, Guatemalans, and Nicaraguans. New York, also with more than 500,000 "other Hispanics," has attracted many Dominicans, Colombians, and Ecuadorans. "Other Hispanics" are also becoming increasingly evident in the Miami and Chicago areas. The "other Hispanics" in New York, New Jersey, Florida, and Illinois are mostly immigrants from Central and South American countries, while it is likely that the "other Hispanics" in Texas, New Mexico, and Colorado are largely Hispanos who prefer not to identify themselves as Mexican-Americans in the census. California's "other Hispanics" are a mixture of Hispanos and Central and South Americans.

The proportion of all Hispanics living in the nine most Hispanic states increased from 82 percent to 85 percent between 1970 and 1980, and the proportion of Puerto Ricans in New York, New Jersey, and Illinois declined from 80 to 67 percent. On the other hand, the percentage of Cubans living in Florida rose from 46 to 49 percent during the 1970s, and the share of "other Hispanics" living in California and New York went up from 28 to 43 percent.

Though perceived by many as rural, Hispanics are a highly urban population. Fully 88 percent live in metropolitan areas, according to the 1980 census, compared with 75 percent of the general population and 81 percent of blacks.[13] Moreover, 50 percent of U.S. Hispanics live in the central cities of metropolitan areas. This is far more than the 30 percent of the general population living in central cities.

Table 1.5 lists the 27 of the nation's 318 Standard Metropolitan Statistical Areas where Hispanics numbered more than 100,000 in 1980. Over 3.5 million lived in the Los Angeles and New York areas alone—almost one-quarter of all Hispanics in the United States. Mexican-Americans are the largest Hispanic group in most of the 27 SMSAs listed in Table 1.5. However, Cubans are the most metropolitan of Hispanics; virtually 100 percent are metro dwellers in the four states with the most Cubans (Florida, New Jersey, New York, and California).

Miami is the undisputed Cuban center. Over half the country's Cuban-Americans live in the Miami area, where Cubans make up 70 percent of Hispanics. The Cuban influence has transformed Miami from a resort town to a year-round commercial center with linkages throughout Latin America and a leading bilingual cultural center. The Los Angeles area is the Mexican-American metropolitan capital. Mexicans comprise 80 percent of Hispanics in the area, 22 percent of the total population, and one-fifth of all Mexican-Americans in the country. San Antonio, however, where Mexican-

Table 1.5
Standard Metropolitan Statistical Areas with 100,000
or More Hispanics in 1980

Standard Metropolitan Statistical Area[a]	Hispanics in SMSA	Hispanics in central city	Largest Hispanic group and its percent of all Hispanics in SMSA
Los Angeles-Long Beach, CA	2,065,727	866,689	Mexican, 80%
New York, NY-NJ	1,493,081	1,405,957	Puerto Rican, 60%
Miami, FL	581,030	194,087	Cuban, 70%
Chicago, IL	580,592	422,061	Mexican, 64%
San Antonio, TX	481,511	421,774	Mexican, 93%
Houston, TX	424,901	281,224	Mexican, 88%
San Franciso-Oakland, CA	351,915	115,864	Mexican, 54%
El Paso, TX	297,001	265,819	Mexican, 95%
Riverside-San Bernardino-Ontario, CA	289,791	81,671	Mexican, 87%
Anaheim-Santa Ana-Garden Grove, CA	286,331	145,253	Mexican, 81%
San Diego, CA	275,176	130,610	Mexican, 83%
Dallas, Ft. Worth, TX	249,613	159,778	Mexican, 89%
McAllen-Pharr-Edinburg, TX	230,212	86,393	Mexican, 96%
San Jose, CA	226,611	140,574	Mexican, 78%
Phoenix, AZ	198,999	115,572	Mexican, 89%
Denver-Boulder, CO	173,362	94,933	Mexican, 63%
Albuquerque, NM	164,200	112,084	Other Hispanic, 56%
Brownsville-Harlingen-San Benito, TX	161,632	116,076	Mexican, 86%
Corpus Christi,TX	158,123	108,175	Mexican, 96%
Fresno, CA	150,820	51,489	Mexican, 93%
Jersey City, NJ	145,163	41,672	Puerto Rican, 38%
Newark, NJ	132,356	61,254	Puerto Rican, 47%
Philadelphia, PA-NJ	116,280	63,570	Puerto Rican, 68%
Oxnard-Simi Valley-Ventura, CA	113,241	64,223	Mexican, 89%
Tucson, AZ	111,418	82,189	Mexican, 90%
Nassau-Suffolk, NY	101,418	[b]	Puerto Rican, 49%
Sacramento, CA	101,692	39,160	Mexican, 77%

Sources: Bureau of the Census. "Standard Metropolitan Statistical Areas and Standard Consolidated Statistical Areas: 1980." *1980 Census of Population*, Supplementary Report, PC80-S1-5, October 1981: and Cheryl Russell. "The News About Hispanics." *American Demographics*, March 1983, p. 17.

[a]A Standard Metropolitan Statistical Area (renamed Metropolitan Statistical Area as of July 1983) is a county with a central city (or urbanized area) of at least 50,000 population, plus adjacent counties that are economically linked with that county.
[b]Does not contain a central city.

Americans make up 93 percent of Hispanics and are also the population majority in the central city, can claim to be the first large U.S. city with a Mexican-American mayor—Henry Cisneros, elected in 1981. Puerto Ricans began flowing into New York City during the 1950s, and with 43 percent of all Puerto Ricans in the country, the New York metropolitan area is the hub of Puerto Rican life in the United States.

FERTILITY

Although immigration may appear to be the major spur to the growth of the U.S. Hispanic population, an estimated two-thirds of that growth actually stems from Hispanics' relatively high fertility, combined with a mortality rate that is probably not higher than that of non-Hispanics. The available data suggest that the fertility of Hispanic women as a group—though lower than it was in the 1960s—is about 60 percent higher than the non-Hispanic average and 50 percent higher than the average for all U.S. women. It is also higher than black fertility. Mexican-American women have the highest fertility among Hispanics, while Cuban women's fertility is far below even that of non-Hispanic women.

Hispanic fertility is difficult to estimate because accurate counts of the "true" Hispanic population are still so elusive and systematic registration of births by Hispanic origin began only in 1978 and so far covers only 22 states (though an estimated 90 percent of the Hispanic population). One clue, however, is the "child-woman ratio," the number of children under age 5 per 1000 women aged 15-44, calculated from the 1980 census. As shown in Table 1.6, this ratio was 462 for Hispanic women, 55 percent higher than the ratio of 298 for non-Hispanic women of childbearing age and 26 percent higher than the black ratio of 366. Also, as already noted, 32 percent of the total Hispanic population counted in the 1980 census were children under age 15. This compares with 29 percent in the black population and 22 percent among all non-Hispanics.

Table 1.7 shows birth rates and fertility rates for 1979 that could be computed by the National Center for Health Statistics (NCHS) for 9 of the 19 states where births were then being recorded by Hispanic origin of father and mother. The most recently published from birth registration information, these 1979 rates cover less than 60 percent of the Hispanic population and exclude the heavily Hispanic states of Texas and New Mexico, which, along with Georgia, began registration of births by Hispanic origin only in 1980.

Table 1.6
Child-Woman Ratio and Percentage of Children Among Hispanics, Non-Hispanics, and Blacks: 1980

Population	Children aged 0-4 per 1,000 women aged 15-44	Percent of population under age 15
Hispanic	462	32.0
Non-Hispanic	298	22.0
Black	366	28.7

Source: Bureau of the Census, "Age, Sex, Race, and Spanish Origin of the Population by Regions, Divisions, and States: 1980," *1980 Census of Population*, Supplementary Report, PC80-S1-1, 1981.

Table 1.7
Birth Rates and Fertility Rates, by Hispanic Origin:
Nine States, 1979

Ethnic group	Births per 1,000 population	Births per 1,000 women aged 15-44
All origins	15.6	66.7
Non-Hispanic	14.7	63.2
All Hispanic	25.5	100.5
Mexican American	29.6	119.3
Puerto Rican	22.6	80.7
Cuban	8.6	39.7
Other Hispanic	25.7	95.9

Source: Stephanie J. Ventura, "Births of Hispanic Parentage, 1979." *Monthly Vital Statistics Report*, Vol. 31, No. 2, Supplement, May 1982.

Note: The nine states are Arizona, California, Colorado, Florida, Illinois, Indiana, New Jersey, New York, and Ohio.

The crude birth rate for all Hispanics of 25.5 births per 1000 population was 73 percent higher than the birth rate of 14.7 per 1000 of the non-Hispanic population. However, the gap was less when measured by the number of births per 1000 women of childbearing age (15-44), a more accurate measure of fertility. In the latter category, the 100.5 rate for Hispanic women as a whole was 59 percent higher than the rate of 63.2 for non-Hispanic women, but only 51 percent higher than the rate of 66.7 births per 1000 among all women aged 15-44 in the nine reporting states. The latter results tally well with results from the Census Bureau's June 1980 *Current Population Survey*. Among the 36,000 women aged 18-44 included in the nationwide sample, there were 197 births per 1000 Hispanic women in the 12 months preceding the survey.[14] This rate was 51 percent higher than the rate for all women—71—and it was 27 percent higher than the black rate of 84.

The Mexican-American rate of 119.3 births per 1000 women aged 15-44 shown in Table 1.7 is the highest among the four Hispanic groups. The rates for Puerto Ricans (80.7) and "other Hispanic" women (95.9) are also much higher than the rates for non-Hispanics (63.2) and for all women (66.7). The Cuban rate of 39.7 is far below all others. Stephanie Ventura, author of the

NCHS report, attributes this partly to the relatively older age of Cuban women in Florida (more of those aged 15-44 are in the low-fertility years of 35-44 than are their Mexican and Puerto Rican counterparts), but it probably also reflects the low family-size preferences of the relatively affluent and better-educated Cuban population.[15]

Reasons for Higher Hispanic Fertility

Except for Cubans, Hispanics have less education and lower family incomes, and are much more likely to be living in poverty than the general U.S. population. This undoubtedly explains much of their higher fertility, for these factors are correlated with relatively high fertility among all U.S. groups. The Census Bureau's June 1980 survey, for example, found a rate of 94 births per 1000 women in families with incomes under $5000 per year, compared with 49 per 1000 women in families with incomes of $25,000 and over. The NCHS found that only 47 percent of all Hispanic women and 37 percent of Mexican-American women reported to have had a birth in 1979 had completed at least 12 years of schooling, compared with 78 percent among the non-Hispanic mothers and 77 percent among Cubans. Ventura comments that these lower levels of schooling among non-Cuban Hispanics are partly due to "the relatively larger proportion of births to teenagers among Hispanic mothers."[16] Fully 19 percent of Hispanic women in the study who had a birth in 1979 were under age 20, compared with 15 percent for all mothers. The proportion of teenage births for Mexican women was 20 percent, and 23 percent for Puerto Rican women.

Traditional preferences for large families in the countries from which most Hispanics originate probably also play a role. Cuba currently has an exceptionally low fertility for a developing country—1.8 births per woman, the same as that of the United States.[17] Puerto Rico's rate of 2.7 is considerably higher, but still well below the Latin American average of 4.3 births per woman. More typical is Mexico's experience. At the beginning of the 1970s, Mexico's fertility rate was over 7 births per woman. However, in less than a decade it has dropped to about 4.7 births per woman in the wake of a vigorous government family-planning program.[18] Other Latin American countries have now launched family-planning programs to reduce population growth, and it is probable that many recent Hispanic immigrants to the United States have had some experience with contraception.

To judge from a 1979 survey of 2100 women of childbearing age living on the U.S. side of the Mexican border, contraceptive use is quite high among Hispanics in the United States, but not so high as for non-Hispanics. Some 66 percent of the currently married Hispanic women surveyed were using contraception, compared with 75 percent among Anglos (white, non-Hispanic).[19] However, the differences were not significant among women under 35, which suggests that younger Hispanic married women may be about as likely to practice contraception as their non-Hispanic counter-parts. Never-married Hispanic women were only half as likely to be using contraception as single Anglo women, however, though equal proportions in both groups (12 percent) reported that they were sexually active.

Closing the Gap

Although Hispanic women's fertility is still well above the national average, there is evidence that it has been falling in concert with that of all U.S. women since the mid-1950s. This suggests that the gap should eventually be closed.

Using census data on "own children," demographers Robert Rindfuss and James Sweet calculated that Hispanic women's fertility dropped by 25 percent between 1955 and 1969. A study by the Centers for Disease Control noted a similar decrease from 1970 to 1977 among Spanish-surnamed women in Texas.[20] Data from the Census Bureau's *Current Population Survey* displayed in Table 1.8 show that the decline continues. In 1973, Hispanic married women aged 30-34 reported that they had 3.3 births to date; by 1981, the average for such women was down to 2.5. In 1981, these women still expected to have an average of 2.8 children during their lifetime, compared with 2.2 for all married women aged 30-34. But young Hispanic married women aged 18-24 in 1981 said they expected an average of 2.3, virtually the same as the 1981 national average of 2.2 for all married women aged 18-24.

Thus, the fertility of U.S. Hispanic women as a group—now probably about 2.5 births apiece—is likely to continue to decline. Actual convergence with the U.S. national average may be somewhat delayed, however, as each year brings a new wave of legal and illegal immigrants reared in traditions of somewhat larger families. From a demographic standpoint, it is also significant that Hispanic fertility is still well above the "replacement" level of about two children per woman needed to stop population growth in the long run, and may remain above that level for some time to come.

MORTALITY AND HEALTH

In mortality levels there may be no overall gap between Hispanics and non-Hispanics; in fact, Hispanic life expectancy may now be even slightly higher than that of U.S. white persons and certainly higher than that of blacks. But this conjecture is based only on studies of Hispanic mortality in Texas and in California. So far, there are no nationally representative mortality data for Hispanics.

This was rectified in 1983, when the NCHS issued a first report on His-panic mortality in the 22 states that now include a question about Hispanic origin on death certificates as well as on birth certificates.[21] This question

Table 1.8
Births to Date and Total Births Expected in Lifetime, Hispanic and All Married Women: 1973, 1975, 1978, 1981
(Numbers are births per currently married woman)

Year and group	Total, aged 18-34		Women 18-24		Women 30-34	
	Births to date	Lifetime births expected	Births to date	Lifetime births expected	Births to date	Lifetime births expected
Hispanic women						
1973	2.1	3.0	1.1	2.6	3.3	3.8
1975	1.9	2.7	1.0	2.2	3.0	3.2
1978	1.8	2.6	1.1	2.4	2.8	3.0
1981	1.9	2.6	1.1	2.3	2.5	2.8
All women						
1973	1.7	2.5	0.9	2.3	2.6	2.8
1975	1.6	2.3	0.8	2.2	2.4	2.6
1978	1.5	2.3	0.8	2.2	2.2	2.4
1981	1.5	2.2	0.9	2.2	2.0	2.2

Source: Carolyn C. Rogers. "Fertility of American Women: June 1981." *Current Population Reports*. Series P-20. No. 378. April 1983. Table 1.

has proven to be more of a problem for death registration, however. Birth certificates are filled out by hospital staff with the mother available to respond to the ethnic query, but death certificates are completed by funeral directors, who must rely on the often less reliable information supplied by relatives, friends, or neighbors, or on their own observation. Compliance with the request for Hispanic-origin information has often been poor or arbitrary. California, for example, has not coded this question for half of its recent death certificates, and in New Mexico all certificates not checked for the ethnic identifier are assumed to be non-Hispanic.

A study based on Texas State Department of Health Data for 1970 revealed life expectancies at birth for the Spanish-surnamed population of the state were very close to those of the national population at the time: 67.2 years, compared with the national average of 67.1 among males, and 73.4 versus 74.8 years among females.[22] Two studies of age-specific death patterns derived from 1970 census data for California and Texas found higher infant mortality and much higher mortality for young adult males among the Spanish-surnamed population than for the U.S. white population.[23] Nevertheless, life expectancies at birth for Hispanics were similar to those of non-Hispanics. The first study based on 1980 census data for the state of Texas suggests, with caveats on the quality of the data, that Hispanic life expectancy may now be higher than that of the total U.S. white population.[24] Among males, life expectancy was 71.4 years for the Texas Spanish-surnamed population, compared with 70.2 for all white males in the United States in 1978; for females the figures were 79.5 and 77.2, respectively. Black life expectancies in 1978 were 64.0 years for males and 72.7 years for females.[25]

For Hispanics other than Mexican-Americans (who predominate in Texas and California) there is only indirect evidence on life expectancy. Puerto Rico and Cuba both have good vital statistics registration data indicating that their life expectancies are near or even above U.S. levels. Thus, immigrants from these countries probably also have mortality rates on a par with U.S. national averages. "Other Hispanics," of course, come from many countries, some with life expectancies well below those of men and women in the United States. Immigrants may be healthier than their compatriots who stay at home, but there is no information on this or on how "other Hispanics" tie into the U.S. health care system.

Considerably more will soon be known about the health of U.S. Hispanics. Beginning in the fall of 1982 by NCHS, the Hispanic Health and Nutrition Examination Survey collected information from a sample of 16,000 Mexican-Americans in the Southwest, Cubans in Miami, and Puerto Ricans in New York City on medical histories, diet, nutrition, physical measurements, and use and need for health services. Results from the two-year study were released in late 1985.

FAMILY AND MARITAL STATUS

Hispanics are less likely than the general U.S. population to be living in married-couple families and much more likely to be in families headed by a single parent, almost always the mother. But in both respects they fare much better than blacks.

In 1981, as Table 1.9 shows, 73 percent of the nation's 3.2 million Hispanic families were headed by a married couple, compared with 82 percent of all families and 54 percent of black families. Fifty-two percent of Hispanic families had children living at home, versus 41 percent among all families.

Single parents with children under 18 comprised 18 percent of all Hispanic families. This was 75 percent higher than the proportion among all families (10 percent) but well below the proportion among blacks (31 percent). Fully 16 percent of Hispanic families in 1981 were maintained by a

Table 1.9
Hispanic, Black, and All Families: 1981

Family type and presence of own children under 18	Hispanic	Black	All families
All families			
Number			
(in thousands)	3,235	6,317	60,309
Percent	100.0	100.0	100.0
Married-couple families	73.1	53.7	81.7
With own children	51.7	30.7	41.3
No own children	21.5	23.0	40.4
Single-parent child families	18.2	30.6	10.4
Mother and own children	16.3	28.9	9.3
Father and own children	1.9	1.8	1.1
Other families	8.7	15.7	7.8

Source: Bureau of the Census, "Household and Family Characteristics: March 1981," *Current Population Reports*, Series P-20, No. 371, May 1982, Tables 12 and 13.

woman alone, compared with 9 percent among all families. Puerto Rican families are far more likely than other Hispanic families to be maintained by a woman—40 percent were in 1979, versus 15 percent among Mexican-Americans and 17 percent among other Hispanics, including Cubans.[26]

Because of their higher fertility, Hispanic family households are larger than the national average. In 1981, Hispanic families averaged 3.9 persons each, compared with 3.3 among all families and 3.7 for blacks.[27]

Marital Status

Although Hispanics marry as readily as all Americans, they are somewhat more likely to separate or divorce, which explains their higher proportion of female-headed families. Fourteen percent of Hispanic women aged 15 and over were separated or divorced in 1981—more than the 10 percent for all women this age but, again, lower than the proportion among black women, which was nearly 20 percent (Table 1.10). In the same year there were 146 divorced Hispanic women for every 1000 Hispanic women who were married and living with their husbands.[28] For all women, the ratio was 129, and for black women, 289. On the other hand, 53 percent of Hispanic women over 15 were married and living with their husbands in 1981, very close to the 55 percent among all women. Hispanics tend to marry somewhat earlier than other Americans do. In 1981, about 25 percent of Hispanic women under age 20 were or had been married, compared with 15 percent among all teenage women and only 7 percent among black women.

Thus, while the marital experience of Hispanics is more similar to the U.S. average than that of blacks, Hispanics are somewhat more likely to dissolve their marriages. This leads to somewhat higher proportions of female-headed households, which is a factor in Hispanics' lower family incomes.

IMMIGRATION

Hispanics' increasing visibility on the American scene reflects a striking shift in the pattern of immigration. From 1930 to 1960, Europeans still dominated the immigrant influx—41 percent from northern and western Europe, and 17 percent from southern and eastern Europe. Latin Americans made up only 15 percent of total legal immigration. Since 1960, Latin Americans have averaged 40 percent of the total. By 1975-79, they were up to 42 percent, outpacing legal immigrants from Asia (39 percent) and Europe (13 percent).[29] The total numbers have also been rising. Immigration and Naturalization Service (INS) statistics put the number of Hispanic immigrants entering the country legally at 956,000 during the 1950s, 1.3 million in the 1960s and 1.4 million in the 1970s. Added to this is a growing, though unknown, number of illegal immigrants from Latin America.

Table 1.10
Marital Status of Hispanic, Black, and All Persons Aged 15 and Over: 1981 (Numbers in percent)

Marital Status	Hispanic		Black		All persons	
	Males	Females	Males	Females	Males	Females
Total	100.0	100.0	100.0	100.0	100.0	100.0
Never married	34.0	26.0	41.0	33.7	29.4	22.5
Married, spouse present	55.2	52.6	41.1	32.8	60.2	54.8
Married, spouse absent	5.2	7.8	7.0	11.4	2.8	3.7
Separated	2.5	6.4	5.8	10.1	1.9	2.9
Other	2.6	1.4	1.2	1.2	0.9	0.8
Widowed	1.6	6.0	3.7	12.7	2.3	11.9
Divorced	4.0	7.7	7.3	9.5	5.3	7.1

Source: Bureau of the Census, 'Marital Status and Living Arrangements: March 1981.' Current Population Reports, Series P-20, No. 372, 1982, Table 1

This shift in the origins of immigrants has had all the more impact on the makeup of the U.S. population because net immigration has become an increasingly important part of annual population growth as fertility has declined. In 1981, for example, it has been estimated that natural increase (births minus deaths) accounted for 57 percent of population growth; 43 percent was contributed by 1.2 million immigrants—480,000 legal immigrants, 217,000 refugees, and an estimated 500,000 illegal immigrants.[30]

Behind the shift are some stark demographic and economic figures. Latin America's labor force is growing by 4 million a year; that of Mexico and the rest of Central America, by 1.2 million a year. Forty percent of their current work force is unemployed or working only a few hours a week or days in the year.[31] Per capita income for all Latin America was $2063 in 1981. For the United States—even as the recession deepened—it was $12,530.[32]

Equally important in the shift to Latin American predominance among immigrants was the change in U.S. policy signaled by passage of the Immigration and Nationality Act of 1965, which came into force in 1968. Responding to an increased influx of Latin American immigrants, it imposed for the first time a numerical limit on legal immigration from the Western Hemisphere—120,000 annual arrivals, admitted on a first-come, first-served basis. At the same time, Eastern Hemisphere countries became subject to a 170,000 overall ceiling, plus a 20,000 annual per-country limit based on a complicated preference system that stressed job skills and reunification with close family members already in the United States. This abolished a quota system in effect since the 1920s that had favored immigrants from northern and western Europe.

The result was an increase in the percentage of legal immigrants from non-European countries. It also left many would-be Mexican migrants without legal means of entry, coming as it did just after Congress had ended the bracero program, which, at its peak, had brought over 400,000 temporary Mexican workers annually.[33] Without the visa preference system, there was little control over legal admissions of Latin Americans. To change this and put Latin America on an "equal footing" with the rest of the world, the United States in 1977 extended the visa preference system and the 20,000 per-country annual limit to the Western Hemisphere, and probably stimulated illegal immigration of persons who did not qualify for a preference or refused to wait the many years it often takes to gain clearance.

In 1978, the hemisphere quotas were replaced with a single worldwide ceiling of 290,000, later changed to 270,000 excluding refugees, with no more than 20,000 from any one country. Immediate relatives of U.S. citizens are admitted in addition to the 270,000 limit, however, which raised the total of legal immigrants to 480,000 in 1981. Another component of the legal influx are refugees, for whom quotas are set annually under the terms of the Refugee Act of 1980; 140,000 refugee slots were allocated in 1982.

The 125,000 Cubans of the Mariel boatlift, along with 10,000 Haitians who sought refuge during 1980, were admitted under still another category as special "entrants."

The growing share of Latin Americans among immigrants has aroused public concern about the impact on American standards and values of an ethnically and culturally distinct group endowed with socioeconomic characteristics perceived as inferior to those of the "average" American. Forgotten are the similar concerns voiced at the turn of the century when immigrants from southern and eastern Europe began to outnumber those from northern and western Europe. The degradation of U.S. society predicted at that time obviously has not come to pass.

One issue unique to Hispanics, however, is that they share a common language. This has helped them develop a group identity and increased leverage in demands for special attention and services. It has also provoked a negative response from those who fear the United States will be forced into bilingualism, or at least the sort of linguistic factionalism most recently evident in Canada. In 1981, Senator S. I. Hayakawa proposed a resolution to amend the U.S. Constitution to make English the country's official language. Voters in Dade County, Florida, where Miami is located, in November 1980 overturned a countywide policy of bilingualism adopted in 1973.

In numbers is strength, however. Thus Hispanics are likely to continue to dominate immigration to the United States, to the disadvantage of white non-Hispanics and blacks from other countries who currently make up little of the flow. The United States became more ethnically and culturally diverse as the result of earlier shifts in the profile of immigrants, and this can be expected to occur again with the increase in Hispanics. Legitimate questions remain about the costs and benefits of reorganizing society and how fast that should happen. More easily influenced by policy makers than are fertility and mortality—the other two variables that shape a country's population growth and composition—immigration is likely to remain a much-debated issue for some time to come.

Legal Immigration Diversity

Each of the four Hispanic groups has its own immigration history and, once arrived, has generally settled in a different region of the United States. There are also differences in the amount that immigration has contributed to each group's growth since 1950—almost all for Cubans and "other Hispanics," and very little since the 1960s for the Puerto Ricans.

Data on legal immigration for Mexicans, Cubans, and other Hispanics are drawn from INS records. Puerto Ricans, who have unrestricted access to the United States, do not appear in INS records. To estimate their net migration, one must use a residual procedure involving two Puerto Rican census counts and registration of births and deaths for the decade they span. Drawing on these two sources, Table 1.11 shows immigration of each of the four groups from 1950 to 1979.

During the 1950s, Puerto Ricans accounted for half of all Hispanic immigration, providing the United States with a net gain of nearly 500,000. This movement, with one of every six Puerto Ricans moving to the mainland during the decade, ranks as one of the most dramatic voluntary exoduses on record. It was driven by the promise of jobs—any jobs—as an escape from the island's stagnant agrarian economy, cheap plane fares, and the freedom of entry accorded Puerto Ricans as U.S. citizens.

A sharp rise in immigration in the last half of the 1950s boosted Mexican immigration to almost 300,000 for the decade. The number grew by about 140,000 in each of the next two decades, yielding a total for the 1970s of just under 570,000. Mexico ranked as the largest single contributor to U.S. legal immigration—over 40 percent of all Hispanic immigration.

Cuban immigration also grew dramatically. Although the INS statistics shown in Table 1.11 add 527,000 Cuban immigrants for 1960-79, the actual number of Cuban arrivals was close to 640,000, with over 70 percent occurring during the 1960s. Such large numbers of Cubans could enter the United States only under a special status, such as political refugee or "parolee." But the INS records such individuals' entries only when their status is adjusted to "immigrant."

Touched off by Castro's rise to power in 1959, Cuban legal immigration subsequently rose and fell in concert with shifts in both U.S. and Cuban government policies—surging in the first years after the revolution and in the late 1960s and early 1970s, ebbing after the 1962 missile crisis and following Castro's cutoff of emigration in 1973. The latest and largest influx of Cubans began when an April 1980 rush on the Peruvian embassy in Havana by a crowd demanding asylum drew a sudden response from Castro that whoever wanted to leave the island was welcome to go. By December 1980, 125,000 had arrived in the United States, transported in a flotilla of boats sent to collect them from the port of El Mariel. These refugees were set off from their predecessors not only by their numbers but also by their socioeconomic characteristics. Most stemmed from "urban working and lower class origins," as had Cubans arriving in the early 1970s, while the first waves of postrevolution refugees had been "displaced bourgeoisie"—well educated, middle- and upper-class professionals and business people alienated by the new regime.[34]

One effect of the timing of the Mariel boatlift, which began just after completion of the 1980 census, was to undermine the relevancy of census data on the Cuban population. Close to 15 percent of the 1981 U.S. Cuban population was not in residence at the time of the April 1, 1980, census.

Comparing the 1980 census count of Cubans (803,000) with the number estimated to have emigrated to the United States from 1959 up to the census

Table 1.11
Hispanic Immigration into the United States,
by Ethnic Group: 1950-79

Ethnic group	1950-59		1960-69		1970-79	
	Number of migrants	Percent of total	Number of migrants	Percent of total	Number of migrants	Percent of total
Mexican	293,000	30.7	431,000	33.2	567,000	40.8
Cuban	71,000	7.4	249,000	19.2	278,000	20.0
Puerto Rican	480,000	50.2	222,000	17.1	41,000	3.0
Other Hispanic	112,000	11.7	397,000	30.6	503,000	36.2

Sources: Mexican, Cuban, Other Hispanic: Immigration and Naturalization Service annual reports 1950-1979, Table 9; Puerto Rican: Estimated from Puerto Rican census and vital statistics.

date (670,000) indicates that some 80 percent of the 1980 population are first-generation immigrants. The Mariel arrivals would, of course, further increase this percentage.

The "other Hispanics" are shown in Table 1.11 to have had the largest gain in immigration over the 30-year interval: from 112,000 and 12 percent of Hispanic immigrants to 503,000 and 36 percent of the total in the 1970s, putting them into second place after Mexicans in their contribution to Hispanic immigration for the decade. For the 1975-79 period, they were actually in first place. Of course this total represents immigration from 16 separate nations. The largest contingents come from the Dominican Republic, Colombia, Argentina, and Ecuador, joined, in recent years, by growing numbers of escapees from the political turmoil in Nicaragua and El Salvador. This increase in "other Hispanic" immigration partly reflects growing population pressures in the countries from which they come. Current population growth in these 16 countries averages over 2 percent a year—a rate at which a population doubles in just 35 years. This alone foretells for this group an every-growing dominance in Hispanic legal immigration totals.

After holding first place during the 1950s, Puerto Rican net immigration dwindled to 41,000 and 3 percent of the total in the 1970s. Why was this? With an island population of less than 2.4 million in 1960 and fertility on the decline, it would have been impossible for Puerto Rico to continue to export 500,000 residents each decade. But other factors also played a role. For one, pressure on the home job market was relieved by the exodus of earlier emigrants. Economic opportunities may still have been brighter on the mainland, but not enough to warrant the wrench of leaving home. Deciding to stay was also made more feasible by increases in U.S. government welfare support, combined with remittances from family members who had ventured to the mainland.

Unique to Puerto Rican immigration, however, is the fact that the net migration figures mask a large movement of people back and forth from the island, which unrestricted entry to the mainland permits. Puerto Ricans have been characterized as having "one foot on the mainland and one on the island." Detailed figures for the 1970s show a new flow back to Puerto Rico of people aged 35 and over and older children aged 5-19, but this was offset by a larger net influx to the mainland of persons aged 20-29 and children under age 5. This suggests that young adults are lured to the mainland with their children by the prospect of better economic opportunities, and later choose to return to the island.

Sex and Age of Legal Immigrants

The characteristic ages and sexes of 1950-79 immigrants, which helped shape the age-sex composition of the 1980 resident Hispanic population, varied among the four groups. Women consistently outnumbered men among immigrants from Cuba and other Hispanic countries, as has been true of immigrants generally since the 1930s. Fifty-seven percent of new arrivals among "other Hispanics" during the 1950s were women—a high proportion that reflects the pattern of rural-to-urban migration in Latin America, where women also outnumber men. By the 1970s this figure had declined somewhat to 54 percent.

Among Cuban immigrants, the proportion of women was 53 percent in the 1950s and 1960s, just before and after the 1959 revolution, and rose to 55 percent in the 1970s. In this case the predominance of women came about because young men of conscription age were not allowed to emigrate. The sex ratio of Cuban immigrants in the 1980s will have changed with the addition of the *marielitos*, 70 percent of whom were men.[35]

Among Mexican and Puerto Rican immigrants, by contrast, men have been more numerous. For Mexicans, the male share was 53 percent during the 1950s, followed by a decline to 50-51 percent in the next two decades. This pattern probably reflects job opportunities in the Southwest. Many legal immigrants in the 1950s may have been former braceros or their relatives who knew of job opportunities for men in the United States.

Among Puerto Ricans, the proportion of men was 54 percent during the 1950s, 56 percent in the 1960s, and 73 percent in the 1970s. The 1970s figure must be viewed cautiously, since it is based on such a small net immigration total. Even so, the increasing predominance of males is obvious. This could be because Puerto Ricans can come to the mainland freely, without the hurdles that face all other Hispanic legal immigrants, and men are thus easily able to come temporarily to take a job without uprooting an entire family.

Two-thirds of immigrants arriving from Mexico and "other Hispanic" countries from 1950 to 1979 were between the ages of 15 and 44. This is typical of most migrant streams, for this is the stage of life when one can expect to profit most from a move to a place promising better economic opportunities. As might be expected, such migrants bring with them a sizable number of young children.

Puerto Rican movement during the 1970s, as noted, stands out for its net influx of migrants aged 20-29 and net emigration at ages above 35. The pattern was similar, if less pronounced, in the earlier decades.

Cuban immigrants of the 1950s were mostly in the typical young adult ages but were much older in the two decades after the revolution. Thirty-three percent in the 1960s and 45 percent in the 1970s were 65 and over, much higher than the 7.1 percent of Cuban women this age counted in the 1980 U.S. census. Demographers Sergio Díaz and Lisandro Pérez point out some reasons for the older, more female Cuban immigration before the Mariel boatlift:

The Cuban government generally prohibited the emigration of males eligible for military conscription. Also persons of working age had to spend time in agricultural labor before being allowed to leave the country. There were no such restrictions for the elderly, a dependent population the revolutionary government was not particularly eager to keep.[36]

Illegal Immigration

Illegal immigration—hard to measure but thought to be on the increase—looms large in any assessment of the impact of recent Hispanic immigration to the United States. Not all illegal immigrants are Hispanics, of course, but the majority probably are. Their motives are no different from those of legal immigrants; most come seeking jobs or to escape political and social turmoil at home. Unfortunately, these legitimate interests often conflict with the interests of current citizens.

Who Are They?

Illegal or undocumented aliens are classified as persons crossing the border "without inspection" or with fraudulent documents, or overstaying a work or student visa. This definition rules out Puerto Ricans, with free access as U.S. citizens, and most Cubans, who have been accorded special refugee status because of the political overtones attached to their movements to the United States. Thus the undocumented Hispanic population is made up almost entirely of Mexicans and other Hispanics.

An estimated 50-60 percent of all illegal aliens are Mexicans,[37] stimulated by the closeness of the border, a long history of moving back and forth to fill the heavy labor needs of the Southwest's agriculture, and erratic U.S. policies. Mexicans were deported when jobs grew scarce during the 1930s" and courted again with the bracero program as labor became short during World War II. Though the bracero program was viewed as a way to stop illegal immigration, it actually served to step up the influx as word got around of jobs to be had across the border. By the 1950s the domestic labor supply was back up to full force, and the INS set out to stanch the illegal flow with "Operation Wetback." (Many Mexicans waded clandestinely across the Rio Grande; hence, "wetback.") At the same time, however, U.S. employers were still allowed to hire illegal entrants who managed to get through. Further illegal Mexican immigration was practically guaranteed by the ending of the bracero program in 1964 and institution of the 120,000-person hemispheric ceiling on immigration in 1968 and the 20,000 per-country limit in 1977. Currently, with unemployment again high in the United States, there is renewed pressure for control of the influx from Mexico, just as pressure mounts on the other side to escape Mexico's deteriorating economy and devalued peso.

Much of the illegal movement from Mexico into the United States is offset by return migration. Workers come north, find jobs, and eventually return to home and family. The Southwest has been the traditional destination for Mexican migrants, but many now make their way as far north as Chicago and Detroit. The farther the search for a job and the more urban the job is, the less likely it is that an undocumented Mexican will move back and forth across the border.

A substantial portion of the other illegal immigrants are from Guatemala, El Salvador, the Dominican Republic, Colombia, Ecuador, and Peru. Many of these are now crossing the Mexican border. Undocumented "other Hispanics," however, more typically enter with a temporary work visa and stay past the expiration date, sticking to large cities to avoid detection. Many Dominicans enter through Puerto Rico. They travel to the island and are virtually unidentifiable among Puerto Ricans in legal transit to the mainland. "Other Hispanic" illegal aliens are more likely than Mexicans to remain in the United States.

How Many?

In the early 1970s, estimates of the number of illegal aliens living in the United States ranged from 2 million to 12 million. Recently a consensus has grown for an estimate of 3.5 million to 6 million, as given in a 1981 report prepared by Census Bureau demographer Jacob Siegel and colleagues for the Select Commission on Immigration and Refugee Policy.[38] A Census Bureau study, unveiled in April 1983, estimated that just over 2 million undocumented persons were included in the 1980 total census count of 226.5 million.[39] This does not reveal how many undocumented residents were missed by the census, but it is difficult to imagine that it was even as many as the number counted, because the Census Bureau made a concerted effort to enumerate the undocumented population and to reach all segments of the Hispanic community.

Of the 2 million, 1.3 million (64 percent) were estimated to be from Latin America. Mexican alone accounted for 931,000. All other Latin American countries with legal immigration to the United States also turn up in the estimate of illegal aliens enumerated in the 1980 census, but none made a substantial contribution.

That the number of illegal aliens arriving each year may be increasing is suggested by figures on deportable aliens apprehended by the INS. This number grew from 420,000 in 1971 to over a million each year in 1977 through 1979, followed by a slight drop to 976,000 in 1981 and 970,000 in 1982.[40] Most apprehensions occur at the Mexican border, where the INS concentrates such efforts. From January through April 1983, there were 377,000 apprehensions at the border, a 46 percent increase over the same period in 1982.[41] Apprehensions, however, are not an accurate count of the actual number of illegal aliens entering each year, since the same person may be apprehended more than once in a year. Nor do they record movements out of the country. Estimates of the annual net increase in the total undocumented population of the United States range from below 100,000 up to 500,000.[42]

Issues and New Legislation

Although the United States has generally approved of immigration as contributing to the country's development, this position may be eroding, according to immigration expert Michael Teitelbaum:

There is a clear risk that growing opposition to immigration and refugee flows that are widely perceived to be excessively large, insufficiently plural, and heavily illegal may overwhelm existing domestic support for a truly humane and generous set of policies.[43]

Particularly sensitive at this time of high unemployment is the claim that illegal aliens take jobs from legal residents, including Hispanics. In fact, many of these jobs are paid so poorly that U.S. workers would not apply. Illegal workers may even promote domestic employment in the sense that they keep alive some manual labor that otherwise might be automated. Some job displacement undoubtedly occurs, but a more important impact on U.S. employment is that illegal workers tend to hold down wages and impede improvements in working conditions. Fearful of deportation, they are characteristically docile and frequently exploited. Some observers believe this lack of access to the rights and protection of the U.S. legal process is the most damaging aspect of illegal immigration. Immigration expert Charles Keely puts it thus: "In terms of its effect on U.S. society, what is likely to prove most disruptive is not the presence of the immigrants but their status as illegal aliens."[44] How better to undermine the fundamental concepts of personal rights, equality of opportunity, and tolerance of cultural diversity than to condone the existence of an illegal underclass? Some direction on this issue was provided by a landmark June 1982 Supreme Court ruling that struck down a Texas law withholding state funds for education of children of illegal aliens. In their decision the justices declared for the first time that illegal aliens are included among persons guaranteed "equal protection of the laws" under the Fourteenth Amendment.

Another concern is the use that illegal aliens make of public services paid for by U.S. taxpayers—welfare payments, unemployment insurance, medical services, public schools. It is known that illegals do use these services to some extent, particularly medical services, but nationwide they may pay more in federal, state, and local taxes than the cost of benefits received. Even if this is true, however, the cost of providing services falls unevenly on such local jurisdictions as Los Angeles County, which had an estimated 300,000-600,000 illegal residents in June 1982.[45]

After years of study and debate by several presidential task forces, congressional commissions, and public interest groups arguing both for and against reform, a comprehensive overhaul of U.S. immigration law appeared to be imminent in June 1983. A highly controversial immigration reform bill was first introduced into Congress by Senator Alan Simpson, Republican of Wyoming, and Representative Romano Mazzoli, Democrat of Kentucky, in 1982. After several years of debate, reformulation, and compromise in Congress, it was finally passed by both houses in 1986 as the Simpson-Rodino bill or the Immigration Reform and Control Act. Even though President Reagan was concerned about the cost of providing services to illegal aliens granted amnesty under the bill, he signed it into law on November 6, 1986.

The general provisions of the new legislation are the following:

- An annual allowance of 350,000 "guest workers" from Mexico to enter this country annually on a temporary basis, but not including refugees, for whom quotas will continue to be set annually by the administration and Congress.
- Penalties for employers who knowingly hire undocumented aliens, and a requirement to verify legal residence before employment.
- Amnesty (legal status) for illegal aliens who entered the United States before January 1, 1982, and who have maintained continuous residence since that date.
- Judicial review for persons ordered to be deported, excluded, or refused asylum under the terms of the legislation.

EDUCATION

Younger Hispanic adults spend more time in school than their elders did, as is now true for all racial and ethnic groups in the United States. But Hispanics still lag behind blacks and far behind whites as a whole in average educational attainment—the key to economic and occupational progress. Some Hispanic groups are more educated than others, however, which reflects differences in immigration histories more than ethnic attitudes toward education.

Cubans, still dominated by the middle-class and professional people who were the first to flee the Castro regime, tend to be better educated than other Hispanics. So, too, are recent legal immigrants from Central and South America. The Mexican-American roots in the United States go far back in history, typically progressing from little education among earlier generations to several college graduates and holders of advanced degrees among the latest generations. However, educational attainment for Mexican-Americans as a whole reflects the much lesser schooling of the majority who are recent legal and illegal immigrants. Average educational attainment is also low for Puerto Ricans, partly stemming from the constant flow back and forth between the island and the mainland. Public education in Puerto Rico suffers from scant funding— just $694 per pupil in 1977—below the $900 of Arkansas, which ranked lowest of U.S. states on this score.[46] Children transferred to schools on the mainland must usually drop to grades lower than the average for their age and often have their schooling disrupted by moves back to the island; some 20,000 pupils a year were transferred back and forth between Puerto Rico and New York City alone during the 1970s. Frustration with the public school system in Puerto Rico prompts many middle- and upper-class professionals to place their children in private schools.

School Enrollment Progress

Hispanics' lesser involvement in education begins early. In 1981, only 25 percent of Spanish-origin three- and four-year-olds were enrolled in school, compared with some 36 percent of both blacks and whites as a whole.[47] These early education programs include public and private nursery schools and Head Start, which are particularly important for children from disadvantaged backgrounds.

Between ages 5 and 15, nearly all Hispanics, along with blacks and whites, attend school, but the gap widens again from age 16, when students are able to leave school legally in most states. In 1981, school enrollment among Hispanics was 83 percent for 16- and 17-year-olds, compared with some 91 percent for blacks and whites, and only 38 percent at ages 18 and 19, in contrast with roughly half for the blacks and whites. Some 36 percent at ages 18 and 19 were not enrolled in school and also were not high school graduates (that is, they were dropouts). This was more than double the figure for whites of that age (16 percent) and almost double that of blacks (19 percent).

Hispanics' high dropout rates are partly due to the fact that many are enrolled in grades below the average for their age, where they can be bored, feel out of place, and be labeled slow learners. In 1976, about 9 percent of Mexican-American and Puerto Rican 8-to-13-year-olds were at least two years behind their "expected" grade in school, compared with 5 percent of white non-Hispanics; at ages 14-20, the figures were 25 percent of Hispanics versus 9 percent for non-Hispanic whites.[48] In New England in the early 1970s, 50 percent of Hispanics were at least two grades behind, and only 12 percent were in their "expected" grade.[49] Delay is particularly serious for transfer students from Puerto Rico; in Boston, for example, students aged 17-19 who were in senior high school in Puerto Rico are often placed in the sixth or seventh grade.

Not surprisingly, Hispanics are much less likely to graduate from high school than are other groups, and the percentage of Hispanic high school graduates who go on to college dropped from 35.4 percent to 29.9 percent between 1975 and 1980.[50]

High School and College Completion

Hispanics aged 25 and over are increasingly likely to be at least high school graduates, like blacks and all white adults, but the gap remains wide, as seen in Figure 1.4. In 1981, 46 percent of Hispanic males, for example, had completed four years of high school or more, up from 33 percent in 1970, but the figure for black males was 53 percent and for white males as a whole, 72 percent. However, younger Hispanics are catching up. Among those aged 25 to 34 in 1981, 47 percent had completed high school. Mexican-Americans and Puerto Rican males have made some gains in high school completion since 1960, according to a study by the U.S. Commission on Civil Rights, but still trailed behind other Hispanic groups as well as blacks and all whites in 1976.[51] There is another gap in high school completion between metropolitan and nonmetropolitan Hispanics; in 1979, only 35 percent of Hispanic adult men living in nonmetropolitan areas had finished high school, compared with 44 percent of men in metropolitan areas.[52]

Scholastic Aptitude Test scores reveal the poorer preparation of Hispanic high school graduates who go on to college. Among entering freshmen in 1979, the average on the verbal part of the test was 356 (out of a possible 800) for Puerto Ricans and 372 for Mexican-Americans, compared with 442 for non-Hispanic whites, and 387 for Puerto Ricans and 413 for Mexican-Americans in math, versus 482 for non-Hispanic whites.[53]

Hispanic college enrollment doubled from 250,000 to 500,000 between 1972 and 1981, but still made up only 4.8 percent of total college enrollment in 1981.[54] Once in college, Hispanics are far more likely than other college students to drop out; 57 percent of Hispanic males and 54 percent of Hispanic females fail to graduate, compared with 34 percent of all white males and females.[55] Figures in 1981 for adults 25 years and over who had completed at least four years of college were only 10 percent for males and 6 percent for females among Hispanics, compared with 22 percent for all white males and 14 percent for white females, and 8 percent for both black males and females.[56] Part of the reason for this disparity is that Hispanic students primarily attend two-year colleges. In 1980, 54 percent of Hispanics enrolled in college, compared with 36 percent of all white students, were attending two-year colleges.[57]

Why the Educational Lag?

Whether he or she was born in the United States makes a difference in a Hispanic's educational attainment. Demographers A. J. Jaffe, Ruth

Figure 1.4
Hispanics, Blacks, Whites, and Total Population Aged 25 and Over
Who Completed Four Years of High School or More: 1970 and 1981

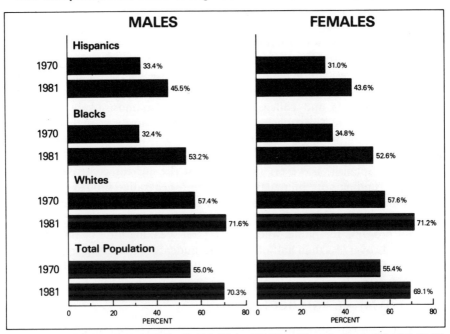

Source: Bureau of the Census, "Population Profile of the United States: 1981," *Current Population Reports*, Series P-20, No. 374, 1982, Table 6-3.

Cullen, and Thomas Boswell found from 1970 census data that Hispanics born in the United States generally attend school longer than their foreign-born parents.[58] Another research team found even greater educational progress between second- and third-generation Mexican-Americans.[59] Thus, like other immigrant groups before them, U.S. Hispanics' educational attainment should improve in time. Meanwhile, there are barriers, as Jaffe and his colleagues point out. "Cultural reinforcement" is one. A constant influx of new arrivals keeps Latin cultural values and the Spanish language alive among Mexican-Americans in the Southwest, Puerto Ricans in the Northeast, and Cubans in Florida, washed by the wave of Marielitos in 1980. A Mexican-American professional in California described how "macho" values can hinder education: "If you drop out [to father a child] or to buy a car, you're a big man. But when I came home with my Ph.D., my friends acted like they didn't know me."[60] Early pregnancy and marriage, poverty that forces teenagers prematurely into the labor force, and the problems of overcrowded, poorly equipped big-city schools that most Hispanics attend also boost dropout rates and discourage education. And, like blacks and unlike earlier immigrant groups, Hispanics in the United States and in its schools have suffered from the discrimination accorded dark-skinned people.

Lack of English clearly retards Hispanics' general educational progress. In 1978, 26 percent of Hispanics in public elementary and secondary schools spoke little or no English.[61] On the other hand, use of Spanish is not necessarily a barrier to education, as proven by Cubans. Though educational levels are generally higher for those who grew up speaking English at home, Cubans, who outpace other Hispanics in high school achievement tests and college entrance, are also most likely to speak Spanish at home. This suggests that factors like more parental education and higher family income determine educational progress more than use of Spanish.[62]

Use of Spanish, however, is an issue in the current controversy over federal funding of bilingual education. Federally funded bilingual programs, in which students are taught academic subjects in their native languages until they can master English, began in 1968 in order to speed school progress for pupils who enter school speaking little or no English. They still cover less than half of Hispanic students in that category; funding was cut from $167 million in fiscal year 1981 to $138 million in 1982.

EMPLOYMENT AND OCCUPATION

From poor education to poor economic and professional standing is but a short step. Though Hispanics' economic status has improved in recent decades, they remain clustered in low-paying blue-collar and semiskilled jobs in fields, like construction and manufacturing, that suffer high seasonal or cyclical unemployment, and thus earn far less and are more likely to be unemployed and live in poverty than the white population as a whole. Again, however, Cubans and Central and South Americans fare better than Mexican-Americans and Puerto Ricans, especially women.

Economist Dennis Roth of the Congressional Research Service points out that Hispanic women aged 20 and over were almost as likely as all adult women to be working or seeking work in 1980 (48.8 percent compared with 51.3 percent), and the labor force participation rate for Hispanic men (85.2 percent) was higher than the rate for all adult men (79.4 percent).[63] But this comparison is misleading. As seen in Table 1.12, within specific age groups, Hispanic women's rates were generally 7.5 to 12 percentage points lower than those of all adult women, and Hispanic men had rates slightly less than those of the total male population, except at ages 20-24 and 55 and over. The overall rates for Hispanics were pushed up because Hispanics are generally younger than the average for the total population, and younger adults are more likely to be in the labor force.

Table 1.12
Labor Force Participation Rates of Hispanics and All
U.S. Adults, by Sex: 1980

| | Percent in labor force | | | |
Age group	All men	Hispanic men	All women	Hispanic women
Total, 20 and over	79.4	85.2	51.3	48.8
20-24	86.0	88.2	69.9	57.1
25-34	95.3	93.5	65.4	53.9
35-44	95.5	94.1	65.5	56.0
45-54	91.2	91.0	59.9	52.0
55-64	72.3	72.5	41.5	32.9
65 and over	19.1	19.4	8.1	4.9

Source: Dennis M. Roth, "Hispanics in the U.S. Labor Force: A Brief Review," in Congressional Research Service, *The Hispanic Population of the United States: An Overview,* report prepared for the Subcommittee on Census and Population of the House Committee on Post Office and Civil Service (Washington,. D.C.: Government Printing Office, 1983) Table 1, p. 60.

Between 1973 and 1981, the number of Hispanic women in the work force surged by 82 percent, outpacing the increase among all women, Roth points out. This was mainly due to an increase in the number of Hispanic women of working age because of continued immigration. But, except for Puerto Ricans, Hispanic women's labor force participation rate also went up nearly nine percentage points—slightly more than that of all women. Meanwhile, the rate for Puerto Rican men dropped more than eight percentage points, while remaining about the same for Hispanic men as a whole. Roth attributes the drop in rates for Puerto Rican men and women to the declining economy in New York City. In 1979, half of all mainland Puerto Ricans of working age lived in New York, where total employment had dropped by 13 percent between 1969 and 1977. By 1982, only 51 percent of adult Puerto Ricans on the mainland were in the labor force, compared with some 62 percent of Cubans and Mexican-Americans, and similar proportions of blacks and all whites.[64] This was primarily due to the low 37 percent of Puerto Rican women who were working or looking for work; among all other women, including Mexican-Americans and Cubans, the figure was about 50 percent.

In an earlier review of Hispanics' work experience, Bureau of Labor

Statistics economist Morris Newman suggests that Puerto Rican women's low labor force participation rate may be a lingering cultural trait—women in Puerto Rico are much less likely to work outside the home than women on the mainland. But this is true of all Latin nations, and yet Mexican women, once in the United States, join the work force in proportions equal to that of all other women, although they are no more educated and have more children than Puerto Rican women, on average.[65]

Unemployment and Underemployment

Hispanics' jobless rate is typically 40 to 50 percent higher than the overall unemployment rate, though not so high as that of blacks, which is usually double the national rate. In the last quarter of 1982, for example, when unemployment rates climbed to the highest levels since the depression of the 1930s, 15.2 percent of Hispanic workers and 20.4 percent of black workers over age 20 were out of work, while the overall unemployment rate for adults was 10.7 percent.[66]

As might be expected, Puerto Ricans have the highest unemployment rate among Hispanics and Cubans the lowest. Dennis Roth credits Cubans' lower rate to their better education and older age—60 percent of Cuban workers are over 35, compared with 36 percent of Puerto Ricans—and joblessness is usually lower among more mature, stable, experienced older workers.

A study by the U.S. Commission on Civil Rights of minorities' work experience from 1971 to 1980 shows that Hispanic men and women— along with blacks and non-Hispanic white women—are more likely to be underemployed than "majority" non-Hispanic white men, and to have higher unemployment rates.[67] Hispanic men and women are more likely than "majority" males to have to accept part-time work when they would rather work full-time. Hispanic men are also more likely to be employed on and off, receive poverty wages, and be overeducated for their jobs, while more Hispanic women than any other minority group are paid inequitably.

Occupations

In 1981, as in earlier years, Hispanic workers were more concentrated in lower-paid, less-skilled occupations than the overall work force. More than 75 percent of employed Mexican-American, Puerto Rican, and Cuban women were clerical workers, machine operators, or "nontransport operatives" (service workers)—three of the lowest-paid occupations— compared with less than two-thirds of all women workers (see Table 1.13). Although the large percentage of Hispanic women employed in clerical positions is similar to that of all working women, their heavy concentration in operatives jobs—dressmakers, assemblers, packers, graders, and the

Table 1.13

Occupations of Hispanic and All Workers, by Sex: 1981

(Numbers in percent of total workers, by sex)

Occupation	All workers		Total Hispanics		Mexican American		Puerto Rican		Cuban	
	Men	Women	Men	Women	Men	Women	Men	Women	Men	Women
Professional and technical	15.9	17.0	7.7	8.8	5.7	8.0	8.5	11.6	12.9	9.9
Managers, Administrators	14.6	7.4	7.8	4.7	6.3	4.3	6.9	6.1	14.5	5.5
Sales	6.1	6.8	3.1	5.1	2.6	5.2	2.6	3.0	6.2	4.9
Clerical	6.3	34.7	6.4	31.9	5.0	32.4	13.1	36.4	9.4	31.9
Craft and kindred workers	20.7	1.9	20.1	2.4	20.9	2.5	15.4	2.5	20.7	2.2
Operatives, except transport	11.1	9.7	18.9	22.0	20.2	21.6	20.6	25.8	12.5	29.7
Transport equipment operatives	5.5	0.7	6.6	0.4	6.8	0.5	6.2	0.5	6.6	—
Nonfarm laborers	7.1	1.3	10.9	1.6	12.7	2.2	8.5	0.5	7.4	1.1
Service workers	8.9	19.4	13.3	21.4	12.2	21.1	17.6	13.1	9.4	14.8
Farm workers	3.9	1.1	5.2	1.6	7.5	2.5	0.3	0.5	0.4	—

Source: Roth, "Hispanics in the U.S. Labor Force" (see Table 1.12), Tables 5 and 6.

like—is striking. Nearly 30 percent of Cuban women, about one-quarter of Puerto Rican women, and more than one-fifth of Mexican-American women worked at these jobs in 1981, compared with one-tenth of all women. Interestingly, Puerto Rican and Cuban women were less likely than women in general to work in services—as cleaners, housekeepers, restaurant helpers, and such.

Among men, Cubans were nearly as likely as all men to be employed in professional and technical jobs or as managers and administrators—27 percent compared with 31 percent. The percentages for Mexican-Americans (12.0) and Puerto Ricans (15.4) in these two highest-paid fields were less than half or barely half the Cuban rate, probably due mostly to their relative youthfulness and low educational attainment. Puerto Rican men were most likely to work in nontransport operatives jobs (21 percent), with large proportions employed as service workers and craft workers. Among Mexican-American and Cuban men, craft jobs were most prevalent, with services and operatives jobs also employing many individuals. Mexican-Americans are often stereotyped as farm workers but, in fact, only 8 percent of employed Mexican-American men were recorded as farm workers in 1981. However, this was double the 4 percent for all male workers in the United States. Probably, also, the actual number of Mexican-American farm workers is understated in the Census Bureau's *Current Population Survey,* which collects these data; illegal immigrants, many of whom work in the fields, probably avoid interviews, and migrant farm workers are hard to locate.[68]

Though Hispanics remain underrepresented in more-skilled, higher-paying occupations, their occupational status has improved since 1973—the earliest year for which suitable data are available—though more for women than for men. Between 1973 and 1981, the proportion of Hispanic men employed as professionals, technicians, managers, and craft workers (which includes often well-paid jobs as construction workers and mechanics) rose from 32 percent to 36 percent, and the percentage of machine operators and farm workers declined. For women there was a similar but more marked shift, plus an increase in clerical workers.

Hispanics have been sharing these shifts with all U.S. workers as lower-skilled, blue-collar jobs lose out to automation and white-collar office jobs increase. However, Roth notes that "Generally speaking, Hispanics improved their labor market status relative to the improvement made by all workers," and observes: "It does appear that Hispanics will be able to further improve their occupational status in the U.S. if past trends continue."[69] Marked improvement, however, will require a gain in Hispanics' educational attainment rapid enough both to narrow the gap with increasingly highly educated white non-Hispanics and to meet the demands of the high-technology age.

INCOME AND POVERTY

If Hispanic workers improved their occupational status relative to all U.S. workers during the 1970s, this gain has not yet shown up in family income statistics. In 1972, the median Hispanic family income was 71 percent of the median for white families, as seen in Table 1.14, which measures Hispanic-white differentials in median family income since 1972 in constant 1981 dollars. In 1981, the median for Hispanic families ($16,401) was just 70 percent of the median for white families as a whole ($23,517) after two years of recession had reduced real incomes for all families. Hispanics fare better than blacks, however, whose median family income in 1981 ($13,266) was just 56 percent of the median for white families, down from 59 percent in 1972. Like blacks, Hispanics' family income must stretch further than that of white families, for family sizes are generally larger. Hispanics' relative youthfulness also depresses family

Table 1.14
Median Income of Hispanic, Black, and White Families: 1972-81 (in constant 1981 dollars)

Year	Median family income			Hispanic family income as percent of white income
	Hispanic	Black	White	
1972	17,790	14,922	25,107	71
1973	17,836	14,877	25,777	69
1974	17,594	14,765	24,728	71
1975	16,140	14,835	24,110	67
1976	16,390	14,766	24,823	66
1977	17,141	14,352	25,124	68
1978	17,518	15,166	25,606	68
1979	18,255	14,590	25,689	71
1980	16,242	13,989	24,176	67
1981	16,401	13,266	23,517	70

Source: Bureau of the Census, "Money Income and Poverty Status of Families and Persons in the United State: 1981 (Advance Data from the March 1982 Current Population Survey)," *Current Population Reports*, Series P-60, No. 134, July 1982, Table 3.

income statistics—younger householders, in general, earn less than older ones.

Hispanics do better when both husband and wife work. In 1981, the median family income for such families was $23,641, almost 80 percent of the median of $29,713 of all married-couple white families with the wife in the paid labor force.[70] The biggest difference in Hispanic-white family income levels comes in female-headed families. In 1981, 23 percent of Hispanic families were headed by a female alone—double the 12 percent among all white families—and their median income ($7586) was just 60 percent of the median income of $12,508 of female-headed families among all whites.

Cubans, as might be expected, have the highest incomes of all Hispanic groups. In 1979, their median family income was $17,538, 86 percent of the white median of $20,502. This was close to double the Puerto Rican median of $9,855, which was the lowest among Hispanic families, and well below the black family median of $11,644.[71] Mexican-American and Central and South American families had intermediate and similar median incomes— $15,171 and $15,470, respectively.

Poverty

In 1981, close to 800,000 Hispanic families—24 percent of all Hispanic families—in the United States were classified as "poor" by the Census Bureau, compared with 8.8 percent of all white families (see Table 1.15). The Census Bureau's poverty threshold varies by family size and age of householder, and is adjusted annually for inflation. It is based only on money income and does not take account of the benefits received by many low-income persons, such as food stamps, Medicaid and Medicare, and housing aid. (In 1981, the average poverty threshold for a family of four was $9287.) On this score, too, Hispanics do better than blacks; nearly 31 percent of black families fell below the poverty threshold in 1981. Also, the rise in the poverty rate was a little less for Hispanics than for other families from 1979 to 1981, as the recession deepened and unemployment rose. However, Hispanic families were still 2.7 times as likely as all white families to be living in poverty in 1981, only marginally improved from the differential in 1973 (3.0), when poverty statistics for the Hispanic population were first calculated.

Thus the statistics for the decade 1973-83 show Hispanics as a group still trailing well behind the general U.S. population on all measures of social and economic well-being. But a decade is hardly time enough to measure genuine progress. The higher educational attainment of younger Hispanics holds out hope that more Hispanics in general, and not just Cubans, will be joining the higher-paid, white-collar work force in the future. And as they do, income levels should increase and unemployment rates fall, along with

Table 1.15
Poverty Rate of Hispanic, Black, and White Families: 1973-81

Year	Percent of families below poverty level			Ratio of Hispanic to white poverty rate
	Hispanic	Black	White	
1973	19.8	28.1	6.6	3.0
1974	21.2	26.9	6.8	3.1
1975	25.1	27.1	7.7	3.3
1976	23.1	27.9	7.1	3.3
1977	21.4	28.2	7.0	3.1
1978	20.4	27.5	6.9	3.0
1979	20.3	27.8	6.9	2.9
1980	23.2	28.9	8.0	2.9
1981	24.0	30.8	8.8	2.7

Source: Bureau of the Census, "Money Income and Poverty Status: 1981" (see Table 1.14), Table 15.

poverty rates. Even with their present income lag behind the general U.S. population, Antonio Guernica and Irene Kasperuk note in *Reaching the Hispanic Market Effectively* that "Hispanics in the United States are the wealthiest Hispanics in the world. The opportunity for economic improvement is the primary reason why legal and illegal Hispanic immigration to the United States continues unabated."[72]

HISPANICS IN AMERICA'S FUTURE

"The one demographic trend above all others that will mold the future of the Hispanic community through the 1980s and beyond is its numerical growth," Guernica and Kasperuk assert.

The table at the bottom of Figure 1.5 presents two sets of projections from 1980 to 2000 and 2020 for the total U.S. population and the four main racial and ethnic groups: white non-Hispanics, blacks, Hispanics, and Asians and others. The chart at the top shows Hispanic population growth based on these projections. The projections are not predictions of U.S. population growth; rather, they present population size as it might be in 2000 and 2020, given reasonable assumptions about fertility, mortality, and immigration experience in this 40-year period.

The first set of projections assumes that annual net immigration to the United States will average 500,000 a year. This is below the net immigration

Figure 1.5
Population 1980 and as Projected for 2000 and 2020: Hispanics, Total U.S. Population, and Four Main Racial/Ethnic Groups

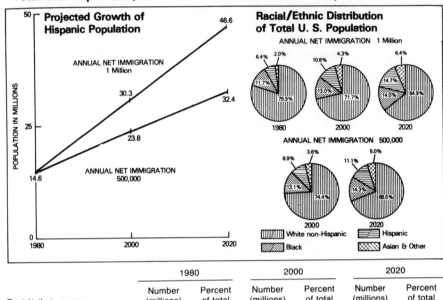

	1980		2000		2020	
Racial/ethnic group	Number (millions)	Percent of total	Number (millions)	Percent of total	Number (millions)	Percent of total
			Annual net immigration = 500,000			
Total U.S. population	226.5	100.0	267.4	100.1	291.5	100.0
White non-Hispanic	181.0	79.9	198.9	74.4	202.7	69.5
Black	26.5	11.7	35.2	13.1	41.7	14.3
Hispanic	14.6	6.4	23.8	8.9	32.4	11.1
Asian and other	4.4	2.0	9.5	3.6	14.7	5.0
			Annual net immigration = 1 million			
Total U.S. population			279.1	100.0	316.9	100.0
White non-Hispanic			200.3	71.7	205.6	64.9
Black			36.4	13.0	44.4	14.0
Hispanic			30.3	10.8	46.6	14.7
Asian and other			12.1	4.3	20.3	6.4

Source: Leon F. Bouvier and Cary B. Davis, *The Future Racial Composition of the United States* (Washington, D.C.: Demographic Informatioin Services Center of the Population Reference Bureau, 1982).

average of 600,000 per year in 1979-81, when refugees from southeast Asia and the sudden influx of Cubans and Haitians in 1980 inflated the number admitted legally to the United States. But it is about what the average will be now that the Immigration Reform and Control Act has been passed with a cap on annual immigrants and if it is rigorously implemented, and allowance is made for refugees. The assumption of 1 million net immigration per year in the second set of projections may appeal to those who wish to add net illegal immigration of at least 500,000 a year—the upper limit of recent net illegal immigration estimates. Both sets of projections assume that the fertility of all racial/ethnic groups will converge in 2030 at the current national average of 1.8 children per woman; for Hispanics, the starting point (1980) was set at about 2.6 children per woman.

With net immigration at 500,000 per year, the Hispanic population is projected to grow to about 32 million and 11 percent of the total U.S. population in 2020. With net immigration at 1 million a year, Hispanics could number some 47 million and nearly 15 percent of the total in 2020, overtaking blacks as the country's largest minority. If all immigration had ceased in 1980, we project the Hispanics would number 24 million in 2020. This is a substantial 9.4 million increase over the 14.6 million of 1980 that would be due solely to the natural increase (births minus deaths) stemming from Hispanics already in the United States in 1980, but far below what the totals would be with the addition of immigrants arriving after 1980 and their subsequent natural increase.

How likely are these projections to materialize? Potential fluctuations in immigration (as well as fertility) make this impossible to tell. Although net immigration of Puerto Ricans dwindled to a trickle in the 1970s, their immigration remains unrestricted and could surge upward again if the island's economy deteriorates and prospects on the mainland improve. Refugee influxes from Cuba depend on the vagaries of Cuban—and U.S.—policy. While immigration from Mexico and other Spanish-speaking countries of Latin America does fall under the control of U.S. immigration law, the open-ended family reunification clause currently allows for more arrivals than the 20,000 per-country annual limit. This will probably change with the passing of the New Immigration Act, but there remains the murky question of illegal immigration.

The ethnic mix of the Hispanic population should remain relatively stable for the remainder of this century, although Hispanics from countries other than Mexico, Cuba, and Puerto Rico may increase their share of the population somewhat. Here, too, the big unknowns are unregulated immigration from Puerto Rico and illegal immigration, as well as changes in U.S. immigration law.

Whatever their future numbers, Hispanics are already a growing force in American society. There are now 14 Hispanic congressmen,[73] one state governor (Bob Martínez of Florida), and Hispanic mayors in Denver, Miami, and San Antonio; and groups like the Southwest Voter Registration Project in San Antonio are working to get out more of the Hispanic vote. Only 30 percent of Hispanics of voting age cast ballots in the 1980 presidential election, compared with the national figure of 59 percent— down from 38 percent in 1972. Hispanics' political and social influence is marshaled by such organizations as the Mexican-American Legal Defense and Educational Fund (MALDEF), the Puerto Rican Legal Defense and Education Fund (PRLDEF), the National Council of La Raza, and the

League of United Latin American Citizens. There are numerous TV and radio stations broadcasting full-time in Spanish and hundred of others scheduling ten or more hours a week in Spanish. And U.S. business has discovered the Hispanic market: J. Walter Thompson and other leading advertising agencies now have Hispanic units; Safeway, Jewel, and other supermarket chains stock Hispanic culinary specialties; and Mattel markets a Hispanic version of a variety of toys.

Many questions about the impact of the growing Hispanic population will be answered only with the passage of time. Will Hispanics assimilate into the U.S. "melting pot" as other immigrant ethnic groups have before them? How much of their identity as a group will they wish to maintain? Whatever the outcome, their arrival has changed the face of America once again.

NOTES

1. W. Fernández and N. McKenney, "Identification of the Hispanic Population: A Review of Census Bureau Experience," unpublished paper of the Population Division, Bureau of the Census, 1980.

2. Bureau of the Census, "Persons of Spanish Origin," *1970 Census of Population,* Subject Reports, PC(2)-1C (1973); and Jacob S. Siegel and Jeffrey S. Passel, "Coverage of the Hispanic Population in the United States 1970 Census," *Current Population Reports,* Special Studies, Series P-23, no. 8w (1979).

3. Select Commission on Immigration and Refugee Policy, *U.S. Immigration Policy and the National Interest* (Washington, DC: U.S. Government Printing Office, 1981).

4. U.S. Commission on Civil Rights, *Puerto Ricans in the Continental United States: An Uncertain Future* (Washington, DC: U.S. Government Printing Office, 1976).

5. Lisandro Pérez, "Cubans," in *Harvard Encyclopedia of American Ethnic Groups* (Cambridge, MA: Belknap Press of Harvard University, 1980).

6. Unpublished tables of immigrants by country of birth, 1950-79, obtained from Immigration and Naturalization Service, Statistics Branch.

7. Bureau of the Census, "Persons of Spanish Origin."

8. Bureau of the Census, "Persons of Spanish Origin in the United States: March 1980 (Advance Report)," *Current Population Reports,* Series P-20, no. 361 (1981), Table 1.

9. Bureau of the Census, "Persons of Spanish Origin by State: 1980," *1980 Census of Population,* Supplementary Report PC80-S1-7 (August 1982).

10. The 14.6 million figure for 1980 is undoubtedly an undercount of Hispanics actually in the United States on April 1, 1980, but the Census Bureau has not yet completed its analysis of this undercount. For 1970, the Bureau estimated that the undercount for Hispanics fell somewhere between that of the white population (1.9 percent) and that of the black population (7.7 percent).

11. Bureau of the Census, *1980 Census of Population, General Population Characteristics,* PC80-1B, various state issues.

12. Immigration and Naturalization Service, annual report, various years.

13. Bureau of the Census, *State and Metropolitan Area Data Book: 1982* (Washington, DC: U.S. Government Printing Office, 1982), Table A.

14. Martin O'Connell and Carolyn Rogers, "Differential Fertility in the United States: 1876-1980," *Family Planning Perspectives* 14, no. 5 (September/October 1982): Table 1, p. 284.

15. Stephanie J. Ventura, "Births of Hispanic Parentage, 1979," *Monthly Vital Statistics Report* 31, no. 2, supplement (May 1982): p. 2; personal communication, June 1983.

16. Ventura, "Births of Hispanic Parentage," p. 3.

17. Population Reference Bureau, *1983 World Population Data Sheet* (Washington, DC: Population Reference Bureau, 1983).

18. Instituto Mexicano del Seguro Social, *Fecundidad y uso de métodos anticonceptivos en México* (Mexico City: The Institute, May 1981).

19. Roger W. Rochat et al., "Family Planning Practices Among Anglo and Hispanic Women in U.S Counties Bordering Mexico," *Family Planning Perspectives* 13, no. 4 (July/August 1981): 176-80.

20. Ronald R. Rindfuss and James S. Sweet, *Postwar Fertility Trends and Differentials in the United States* (New York: Academic Press, 1977); Centers for Disease Control, *Texas Fertility, 1950-1977: Childbearing Patterns and Trends* (Atlanta: CDC, 1980).

21. Fernando Trevino, "Vital and Health Statistics for the U.S. Hispanic Population," *American Journal of Public Health* 72, no. 9 (September 1982): 979-83.

22. Siegel and Passel, "Coverage of the Hispanic Population in the United States 1970 Census."

23. Benjamin S. Bradshaw and Edwin Fonner, Jr., "The Mortality of Spanish-Surnamed Persons in Texas: 1969-71," in Frank D. Bean and W. Parker Frisbie (eds.), *The Demography of Racial and Ethnic Groups* (New York: Academic Press, 1978); R. Schoen and V. E. Nelson, "Mortality by Cause Among Spanish-Surnamed Californians: 1969-71," *Social Science Quarterly* 62, no. 2 (June 1981): 259-74.

24. Francis P. Gillespie and Teresa A. Sullivan, "What Do Current Estimates of Hispanic Mortality Really Tell Us?" paper presented at the annual meeting of the Population Association of America, Pittsburgh, April 1983.

25. Bureau of the Census, *Statistical Abstract of the United States: 1982-83* (Washington, DC: U.S. Government Printing Office, 1982), Table 106, p. 71.

26. Bureau of the Census, "Persons of Spanish Origin in the United States: March 1979," *Current Population Reports,* Series P-20, no. 354 (1980), Table 18.

27. Bureau of the Census, "Household and Family Characteristics: March 1981," *Current Population Reports,* Series P-20, no. 371 (1982), Table 18.

28. Bureau of the Census, "Marital Status and Living Arrangements: March 1981," *Current Population Reports,* Series P-20, no. 372 (1982), Table C.

29. Leon F. Bouvier, "Immigration and Its Impact on U.S. Society," *Population Trends and Public Policy*, no. 2 (Washington, DC: Population Reference Bureau, 1981).

30. Elaine M. Murphy and Patricia Cancellier, "Immigration: Questions and Answers" (Washington, DC: Population Reference Bureau, 1982), p. 1.

31. Robert W. Fox, Inter-American Development Bank, personal communication, June 1983.

32. Population Reference Bureau, *1983 World Population Data Sheet.*

33. Mary Barberis, "Hispanic America," *Editorial Research Reports* 11, no. 4 (July 30, 1982): 561-62.

34. Sergio Díaz-Briquets and Lisandro Pérez, "Cuba: The Demography of Revolution," *Population Bulletin* 36, no. 2 (April 1981): 2-41.

35. U.S. Department of Health and Human Services, *Cuban-Haitian Task Force, Monthly Extract Data Report for March 1981*, Table 7.

36. Díaz-Briquets and Pérez, "Cuba," p. 31.

37. Michael S. Teitelbaum, "Right Versus Right: Immigration and Refugee Policy in the United States," *Foreign Affairs* 59, no. 1 (Fall 1980): 23.

38. Jacob S. Siegel et al., "Preliminary Review of Existing Studies of the Number of Illegal Residents in the United States," prepared by Bureau of the Census for the staff of the Select Commission of on Immigration and Refugee Policy, January 30, 1981.

39. Robert Warren and Jeffrey Passel, "Estimates of Illegal Aliens from Mexico Counted in the 1980 United States Census," paper presented at the annual meeting of the Population Association of America, Pittsburgh, April 1983.

40. Immigration and Naturalization Service, *1979 Statistical Yearbook,* Table 23; personal communication, June 1983.

41. Robert Pear, "Immigration Reform Is Alive and Well," *New York Times,* May 22, 1983.

42. David Heer, "What Is the Annual Net Flow of Undocumented Mexican Immigrants to the United States?" *Demography* 16, no. 3 (August 1979): 417-22; Charles B. Keely, "Illegal Immigration," *Scientific American,* 246, no. 3 (March 1982): 41; Teitelbaum, "Right Versus Right," p. 25.

43. Teitelbaum, "Right Versus Right," p. 44.

44. Keely, "Illegal Immigration," p. 46.

45. *Wall Street Journal,* June 16, 1982, cited in Barberis, "Hispanic America," p. 566.

46. Frank Bonilla and Ricardo Campos, "A Wealth of Poor: Puerto Ricans in the New Economic Order," *Daedalus* (Spring 1981): 163.

47. Bureau of the Census, "School Enrollment—Social and Economic Characteristics of Students: October 1981 (Advance Report)," *Current Population Reports*, Series P-20, no. 373 (February 1983).

48. National Center for Education Statistics (NCES), *The Condition of Education for Hispanic Americans* (Washington, DC: NCES, 1981), Table 2.21.

49. U.S. Commission on Civil Rights, *Puerto Ricans*, p. 101.

50. Rafael J. Magallan, "Hispanics: Resume/Overview," Council for Advancement and Support of Education, *CASE Currents* (April 1983): 9.

51. U.S. Commission on Civil Rights, *Social Indicators of Equality for Minorities and Women* (Washington, DC: The Commission, 1978).

52. Frank A. Fratoe, *The Education of Nonmetro Hispanics,* Rural Development Research Report no. 31 (Washington, DC: Economic Research Service, U.S. Department of Agriculture, 1981), Table 4.

53. Richard P. Duran, *Hispanics' Education and Background: Predictors of College Achievement* (New York: College Entrance Examination Board, 1983), p. 59.

54. Bureau of the Census, "School Enrollment . . . October 1981."

55. Magallan, "Hispanics: . . . Overview," p. 9.

56. Bureau of the Census, "Population Profile of the United States: 1981," *Current Population Reports,* Series P-20, no. 374 (September 1982), Table 6-3.

57. Magallan, "Hispanics: . . . Overview," p. 9.

58. A. J. Jaffe, Ruth M. Cullen, and Thomas D. Boswell, *The Changing Demography of Spanish Americans* (New York: Academic Press, 1980), p. 33.

59. L. Grebler, J. M. Moore, and R. C. Guzmán, *The Mexican-American People* (New York: Free Press, 1970), p. 149.

60. Quoted in Marilyn Chase, "Latins Rise in Numbers in U.S. but Don't Win Influence or Affluence," *Wall Street Journal,* June 9, 1982.

61. NCES, *Condition of Education for Hispanic Americans.*

62. Duran, *Hispanics' Education and Background,* p. 109; Susan H. Boren, "Education of Hispanics: Access and Achievement," in Congressional Research Service, *The Hispanic Population of the United States: An Overview,* report prepared for the Subcommittee on Census and Population of the House Committee on Post Office and Civil Service (Washington, DC: U.S. Government Printing Office, 1983), pp. 26-27.

63. Dennis M. Roth, "Hispanics in the U.S. Labor Force: A Brief Examination," in Congressional Research Service, *Hispanic Population of the United States,* p. 59.

64. U.S. Department of Labor, Bureau of Labor Statistics, *Employment and Earnings* (January 1983): Table 45.

65. Morris J. Newman, "A Profile of Hispanics in the U.S. Work Force," *Monthly Labor Review* 101, no. 12 (December 1978): 5.

66. Michael A. Urquhart and Marilyn A. Hewson, "Unemployment Continued to Rise in 1982 as Recession Deepened," *Monthly Labor Review* 106, no. 2 (February 1983): Table 3, p. 8.

67. Henry A. Gordon, Constance A. Hamilton, and Havens C. Tipps, *Unemployment and Underemployment Among Blacks, Hispanics, and Women* (Washington, DC: U.S. Commission on Civil Rights, 1982), pp. 56-57.

68. Newman, "Profile of Hispanics in the U.S. Work Force," p. 11.

69. Roth, "Hispanics in the U.S. Labor Force," pp. 69, 72.

70. Bureau of the Census, "Money Income and Poverty Status of Families and Persons in the United States: 1981 (Advance Data from the March 1982 Current Population Survey)," *Current Population Reports,* Series P-60, no. 134 (July 1982), Table 1.

71. Bureau of the Census, "Persons of Spanish Origin in the United States: March 1980 (Advance Report)," *Current Population Reports,* Series P-20, no. 361 (May 1981), Table 1.

72. Quoted in Cheryl Russell, "The News About Hispanics," *American Demographics,* 5, no. 3 (March 1983): 24.

73. The congressmen are Robert García (D-New York), Kika de la Garza (D-Texas), Henry González (D-Texas), Manuel Luján, Jr. (R-New Mexico), Matthew Martínez Jr. (D-California), Salomon Ortiz (D-Texas), Bill Richardson (D-New Mexico), Edward Roybal (D-California), Esteban Torres (D-California), Albert Bustamante (D-Texas), Tony Coello (D-California), Jaime Fuster (D-Puerto Rico), Ben Blass (R-Guam), and Ron de Lugo (D-Virgin Islands).

2

New York Hispanics:
A Demographic Overview

Douglas T. Gurak

INTRODUCTION

New York City is synonymous with change in almost any area one may choose to examine. One element of this change has been the relative and absolute growth of the city's Hispanic population. The 1980 census showed an increase of over 300,000 since 1970. This increase occurred in the midst of an overall decline in the city's population. Perhaps of greater importance is the fact that the composition of the Hispanic population underwent a major transformation: during the 1970s the Puerto Rican population essentially stayed at its 1970 level, while the numbers of Dominicans, Colombians, and other South and Central Americans increased dramatically.

In 1980, the Puerto Rican population was 860,552, according to the New York census. This number reflected a net loss due to migration and a corresponding gain due to natural increase. These two effects essentially canceled each other, leaving the loci of Hispanic growth in the city to other groups. Table 2.1 provides a rough breakdown of the census counts of major Hispanic ethnic groups in New York. Puerto Ricans still make up around 60 percent of the city's Hispanic population. That percentage will continue to decline as long as the current strong immigration of Dominicans and South and Central Americans continues.

The recency of arrival of the non-Puerto Rican immigrants can be seen more clearly by examining the generational status and year of immigration

This chapter is based on a paper presented at the conference "The Changing Hispanic Community" at SUNY-Albany (April 1985). It also appeared in Lester B. Brown, John Oliver, and J. Jorge Klor de Alva, eds., *Sociocultural and Service Issues in Working with Hispanic American Clients* (Albany, N.Y.: Rockefeller College Press, 1985). Reprinted with author's and publisher's permission.

Table 2.1
Distribution of New York City's Hispanic Population According to the 1980 Census

Group by Origin or Descent:	Number	Percent
Total	1,406,024	100.0
Puerto Rican	860,552	61.2
Cuban	60,930	4.3
Mexican	22,577	1.6
Other Hispanic:	461,965	32.9
(Dominican)	(119,965)	(8.5)
(Colombian)	(42,986)	(3.0)
("Other")	(299,014)	(21.3)

Source: Mann and Salvo, 1984.

of the foreign-born for several Hispanic ethnic groups. While 48 percent of Puerto Ricans in New York were born in Puerto Rico (see Table 2.2), 66.5 percent of non-Puerto Rican Hispanics were foreign-born in 1980. Dominicans and Colombians are quite concentrated in the foreign-born generation: 74.9 percent of the former and 81.4 percent of the latter were born outside the United States. Also, 61.7 percent of foreign-born Dominicans have arrived in the United States since 1965; the corresponding figure for Colombians is 67 percent. The recency of arrival is further emphasized if we look only at the most mobile age range of 20-45 (82.4 percent and 92.7 percent, respectively, have arrived since 1965).

Looking beyond the proportion of foreign-born, one should note that several of the Hispanic groups are present in quite large numbers. For example, Dominicans, Cubans, and Colombians, to mention only those we know the most about at present, constitute large communities with social and economic lives that display a great degree of independence from the Puerto Rican community. Each Hispanic ethnic group has developed distinct patterns of adaptation in areas such as residential settlement patterns and economic activity. In the pages that follow, Hispanic diversity with respect to social and economic factors is described in some detail. In New York City, this diversity is underlined by the distinct residential settlement patterns of Puerto Ricans, Dominicans, Cubans, Colombians, and other South Americans. Puerto Ricans are most heavily settled in Brooklyn and the Bronx. Insofar as concentrations of Colombians exist, they are in Queens. Cubans and many South Americans are quite dispersed

Table 2.2
Age, Sex Composition, Generational Status and Percent Immigrated since 1965 for Hispanic Groups in New York City: 1980 and 1981

	Puerto Rican	Other Hispanic	Dominican	Colombian
Median Age	25.4	26.7	25.4 (31.0)	29.9 (32.0)
Percent Female	56.0	55.1	55.8 (60.0)	55.0 (53.8)
Percent Foreign Or Puerto Rican Born	48.0	66.5	74.9 (100.0)	81.4 (100.0)
Percent Immigrated Since 1965	—	79.6	61.7 (82.4)	67.0 (92.7)

Source: Derived from Mann and Salvo (1984) analysis of 1980 U.S. Census PUMS data. Figures in parentheses are from Gurak 1981 Survey of Dominican and Colombian Immigrants in New York City, foreign born only.

throughout the metropolitan region. Dominicans are heavily concentrated in the northern half of Manhattan and in Queens. While Puerto Ricans, along with Dominicans, reside in Manhattan in large numbers, the Dominican and Puerto Rican locales are quite distinct. All of this does not mean that members of different Hispanic groups do not get along with each other. They do have many close ties. Nevertheless, they also have distinct cultures and distinct histories that include entering the United States in distinct historical periods. These periods vary in many ways, and the conditions of the housing markets in distinct areas of the city represent one of these differences.

A common error one can make when assessing the status of Hispanics in the United States or in a region such as New York is ignoring the tremendous diversity that distinguishes Hispanic ethnic groups. Important commonalities exist well beyond the realm of language, but a brief examination of factors such as family structure, fertility, education, labor force activity, and degree of integration into North American society clearly reinforces the view that country-of-origin differences exist and have been magnified by selectivity mechanisms in the migration process.

New York provides an excellent vehicle for the examination of this diversity. Not only is the population large and diverse in terms of national origins, but it also provides a counterweight to images of the Hispanic population of the United

States produced by focusing on the Mexican population. The 1980 census counted only 22,577 Mexicans in New York City.

The comments that follow are not meant to argue for any particular position. Having mentioned diversity, it is left to the reader to determine whether too much is being made of differences and not enough of similarities. The conclusion will, and should, be influenced by the purposes underlying the examination. This chapter is unabashedly descriptive, focusing primarily on major demographic and socioeconomic aspects of the largest Hispanic groups in New York. It will close with a brief examination of structural integration.

The groups to be examined are categorized as follows. Puerto Ricans and all non-Puerto Rican Hispanics ("other Hispanics") form two principal categories. The data source for these two groups consists of tabulations from the 1980 U.S. Census produced from public use microdata and summary tape files by Mann and Salvo (1984). That same source provides some data on Dominicans and Colombians, though these tabulations are less detailed. Since Dominicans and Colombians represent two of the larger and faster-growing recent immigrant groups, it was clearly desirable to provide more detail on them. This was done by producing similar tabulations from a 1981 probability survey of Dominican and Colombian immigrants residing in Queens and Manhattan. That survey is restricted to first-generation individuals aged 20-45. Hence some variations will be due to data base differences. Nevertheless, the Census and survey tabulations that should be similar, generally are. It should be noted that the survey data were generated to permit a more in-depth analysis of the migration and integration experience than can be produced from Census data. Consequently, the chapter does not make full use of the data's potential.

FAMILY COMPOSITION AND FERTILITY

Many social forces mold the basic structure of the family environment. These include secular trends involving factors such as a rising divorce rate for all sectors of society, but also special forces experienced by minorities living in disadvantaged social and economic conditions. Beyond these factors, long-distance migration can reasonably be assumed to affect the composition of families and households. Table 2.3 provides information on the distributions of six major types of family configurations: married couples, with and without children present; males without spouse present, with and without children; and females without spouse present, with and without children. This is done for each of the four categories of Hispanic groups.

Among families with children present, the married-couple family clearly predominates. Fully 83 percent of Colombian families with own children 18 years of age or less present are of the married-couple type. This is true for only 58.4 percent of similar Dominican families, and only 46.8 percent of children-present Puerto Rican families. The range of more than 36 percentage points is striking. It becomes all the more striking when it is noted that there exists a

Table 2.3
**Percent Distributions of Family Type and Presence of Children
(a) for Puerto Ricans, Other Hispanics, Dominicans, and
Colombians: New York City, 1980 and 1981**

	Puerto Rican (b)	Other (b) Hispanic	Dominican (c)	Colombian (c)
Total Families (d)	100.0	100.0	100.0	100.0
With Own Children	100.0	100.0	100.0	100.0
W/O Own Children	100.0	100.0	100.0	100.0
Married Couple				
Families	51.3	61.5	47.7	54.9
With Own Children	46.8	61.9	58.4	83.0
W/O Own Children	61.1	61.0	33.2	24.3
Male Householder				
(No Spouse)	5.2	6.4	17.7	22.3
With Own Children	3.3	3.3	2.5	2.7
W/O Own Children	9.5	12.0	39.9	44.7
Female Householder				
(No Spouse)	43.5	32.1	34.6	41.5
With Own Children	49.8	34.9	40.3	16.1
W/O Own Children	29.4	27.1	27.4	31.7

(a) Own children consist of those in household and less than 18 years old.

(b) Puerto Rican and Other Hispanic Columns are 1980 Census figures from Mann and Slavo (1984).

(c) Dominican and Colombian columns are from 1981 Gurak survey of Dominicans and Colombians in New York City.

(d) Columns of corresponding rows add to 100 percent. For example, the last three "With Own Children" figures within any column add to 100 percent.

complementary difference in the incidence of female householders with own children. The percentage of families with children that are headed by a woman without a spouse present ranges from 16.1 percent for Colombians to 49.8 percent for Puerto Ricans.

The high incidence of female-headed households among Puerto Ricans is not news, though the actual percentage is always startling. The relatively high incidence among Dominican women (40.3 percent of families with children) represents a datum that is not widely known. The range of incidence among Hispanics clearly demonstrates that much more than being Hispanic or the interaction of being Hispanic and being in the United States is at work. Similarly, the range of 24 points between Dominicans and

Colombians demonstrates that much more than recency of immigration is at work.

It is not possible to do more than speculate about the causes of these patterns. The Puerto Rican pattern results in part from high rates of teenage pregnancy, but other factors have been at work to weaken the viability of the nuclear family among Puerto Ricans in New York. The tendency for Dominican women to support children without the help of a spouse is more closely related to the dynamics of migration. Many Dominican women migrate to the United States after marital disruptions, evidently in an effort to provide for their children and attain greater autonomy than is possible in their home country. The prevalence of nuclear households among Colombians may reflect differences in values, but more likely it results from the selectivity of the migrants from that country. They are of higher socioeconomic status than Dominicans and Puerto Ricans. Further, Colombian migration to the United States is a secondary migration. That is, most emigrants from Colombia settle in Venezuela. Those coming to the United States probably have greater resources and have had more time to plan the migration as a family move. It cannot be overemphasized that these are speculations. While the speculations are consistent with empirical data, they are not well substantiated.

Table 2.3 provides other glimpses at the family situations of diverse Hispanic groups in New York City. None is as important or clear-cut as the situation described in the above paragraphs. One pattern deserves some mention, however. The relatively high proportion of Dominican and Colombian male householders without children is produced by several causes. In part it is due to a real higher incidence of males living by themselves, in group quarters, or as unrelated individuals in other households. This higher incidence is to be expected in a population of recent immigrants. However, part of this high incidence results from differences in the way the category "male householder" is derived from the Census data and from the New York survey data. Many of the males in this category are adult sons living with one or both parents. Future work will control for this difference. It should be noted that the higher incidence of adult children living with parents is itself produced in part by the process of migration. In many cases the parents have been brought here by sons or daughters who arrived first.

In 1983 the U.S. Census Bureau issued a report that produced headlines about high Hispanic fertility. The problem with the headline was that it did not acknowledge that it was reporting primarily high Mexican fertility. Several of the Hispanic ethnic groups have extremely low fertility. The best example of this extreme is the Cubans. Nevertheless, most Hispanic immigrants come from countries that have relatively to very high fertility (such as the Dominican Republic and Colombia); and many observers of immigration and its consequences are concerned with the potentially hidden population growth that the immigration of high-fertility groups can cause. What is the fertility situation among Hispanics in New York?

Table 2.4 presents data on the number of children ever born to women in three broad age groups for each of the four Hispanic categories. A quick reading of the table indicates that (1) there is not too much diversity here and (2) Hispanic fertility in New York is similar to that of Puerto Ricans—which means that it is significantly higher than the below-replacement fertility of the native-born non-Hispanic population, and significantly lower than that of Mexican-Americans (see Gurak, 1978).

The Census data for all non-Puerto Rican Hispanics indicate that this category does have markedly lower fertility than do Puerto Ricans for each of the three age groups. The higher fertility of Dominicans and Colombians appears to be due in part to several factors. Among those aged 15-24, these data are biased upward for Dominicans and Colombians, since only those aged 20-24 are included for those groups. This is especially significant if one notes the lower fertility of Colombians in the 25-34 group. Evidently, younger Colombians do have relatively low fertility, at least in comparison with other Hispanics. Their higher fertility among the 35-44 cohort may be an indication of higher future completed fertility, but more likely reflects the past higher fertility of Colombians (Colombia experienced a dramatic decline in fertility during the 1970s).

The fertility of Hispanic ethnic groups in New York appears to be higher than the U.S. national norm, but not very much higher. Further, there is

Table 2.4
Children Ever Born for Females by Age, Marital Status and Ethnicity: New York City, 1980 and 1981

Females by Age:	Puerto Rican	Other Hispanic	Dominican	Colombian
15-24	.52	.38	.73	.60
Single	.29	.14	.11	.08
Ever Married	1.14	.93	1.24	1.42
25-34	1.87	1.50	1.84	1.65
Single	1.35	.64	.43	.17
Ever Married	2.06	1.71	2.07	1.43
35-44	3.03	2.35 (2.82)	2.94 (1.93)	2.91
Single	2.51	1.01	—	—
Ever Married	3.11	2.54	2.97	3.10

Source of data for Puerto Rican and Other Hispanic categories is the same as in note (b) of Table 2.3. Source of Dominican and Colombian data is the same as in note (c) of Table 2.3, except that figures in parentheses for the 35-44 cohort are Census figures from Mann and Salvo (1984).

evidence of marked declines among some components of the population. The degree of diversity on this point is not nearly as dramatic as in the case of family composition, but some does exist. In addition to the points just made, it should be noted that the number of children ever born to single, never-married Puerto Rican women far exceeds the averages of each of the other groups. This reflects the high incidence of teen pregnancy for Puerto Rican females. If we knew why teen pregnancy was so prevalent among Puerto Ricans and not a major problem for other Hispanic groups, we would be in an enviable position relative to our ability to improve the social situation of these young women. Efforts to determine the causes of recent increases in teen pregnancy are currently using large amounts of research resources. It is to be hoped that these efforts will shed some light on the issue.

GENERAL INDICATORS OF SOCIOECONOMIC SITUATION

On average, each of the Hispanic groups can be characterized as having relatively low or modest levels of educational attainment, and quite low household incomes. This statement flows naturally from a quick reading of Table 2.5. Even at this very basic descriptive level some variations are worth noting. Colombians, especially Colombian males, have completed more years of education than other New York Hispanics. Colombian males completed an average of over 12 years of formal education, while the corresponding figure for the broad "Other Hispanic" category is 11.6, for Dominicans is 8.9, and for Puerto Ricans is 10.3. The pattern for females is essentially the same, though their levels of attainment are somewhat lower.

These relatively modest educational differentials must be viewed in context. For each of the non-Puerto Rican groups a large component of the population obtained most of its education before migrating to the United States. The levels of education reported for Dominicans, for example, are above average for the total native Dominican population. If we view education as an indicator of class position, then these data indicate that the Dominican migration flow tends to consist of those who were doing better than average in the country of origin. This appears to be the case for each of the immigrant groups. That the more established Puerto Rican population, which includes a high proportion of mainland-educated individuals, has a low level of educational attainment is striking. Whether this reflects the special history of Puerto Ricans, the destructive impact of the U.S. educational system, the urban milieu, or something else deserves some careful consideration.

Median household income ranges from a high of $13,972 for Colombian households to a low of $8913 for Puerto Ricans. It must be remembered that the absolute dollar amounts do not mean all that much, since income is one of the more complex and more sensitive aspects of social life that we

Table 2.5
Indicators of Socioeconomic and Labor Force Status
by Ethnicity and Sex: 1980 and 1981

	Puerto Rican	Other Hispanic	Dominican		Colombian	
MALES						
Education	10.3	11.6	8.9	(10.0)	12.2	(11.0)
% in Labor Force	65.9	76.7	75.4	(83.9)	83.7	(93.4)
% Unemployed	7.6	6.8	8.4	(8.7)	4.6	(3.3)
Unemployment Rate (a)	11.6	8.9	11.1	(10.4)	5.5	(3.5)
% Not in Labor Force	34.1	23.3	16.2	(7.4)	11.7	(3.3)
FEMALES						
Education	9.7	10.3	8.3	(9.0)	11.9	(9.0)
% in Labor Force	33.8	51.5	46.6	(51.7)	58.8	(67.4)
% Unemployed	4.4	5.8	6.3	(5.2)	7.2	(9.9)
Unemployment Rate (a)	12.9	11.3	13.5	(10.0)	12.2	(14.7)
% Not in Labor Force	66.2	48.5	47.1	(43.1)	34.0	(22.7)
Median Household Income of All Families	8,913	12,400	9,367	(9,237)	13,972	(10,750)

Source of figures in parentheses is the 1981 survey of Dominicans and Colombians in New York City. All other data derived from Mann and Salvo (1984) 1980 Census data. 1980 figures are based on the non-institutionalized population of individuals 16 years of age and older. The 1981 data are restricted to adults 20-45 years of age.

(a) Unemployed as a percentage of the same-sex labor force category.

routinely seek to measure. People often are not in a position to accurately report income in the form that data collectors would like to have it. For example, people involved in small businesses may confuse cash flow and net income if they are not the accountants. Further, many people may be involved in income-earning activities that are not reported to the IRS. Consequently they may tend to underreport income to outside interviewers, or even fail to routinely let family members know what the actual dollar amounts are. These are general problems in measuring income, but there is no reason to believe that they are any less severe among immigrants. Nevertheless, the general rank order of average household incomes of groups is quite probably reliable. That is, there is no reason to believe that it is more difficult to measure income among one group than among another. Therefore, while the absolute dollar amounts are almost certainly underestimates, those groups with higher reported average income almost certainly do earn more on average.

The low Puerto Rican household income is in large part due to the smaller number of earners in the average Puerto Rican household. The discussion of Table 2.3 provides some of the background for this claim. The typical Puerto Rican household will have fewer earners, in part because the odds are higher for this group that only one spouse will be present in the household. As we shall see, however, male and female Puerto Ricans are less likely to be in the labor force than are other Hispanics.

The income figure for Puerto Ricans is in some ways even lower than it looks. The Census figure includes reports on income from all sources, including public assistance. If we contrast the Puerto Rican figure (Census-derived) with the $9237 household income figure (survey-derived) for foreign-born Dominicans (in parentheses) the poor income situation of New York's Puerto Rican households comes into clearer focus. The Dominican figure represents only reported earned income. It involves extensive underreporting and does not include any other source of income, despite the fact that Dominicans do make extensive use of various forms of public assistance. Nevertheless, the relatively underreported income of recently immigrated Dominican households exceeds that of the two-generation Puerto Rican population for which income reporting is more complete.

The most striking evidence of diversity to be found in Table 2.5 concerns levels of labor force participation. Among males, this ranges from a high of 83.7 percent of the 16-and-older population (93.4 percent for the 20-44 group) among Colombians to a low of 65.9 among Puerto Ricans. Among females, the range is from 58.8 percent (67.4) for Colombians to 33.8 percent for Puerto Ricans. Part of this difference is due to the younger average age of Puerto Ricans, but most of the explanation must be sought elsewhere. One avenue of thought involves focusing more on the exceptionally high rates of participation among the non-Puerto Rican immigrants. It is quite clear that recent immigrants have come here to seek employment. Recency of arrival is associated with a higher incidence of multiple-earner households. Nevertheless, the exceedingly low rate of participation of Puerto Rican females is as striking as the high rates for Colombians.

OCCUPATIONAL AND INDUSTRY LOCATIONS
OF THE EMPLOYED

Restricting our focus to those who were employed at some time during the year prior to the Census or survey, an informative picture of the types of economic activity of the various Hispanic groups emerges. For both sexes and all groups there is a relatively heavy concentration in blue-collar jobs (see Tables 2.6 and 2.7). Within this area, semiskilled operative occupations

Table 2.6
Occupational Distribution of Puerto Rican, Other Hispanic, Dominican, and Colombian Males, 1980 and 1981

Occupational Category	Puerto Rican	Other Hispanic	Dominican	Colombian
Managerial	6.9	7.5	7.0	10.5
Professional/ Technical	5.77	6.6	7.0	6.2
Clerical	15.4	11.6	6.5	8.8
Sales	6.8	6.1	5.6	7.0
Private Household Services	0.1	0.1	0.5	0.9
Other Services	22.0	21.9	20.0	20.4
Farming/Forestry/ Fishing	0.6	0.5	0.0	0.0
Crafts/Skilled Blue Collar	14.3	16.4	7.0	9.8
Operatives/Semi- Skilled	20.5	22.3	34.9	29.9
Laborers/Unskilled	7.8	7.1	11.6	6.4
TOTALS	100.1	100.1	100.1	99.9

Figures for Puerto Ricans and Other Hispanics are derived from 1980 Census data reported in Mann and Salvo (1984); those for Dominicans and Colombians are from the 1981 Survey of those groups conducted by Gurak. For the Census data, the data are for individuals 16 years of age or older. For the 1981 survey data, the populations represented is that of 20 to 45 year olds. All figures are percentages.

Table 2.7
Occupational Distribution of Puerto Rican, Other Hispanic, Dominican, and Colombian Females, 1980 and 1981

Occupational Category	Puerto Rican	Other Hispanic	Dominican	Colombian
Managerial	4.4	3.7	2.0	1.1
Professional/ Technical	9.5	7.0	7.5	4.3
Clerical	36.6	23.2	12.4	9.8
Sales	7.8	6.4	3.1	0.0
Private Household Services	0.8	3.4	7.6	5.4
Other Services	12.8	14.3	7.2	19.6
Farming/Forestry/ Fishing	0.1	0.1	0.5	0.0
Crafts/Skilled Blue Collar	3.5	4.7	2.2	6.5
Operatives/Semi-Skilled	20.9	33.0	42.9	45.7
Laborers/Unskilled	3.5	4.1	14.5	7.6
TOTALS	99.9	99.9	99.9	100.0

Figures for Puerto Ricans and Other Hispanics are derived from 1980 Census data reported in Mann and Salvo (1984); those for Dominicans and Colombians are from the 1981 Survey of those groups conducted by Gurak. For the Census data, the data are for individuals 16 years of age or older. For the 1981 survey data, the populations represented is that of 20 to 45 year olds. All figures are percentages.

prevail. The concentration in blue-collar jobs in general and semiskilled operative positions in particular is most marked for females (see Table 2.7).

Puerto Ricans who are employed have better occupational distributions than do other Hispanics. This situation contrasts with other indicators of socioeconomic status, such as education and income. Only 28.3 percent of Puerto Rican employed men (see Table 2.6) and 24.4 percent of employed women (see Table 2.7) had occupations falling in the operative or laborer category. This contrasts with 46.5 percent and 57.4 percent for Dominican males and females; and with 36.3 and 53.3 percent for Colombian males and females. This relative advantage should not be overinterpreted, since the corresponding national figures are 7.4 and 3.1 percent for all U.S. males and females (Gurak and Kritz, 1984). Hispanics are concentrated in medium- and low-skilled blue-collar positions but this concentration is less for Puerto Ricans in the labor force.

While Puerto Ricans are more likely to be found in managerial and professional occupations than are other Hispanics, this advantage is a thin one (see Tables 2.6 and 2.7). Puerto Rican males are more likely than other Hispanics to hold clerical/administrative and skilled/craft positions. The same relative advantage holds for Puerto Rican females except for skilled blue-collar positions, where higher proportions of Colombian and "other Hispanic" women are to be found.

For all groups, there is an additional concentration of employment in the area of nonprivate-household services. Approximately one-fifth of the male Hispanic labor force hold this category of job, along with between one-eighth (Puerto Rican) and one-fifth (Colombian) of the Hispanic female labor force. Domestic service occupations are almost nonexistent among males, (less than 1 percent of males in each group) and relatively uncommon among females (from 0.8 percent of Puerto Rican to 7.6 percent of Dominican women). Nevertheless, there is a clear tendency for this type of job to be held by recent immigrants when it is held at all (7.6 percent of Dominican and 5.4 percent of Colombian females, compared with 0.8 percent of Puerto Rican females).

The broad range of occupations held by Hispanics in New York is somewhat inconsistent with stereotypes of their occupational distributions. As with most stereotypes, there is some basis in fact for the exaggeration of the disadvantaged position of Hispanics, but the diversity of reality within and between groups should be considered. A very widely held view in the general population is that the vast majority of recent immigrants to New York work in the garment industry. This, it turns out, is the most common form of employment for females, but the garment industry employs only a minority of the Hispanic immigrants. A brief examination of the industry location of Hispanics is called for.

Between 25.5 percent (Puerto Ricans) and 45.1 percent (Dominicans) of Hispanic males are located in the manufacturing sector. Overall, the tendency is for these jobs to be in the area of nondurable goods manufacturing (Table 2.8). Using the 1981 survey of Dominicans and Colombians, further diversity appears. Twenty percent of Dominican males were employed in the garment industry, while only 6.1 percent of Colombian males were so employed. We do not have the comparable data for Puerto Ricans, but the maximum possible figure would be the 13.3 percent in nondurable manufacturing.

Table 2.8
**Industrial Sector Distributions of Puerto Rican, Other Hispanic,
Dominican, and Colombian Males, New York, 1980 and 1981**

Industrial Sector	Puerto Rican	Other Hispanic	Dominican	Colombian
Manufacturing	25.5	29.4	45.1	35.0
Durable	12.3	13.9	16.3	19.3
Non-Durable	13.3	15.5	8.8	9.6
Garment (a)	—	—	20.0	6.1
Transportation/ Utilities	10.9	8.4	8.8	10.5
Wholesale and Retail Trade	20.8	24.1	7.9	10.5
Hotels and Restaurants (a)	—	—	13.0	11.4
Finance/Real Estate/ Communications	11.1	8.9	3.3	4.4
Business Services	6.8	8.0	1.9	9.6
Other Services	4.5	5.7	12.6	12.3
Public Administration/ Education/Social Services	16.9	11.3	7.4	6.1
Other	3.5	4.2	—	0.2
TOTALS	100.0	100.0	100.0	100.0

Figures for Puerto Ricans and Other Hispanics are derived from 1980 Census data reported in Mann and Salvo (1984); those for Dominicans and Colombians are from the 1981 Survey of those groups conducted by Gurak. For the Census data, the data are for individuals 16 years of age or older. For the 1981 survey data, the populations represented is that of 20 to 45 year olds. All figures are percentages.

(a) For Dominicans and Colombians, the total non-durable manufacturing category is the sum of Non-Durable and Garment. Data on Garment Manufacturing was not reported in Mann and Salvo (1984) as it was not for the Hotel and Restaurant sectors. Workers in those sectors would be classified in various categories for Puerto Ricans and Other Hispanics, but principally in Trade and Services.

Females are relatively concentrated in nondurable manufacturing, with approximately 40 percent of employed Dominican and Colombian females being in the garment industry (Table 2.9). The maximum possible concentration of employed Puerto Rican females in the garment industry is 21.2

Table 2.9

Industrial Sector Distributions of Puerto Rican, Other Hispanic, Dominican, and Colombian Females, New York, 1980 and 1981

Industrial Sector	Puerto Rican	Other Hispanic	Dominican	Colombian
Manufacturing	29.9	43.1	62.2	55.4
Durable	8.7	11.9	12.4	9.8
Non-Durable	21.2	31.2	8.0	7.6
Garment (a)	—	—	41.8	38.0
Transportation/ Utilities	3.7	3.6	1.0	2.2
Wholesale and Retail Trade	14.0	13.0	7.5	1.1
Hotels and Restaurants (a)	—	—	2.5	5.4
Finance/Real Estate/ Communications	11.6	8.2	4.0	3.3
Business Services	3.7	4.0	1.5	10.9
Other Services	4.2	8.8	8.5	12.0
Public Administration/ Education/Social Services	32.3	19.0	10.9	7.6
Other	0.6	0.3	2.0	2.2
TOTALS	100.0	100.0	100.0	100.0

Figures for Puerto Ricans and Other Hispanics are derived from 1980 Census data reported in Mann and Salvo (1984); those for Dominicans and Colombians are from the 1981 Survey of those groups conducted by Gurak. For the Census data, the data are for individuals 16 years of age or older. For the 1981 survey data, the populations represented is that of 20 to 45 year olds. All figures are percentages.

(a) For Dominicans and Colombians, the total non-durable manufacturing category is the sum of Non-Durable and Garment. Data on Garment Manufacturing was not reported in Mann and Salvo (1984) as it was not for the Hotel and Restaurant sectors. Workers in those sectors would be classified in various categories for Puerto Ricans and Other Hispanics, but principally in Trade and Services.

percent. Clearly, recent immigrants are disproportionately employed in this sector. It appears quite clear that the stereotype of the Hispanic worker being a garment worker has some basis in fact, but even among women, the majority of employed individuals are in other sectors of the economy.

Those not employed in manufacturing fill occupations in a broad range of other industries. Transportation, wholesale and retail trade (restaurants and hotels for Dominican and Colombian males), services, and public administration/education/social services are among the sectors with significant proportions of the Hispanic labor force. Puerto Ricans (males and females) are more likely than other Hispanics to hold jobs in the areas of finance/real estate and public administration/education/social services (28 percent of Puerto Rican males and 43.9 percent of Puerto Rican females, as opposed to between 10 and 15 percent for other groups). Dominicans and Colombians are more likely to be employed in business and other types of services, with Colombians being much more likely than other groups to be in business services (accounting, security, maintenance).

Several points need to be summarized. Hispanics in New York are highly concentrated in manufacturing. Non-Puerto Rican females and Dominican males are relatively concentrated in the garment industry. Despite this concentration, Hispanics occupy positions in a wide range of industrial sectors in significant numbers. Puerto Ricans in the labor force display occupational and sector distributions that are advantageous relative to those of other Hispanic groups. This seems to reflect both a language advantage and the effects of longer residence, in that clerical, finance, and public administration/education/service jobs generally require greater English-language facility and characteristically have more formalized entrance requirements.

The advantage of Puerto Ricans with respect to occupations contrasts with their relative disadvantage when other indicators of demographic and socioeconomic status are examined. In large part this apparent contradiction results from a bifurcation of the Puerto Rican population into an "in the labor force" group and a "not in the labor force" group. Puerto Ricans in the labor force display advantages that one would expect when comparing a more established minority with a group of recent immigrants. The reasons for the low rates of labor force participation of Puerto Ricans merit careful investigation.

CONCLUSION: SOME COMMENTS ON STRUCTURAL INTEGRATION

This demographic overview has sought to fulfill a need for description of social and demographic aspects of Hispanic populations in New York City. In doing so, it has emphasized some of the dimensions of diversity that distinguish various Hispanic ethnic groups and that constitute the basis of heterogeneity within single groups. Clearly, this diversity exists. It is quite marked in family structure, education, income, and labor force participation. The distinctiveness of the Puerto Rican pattern stands out, but that is only one of several loci of diversity. Some of the diversity results from migratory selectivity, some from factors such as the recency of immigration of a group, and some from complex interactions of the host society and the particular group. This last category includes situations such as the following. Puerto Ricans are citizens of the United States; this renders travel to and from the mainland easier and may, among other outcomes, reduce commitment to economic activity in New York. Citizenship also affects eligibility for public assistance programs. For other Hispanic groups, integration experiences could be affected by the condition of the economy, the housing market, the legal climate, and public opinion at the time of peak immigration. Finally, for all groups, racial composition may affect the initial and subsequent experiences in the United States.

Given these findings on Hispanic diversity, it seems appropriate to look at some indicators of structural assimilation that focus directly on intergroup contact. The vehicle for this discussion consists of studies of intermarriage of Hispanics in New York City (Fitzpatrick and Gurak, 1979; Gurak and Fitzpatrick, 1982). Some attention is also given to residential segregation.

Intermarriage provides an excellent indicator of intergroup contact patterns. The fundamental reason for this is that high rates of intermarriage require the routine, nonhostile interaction of a large segment of the relevant populations across a range of social settings (a necessary but not sufficient cause). Tables 2.10 and 2.11 show that out-group marriage is quite common for Hispanics in New York City. By standards of generation of residence, the out-marriage rate is fairly high for all groups except Puerto Ricans. Considering only marriages of second-generation residents for the moment, between 62 and 95 percent of 1975 marriages of various non-Puerto Rican Hispanic ethnic groups were with members of other ethnic groups (Table 2.11). For these same subgroups, approximately one-third of the marriages were with third-generation residents of the United States. For example, 38.8 percent of U.S-born Cuban grooms in 1975 married third-generation Americans. The corresponding figures for Central Americans, Dominicans, and South Americans were 34.9, 33.3, and 31.9 percent, respectively. Of mainland-born Puerto Rican grooms, only 5.2 percent married third-generation Americans. Due to the small size of the adult third-generation Hispanic population in New York, these marriages are almost certainly with non-Hispanics.

Puerto Ricans have lower out-marriage rates than do non-Puerto Rican Hispanics, regardless of generation of residence in the mainland United States: 72.7 percent of all Puerto Rican grooms and 68.5 percent of all Puerto Rican brides in 1975 married others of Puerto Rican heritage (Table 2.10: diagonal). This in-group tendency was considerably less marked for each of the other Hispanic groups, despite the relatively smaller proportion of each of the non-Puerto Rican groups being U.S.-born. For example, just over one-third of Cubans married other Cubans. Approximately 62 percent of Dominicans married other Dominicans, rendering them the only group to approach the Puerto Rican tendency to marry within their own group.

Table 2.10
Distribution of Ethnicity of Spouses for Hispanic Brides and Grooms, New York City, 1975

GROOMS	BRIDES							
	Puerto Ricans	South Americans	Dominicans	Central Americans	Cubans	Third-generation Americans	Others	
Puerto Ricans	72.7 *68.5*	6.1 *17.9*	4.8 *19.8*	3.4 *22.2*	1.1 *13.5*	8.6 —	3.4 —	100%/ —
South Americans	23.3 *7.8*	50.5 *52.8*	4.0 *5.8*	3.1 *7.2*	2.9 *13.1*	9.4 —	6.7 —	100%/ —
Dominicans	24.6 *5.6*	3.8 *2.7*	62.0 *62.3*	2.4 *3.8*	1.1 *3.4*	3.8 —	2.2 —	100%/ —
Central Americans	20.4 *2.8*	4.7 *2.0*	4.5 *2.6*	45.7 *42.3*	1.0 *1.9*	14.8 —	8.9 —	100%/ —
Cubans	21.1 *1.5*	10.0 *2.2*	5.1 *1.6*	3.3 *1.6*	37.5 *35.9*	15.0 —	7.8 —	100%/ —
Third-generation Americans	— *8.2*	— *9.2*	— *4.4*	— *10.8*	— *13.5*			—/100%
Others	— *6.8*	— *13.1*	— *3.4*	— *12.1*	— *18.9*			—/100%
	—/100%	—/100%	—/100%	—/100%	—/100%			

The percentage distribution of brides' marriage choices is obtained by reading the *italic* figures, organized in columns. The figures for grooms, which are not italicized, are organized in rows situated to the left of the figures for the brides. For example, 6.1 percent of Puerto Rican grooms married South American brides, and 7.8 percent of Puerto Rican brides married South American grooms. Data on third generation and "other ethnicity" are provided only when the individual is a spouse of a Hispanic; we do not have data on all marriage choices of non-Hispanics.

Table 2.11

Distribution of Types of Marriages of First- and Second-Generation Hispanics, New York City, 1975

**Outgroup Marriage Choices of Hispanics
New York City, 1975**

	Puerto Ricans	South Americans	Dominicans	Central Americans	Cubans
BRIDES (N)	**(7,954)**	**(2,554)**	**(1,816)**	**(1,162)**	**(594)**
Endogamous	68.5	52.8	62.3	42.3	35.9
Exogamous	31.5	47.2	37.7	57.7	64.1
With Hispanics	16.5	24.9	29.9	34.8	31.7
With third-generation Americans	6.8	13.1	3.4	12.1	18.9
With others	8.2	9.2	4.4	10.8	13.5
GROOMS (N)	**(7,497)**	**(2,669)**	**(1,823)**	**(1,075)**	**(568)**
Endogamous	72.7	50.5	62.0	45.7	37.5
Exogamous	27.3	49.5	38.0	54.3	62.5
With Hispanics	15.4	33.4	32.0	30.6	39.7
With third-generation Americans	8.5	9.4	3.8	14.8	15.0
With others	3.4	6.7	2.2	8.9	7.8

**Distribution of Types of Marriages
of Second-Generation Hispanics, New York City, 1975**

	Puerto Ricans	South Americans	Dominicans	Central Americans	Cubans
BRIDES (N)	**(3,247)**	**(62)**	**(37)**	**(80)**	**(104)**
Endogamous	69.8	19.4	24.3	7.5	5.8
Exogamous	30.2	80.6	75.7	92.5	94.2
With Hispanics	12.0	27.4	43.3	28.6	34.5
With third-generation Americans	5.7	19.3	8.1	23.9	26.0
With others	12.5	33.9	24.3	40.0	33.7
GROOMS (N)	**(2,443)**	**(72)**	**(39)**	**(63)**	**(103)**
Endogamous	72.3	8.3	37.3	4.8	10.7
Exogamous	27.7	91.7	62.7	95.2	89.3
With Hispanics	19.6	39.0	26.8	46.7	40.8
With third-generation Americans	5.2	31.9	33.3	34.9	38.8
With others	2.9	20.8	2.6	13.6	9.7

Figures represent the percentages of an ethnic group which married endogamously or exogamously. The figures for endogamous and total exogamous individuals add up to 100 percent; the last three figures in each column add up to the total percent of exogamous individuals. For example, 68.5 percent of Puerto Rican brides were endogamous and 31.5 percent were exogamous. Among the exogamous Puerto Rican brides, 16.5 percent married other Hispanics, 6.8 percent married third-generation Americans, and 8.2 percent married others. The last three figures sum up to 31.5 percent, the total exogamous figure.

Only among Puerto Ricans is there no trend toward higher rates of out-marriage among the second-generation component of the population. If we compare Puerto Rican grooms with Dominican grooms (the only group to be similar to Puerto Ricans when generation of residence is not considered), this point becomes quite clear. Whereas 62 percent of all Dominican grooms married Dominican brides, only 37.3 percent of U.S.-born Dominican grooms did so (Table 2.11). The overall figure for Puerto Rican grooms is 72.7 percent, while that for mainland-born grooms is an almost identical 72.3 percent.

Once again it is clear that the experience of Puerto Ricans in New York City is quite distinct from those of other Hispanic groups in that same urban environment. Even among Puerto Ricans, the rate of out-marriage is not that low when compared with rates for Mexican-Americans in Texas, for example. Rather, the rates for other Hispanic groups are startlingly high. Nevertheless, the absence of the usual trend toward increased out-marriage for Puerto Ricans does distinguish their experience from that of most immigrant groups. One might choose to argue that this reflects conscious efforts to preserve a culture, and there is undoubtedly some truth to this position. Nevertheless, it should not be overlooked that the lower degree of structural integration, indicated by the intermarriage data, correlates with a poorer socioeconomic situation.

The picture presented by the intermarriage data fits the image created more indirectly by the description of the socioeconomic situation of the non-Puerto Rican Hispanics in New York. They constitute a highly mobile, economically active group that is rapidly assimilating into American society. The Puerto Rican situation may be an anomaly, or it may indicate that not all trends are linear. We cannot assume that current trends simply can be projected into the future. An earlier study of Puerto Rican intermarriage (Fitzpatrick, 1966) found that as of 1960, Puerto Ricans were marrying non-Puerto Ricans at a rate similar to the experience of earlier immigrant groups. Further, the second-generation Puerto Ricans demonstrated a strong tendency to marry outside their ethnic group.

By 1975, no further increase in the out-group marriage rate had occurred, and the second-generation rate of out-group marriage had actually declined. Nevertheless, it should be pointed out that these results do not necessarily mean that a profound change has occurred in the way Puerto Ricans are treated by non-Puerto Ricans, or the way Puerto Ricans regard non-Puerto Ricans. They may reflect changes in Puerto Rican migration patterns in which New York has increasingly become the home of Puerto Ricans who are less able or less willing to integrate into mainstream culture. The Puerto Rican intermarriage history does dictate caution in interpreting the integration tendencies of non-Puerto Rican Hispanics. It will be important to monitor their progress over the next decade in order to determine whether shifting migration patterns and changes in other conditions have altered the pattern described here.

The extent to which members of different ethnic groups reside in the same locales provides us with another powerful indicator of the degree of social distance separating the groups. For several decades various aspects of the residential segregation patterns of blacks from whites have been subjected to careful scrutiny. Recent studies of U.S. residential segregation patterns have begun to consider the situation of Hispanics. The 1980 Census will yield significant new insights in this area because that Census included a Hispanic identifier on the short-form questionnaire that permits small-area analysis in greater detail than ever before. Much of the important work in this area has been conducted by Massey (1979, 1983). Studies of residential segregation utilize several methods to determine the extent to which members of different groups do or do not reside in close proximity. In general, these studies rely most on a measure that determines the evenness of the residential distributions across a city or metropolitan area. Thus, if a particular group constitutes 20 percent of a city's population, in a situation of absolutely no segregation, that group should constitute about 20 percent of each block within the city. In such a situation we would assign a segregation score of 0. If all members of a group lived on blocks where members of the comparison group (such as whites) did not reside, the score would be 100.

The results to date indicate that Hispanics in general are no more segregated from non-Hispanic whites than were earlier European immigrants: the segregation scores range between 30 and 50 for different cities. Such scores are typical for first- and second-generation European immigrants earlier in this century. Further, Hispanics are resettling in the suburban rings of metropolitan areas, and in a broader set of regions; and the level of segregation is less in those areas. Once again, the Puerto Rican pattern stands out. While nowhere as segregated as are blacks (whose scores are in the 80s and 90s), they are far more segregated than are other Hispanics. This is mentioned here not only because of the value of residential patterns as indicators of intergroup contact, but also because those patterns have implications in employment and schooling.

In conclusion, it should be that the purpose of this chapter was to document general situations and the extent of diversity in these situations. We really understand very little about the causes of some of the observed variation. Insofar as one is concerned with a particular situation, such as that of Puerto Ricans, it appears important to study that group in comparison with other groups rather than focusing on Hispanics in general.

REFERENCES

Fitzpatrick, Joseph P. 1966. "Intermarriage of Puerto Ricans in New York City." *American Journal of Sociology* 71 (January):395-406.
Fitzpatrick, Joseph P., and Douglas T. Gurak. 1979. *Hispanic Intermarriage in New*

York City: 1975. New York: Hispanic Research Center, Fordham University. Monograph no. 2.

Gurak, Douglas T. 1978. "Sources of Ethnic Fertility Differences: An Examination of Five Minority Groups." *Social Science Quarterly* 59, no. 2 (September): 295-310.

Gurak, Douglas T., and Joseph P. Fitzpatrick. 1982. "Intermarriage Among Hispanic Ethnic Groups in New York City." *American Journal of Sociology* 87, no. 4 (January):921-934.

Gurak, Douglas T., and Mary M. Kritz. 1982a. "Socioeconomic Mobility Among Women in New York City." *Migration Today* 10, no. 3/4 (Fall):6-14.

Gurak, Douglas T., and Mary M. Kritz. 1982b. "Socioeconomic Mobility Among Dominican and Colombian Immigrants in New York City." Paper presented at the Annual Meetings of the American Sociological Association, San Antonio, Texas (August).

Mann, Evelyn S., and Joseph J. Salvo. 1984. "Characteristics of New Hispanic Immigrants to New York City: A Comparison of Puerto Rican and Non-Puerto Rican Hispanics." Paper presented at the Annual Meetings of the Population Association of America, Minneapolis (May).

Massey, Douglas S. 1979. "Residential Segregation of Spanish Americans in United States Urbanized Areas." *Demography* 16, no. 4 (November):553-563.

Massey, Douglas S. 1983. "A Research Note on Residential Succession: The Hispanic Case." *Social Forces* 61, no. 3 (March):825-833.

II

IMMIGRATION, ASSIMILATION, AND CULTURAL IDENTITY

3

From Settlers to Newcomers: The Hispanic Legacy in the United States

Edna Acosta-Belén

INTRODUCTION

On September 17, 1968, the U.S. Congress passed a joint resolution requesting that the president issue an annual proclamation designating the week of September 15 as National Hispanic Heritage Week. This proclamation was a symbolic recognition of the major role played by Hispanic groups in the past and present of this nation, from the early days of exploration, conquest, and colonization of the Americas to the modern technological world of today.

The influx of Hispanics from diverse cultural backgrounds into the United States is, therefore, both history and current reality, and leads us to one of the major revelations of the 1980 population census: Hispanics constitute the fastest-growing minority group in U.S. society. Between 1950 and 1980 the Hispanic population increased 265 percent, compared with just under 50 percent for the total U.S. population (see Chapter 1). Currently numbering over 18.8 million, according to demographic projections they could well become the largest minority group in the United States by the year 2000, if current growth rates continue. This projection is based on 1980 census data of 14.5 million Hispanics and is still accurate, since by 1987 the Hispanic population had increased by 30 percent, five times as fast as the rest of the U.S. population (Pear, 1987). Guernica and Kasperuk argue that "the one demographic trend above all others that will mold the future of the Hispanic community through the 1980s and beyond is its numerical growth" (Russell, 1983:24).

The umbrella term "Hispanic" embraces a diverse population found throughout the United States but concentrated in a few geographical regions: Puerto-Ricans in New York and other Northeast and Midwest cities; Mexicans in the Southwest; Cubans in Florida and the Northeast (see Figures 3.1 and 3.2). There are long-time residents and new ones, including

Figure 3.1
Hispanics in the United States

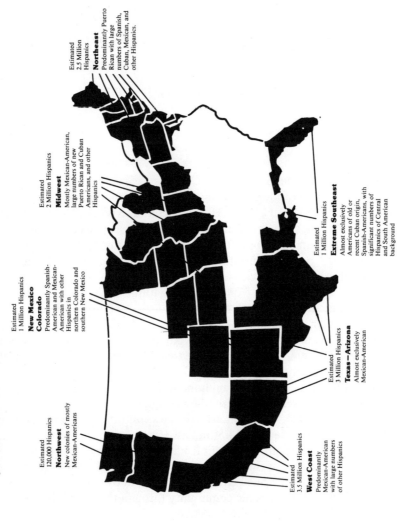

Estimated
1 Million Hispanics
New Mexico
Colorado
Predominantly Spanish-
American and Mexican-
American with other
Hispanics in
northern Colorado and
southern New Mexico

Estimated
2 Million Hispanics
Midwest
Mostly Mexican-American,
large numbers of new
Puerto Rican and Cuban
Americans, and other
Hispanics

Estimated
2.5 Million
Hispanics
Northeast
Predominantly Puerto
Rican with large
numbers of Spanish,
Cuban, Mexican, and
other Hispanics.

Estimated
120,000 Hispanics
Northwest
New colonies of mostly
Mexican-Americans

Estimated
3 Million Hispanics
Texas — Arizona
Almost exclusively
Mexican-American

Estimated
1 Million Hispanics
Extreme Southeast
Almost exclusively
Americans of old or
recent Cuban origin,
Spanish-Americans, with
significant numbers of
Hispanics of Central
and South American
background

Estimated
3.5 Million Hispanics
West Coast
Predominantly
Mexican-American
with large numbers
of other Hispanics

Reprinted from *Hispanics and Grantmakers: A Special Report of Foundation News.* Washington, D.C.: Council of Foundations, 1981, pp 28-29. First published in *La Luz* (August - Sept., 1980).

Figure 3.2
Where Most Hispanics Live

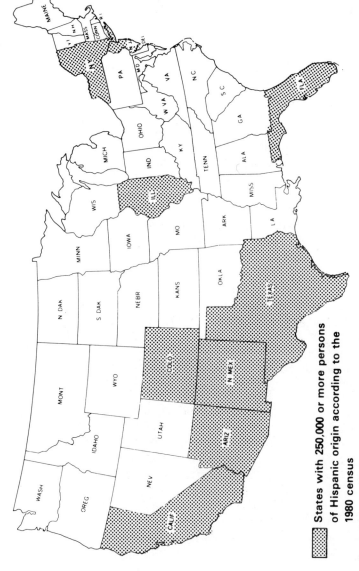

States with 250,000 or more persons of Hispanic origin according to the 1980 census

Some 85 percent of the 14.6 million Hispanics counted in the 1980 U.S. census lived in these nine states. Mexican Americans. the largest Hispanic group. are concentrated in the Southwest, particularly California and Texas. Most Puerto Ricans live in New York and New Jersey. Cubans are headquartered in Florida.. The largest numbers of the fourth. more scattered "Other Hispanic" group are found in California and New York.

Source: *Population Bulletin* 38, no. 3 (June 1983): 2. Reprinted with publisher's permission.

an increasing number of arrivals from Spain and from other Spanish-speaking countries in the Caribbean and Central and South America who have joined the communities established by the major groups. Their Spanish language has been used by census demographers to lump them all together as "Hispanics," creating a false image of homogeneity and unity, and mystifying cultural, racial, and class differences and disparities among individual groups.

The fact that Hispanics might not define or identify themselves with this collective label becomes less true every day. The shorthand label is turning into a symbol of cultural affirmation and identity in an alienating society that traditionally has been hostile and prejudicial to cultural and racial differences, and unresponsive to the socioeconomic and educational needs of a large segment of the Hispanic population. The classification has also proven to be useful in the political articulation of those collective needs and priorities to the larger society. Furthermore, one of the most remarkable traits of Hispanic groups in the United States happens to be the retention of the Spanish language in the midst of all the assimilative pressures exerted by the U.S. majority culture against bilingualism and ethnic cultural preservation. Nearly 90 percent of all Hispanics still speak Spanish with some degree of fluency (Estrada, 1981), and at least two-thirds of all Hispanics are first-generation immigrants. Even though each Hispanic group has a different sense of its own identity, the *latinos* or *hispanos* (as they frequently call themselves in Spanish) are finding that their commonalities provide them with a more effective political voice.

In 1877, the American poet Walt Whitman wrote:

I have an idea that there is much importance about the Latin race's contributions to the American nationality that will never be put with sympathetic understanding and tact on the record.

As has traditionally been the case with women, there is still a great deal of unrecorded or unknown history about the legacy, achievements, and contributions of Hispanics to this nation. This chapter is an ambitious attempt to improve the record by providing a comprehensive overview of almost five centuries of Hispanic presence on the North American continent.

THE SETTLERS

Hispanics are not newcomers to the United States. Their history in this land began long before the arrival of the Pilgrims at Plymouth Rock and the founding of the 13 British colonies. Hence, it is fitting to say that the first wheels that turned on American soil were Spanish in origin.

Almost 500 years ago Christopher Columbus, representing the Spanish Crown, arrived in 1492 in what later became the New World, or America.

He claimed the "discovered" lands for Spain, which at the time was consolidating its political, economic, and religious hegemony within its own territory. This effort culminated in 1492 under the monarchy of the Catholic rulers Ferdinand and Isabella, with the expulsion of the Jews and the defeat of the Moors in Granada. Inspired by Marco Polo's adventures in the lands of the Great Khan two centuries before, and by a crusader's sense of mission to spread the Catholic faith, find new wealth and commercial routes to the Orient, and prove his own navigational theories, Columbus believed that he had arrived in the exotic islands of the Far East known as the Indies. Instead, he had opened up a new continent to European explorers, adventurers, merchants, and immigrants in search of wealth and prosperity.

When the Spanish explored the new lands, they found a wide variety of aboriginal groups exhibiting varying degrees of cultural and socioeconomic development. From the magnificence of the Maya, Aztec, and Inca civilizations—civilizations much older than those of Europe—to the more rudimentary lives of the Tainos or the Caribs, Indian groups experienced the conquest as one of the largest immolations to be recorded in human history. War, forced labor, mistreatment, illness, and suicide all played a substantial role in the decimation of the native populations of the New World.

In areas where the indigenous populations had been larger, their descendants survived and amalgamated to a large extent with the Spanish conquerors; in other areas, such as the Caribbean islands, the Indian populations were almost totally extinct by the end of the first century of colonization. Slaves from Africa were introduced early in the sixteenth century to replace or supplement the decreasing Indian labor force in agriculture, mining, and domestic service. Black slaves also intermingled with the Spanish and Indian groups, creating through the centuries new cultures and a mixed population in the Americas that integrated the three races to varying degrees. The *mestizaje* (race mixture) produced by the fusion of the white, Indian, and black races and cultures is one of the most distinctive features of the Spanish conquest and colonization of the Americas, and hence of Latin American and U.S. Hispanic cultures.

The mentality of the Spanish conquistador was one permeated with myths, legends, and preconceptions from a variety of sources, among which were chivalry novels, medieval legends, classical myths, and biblical tales (Leonard, 1953). The mythological world of the indigenous populations also fed into those preconceptions, and propelled many explorers into a chivalric view of the conquest—a world of adventure, danger, and heroism where monsters were often seen, where there were windmills blurring the line between fantasy and reality. Others were motivated primarily by greed, and the gold and wealth they found in some of the first explored territories only increased their thirst for more.

Spanish exploration and colonization of the North and South American continents extended across a large portion of the territory that constitutes the United States as we know it today. In 1513, Juan Ponce de León, then governor of the island of San Juan Bautista (later known as Puerto Rico), brought an expedition to a land he called "la Pascua florida" (Spanish for Easter, the day of his arrival), in search of the legendary fountain of youth. In the area explored by Ponce de León, the Spanish founded St. Augustine in 1565, the first city of North America which later became one of the most important Spanish military garrisons on that part of the continent. (The San Marcos Castle, built between 1672 and 1756, stands today as a monument to the Spanish colonization and settlement of this region.)

In 1527-28 Pánfilo de Narváez led an ill-fated expedition to the lands of the north and reached the Gulf Coast. Caught by a storm, his ships were destroyed and most of his men perished. One of the few men who survived the shipwreck, Álvar Núñez Cabeza de Vaca, faced all kinds of calamities (among them being captured by the Indians) before he made his 3000-mile journey by foot, which lasted almost nine years, through territories on both sides of the Mississippi River and a good part of what is known today as the U.S. Southwest. He wrote about his odyssey in his *Naufragios*, first published in 1542, a work that has become one of the most important and interesting narratives in the body of literature known as the Chronicles of the Indies. His adventures in the vast wilderness inspired other explorers to follow his footsteps. One of them, Francisco Vásquez de Coronado, searched for the Seven Cities of Cíbola, the seven cities of great splendor where, according to the tales of the time, gold was abundant. In 1540, he reached the territories that later became New Mexico and Colorado. Instead of seven cities of gold, however, he found the villages of the Pueblo Indians. The year before, Hernando de Soto headed an expedition through the territories along the Mississippi River, where he met his death. During the same period, Hernando de Alarcón arrived in a land that was named California because it reminded its explorers of the marvelous imaginary island of the same name inhabited by Amazons, which they had read about in a popular chivalry novel.

These pioneer explorations opened the door to Spanish civilization on the North American continent and to what would become, more than two centuries later, the United States of America.

Settlement of some of the explored territories to the north was largely due to the efforts of Spanish missionary friars. The scattered missions they established in California, Arizona, and New Mexico during the seventeenth and eighteenth centuries began to open up the territories to the west for more settlement. One of the most remembered missionaries is Fray Junípero Serra, who established a mission in 1776 where the majestic city of San Francisco stands today. The missions were crucial to the settlement process, since most major cities were built around them. They contributed to the pacification, Christianization, and education of the Indians, and the development and spread of methods for the cultivation and irrigation of arid lands.

Spanish policies of subjugation of native populations and religious conversion aroused hostilities among many of the North American Indian groups who resisted the conquistadors. Among those groups that were subdued, a process of *mestizaje* took place; and in New Mexico, for instance, the Spanish built their settlements on Indian foundations, causing a degree of Hispanization among the Pueblo Indians.

By the early nineteenth century, the border of the Spanish empire extended to the Mississippi River and far into California and the current U.S. Southwest. Much has been written about the inability of the Spaniards to administer their New World colonies effectively and the neglect to which they relegated the remote territories north of Mexico City, but they occupied and settled areas in New Mexico, Arizona, California, and Florida that later became major centers of economic activity. In New Mexico in 1609, the Spaniards founded Santa Fe, a city that was a center for trade and commercial activity during the next three centuries, particularly after 1821, when the Santa Fe Trail was opened. They also founded San Antonio, El Paso, Tucson, San Diego, Los Angeles, and dozens of other strategically located settlements that are now cities.

The Mexican settlers who came to California during the early 1800s (they called themselves *californios*) became the rancheros who introduced sheep, cattle, and horse grazing to this territory, making the area an important stop for traders who came by sea. In Texas, the cattle ranches gave birth to the vaqueros, the first cowboys. These Spanish pioneers made a considerable contribution to the development of the region by establishing sheep and cattle ranches, introducing horses and other animals, new crops, irrigation and mining techniques, and the now traditional adobe construction (Gann and Duignan, 1986). The Spanish gave the Southwest its distinctive character and, more than any other U.S. region, the territory bears to this day a distinctive Hispanic imprint.

Spain maintained control of its North American territories until the first half of the nineteenth century. By then, the 13 British colonies had shared the North American continent with the Spanish, the Dutch, and the French for more than a century. The relationship between the Spanish and the English colonists had been strained at times because of their economic rivalry, their concern with territorial encroachment, and their religious differences. In 1776, the colonies declared their independence from England, and after the Revolutionary War, in which England was defeated, they constituted themselves in 1787 into the federation of the United States of America.

One of the most downplayed facts in U.S. history is the large degree of Spanish participation in the Revolutionary War. When the colonists declared their desire to be free of British colonial rule in 1776, both Spain and France became major supporters of the revolutionaries, anticipating mutual economic benefits from trade with the new nation. During the first two years of the war, Spain's support of the colonists was tacit and most aid was covert, in order to avoid its own war with the English.

A great deal of recognition has been given to the role of the Marquis de Lafayette in the success of the Revolutionary War. In contrast, the figure of Bernardo de Gálvez, Spanish governor of Louisiana, has not received the same prominence. Between 1779 and 1781, he commanded an army that defeated the English in Louisiana, Alabama, and Florida. His mestizo army included not only Spanish but also Indian and black soldiers, and its military actions kept major Gulf ports open for communications and the flow of weapons and other supplies to the colonists. The Spanish also gained command of Mississippi, frustrating British attempts to encircle and isolate the southern front of the 13 colonies. From the early stages of the American Revolution, money and supplies from Spain and its colonies contributed to turning the tide in favor of the revolutionary forces. The Spanish colonies of Cuba and Puerto Rico were granted permission by Spain to trade with the American colonists, particularly in products such as sugar, which had been available to them before the war from the British-controlled West Indies. Toward the end of the war, Cuban citizens supplied funds that helped Washington's troops in the decisive Battle of Yorktown.

A few decades after the American Revolution, Spain faced wars of independence waged by its New World colonies. Liberalism and its democratic ideals of equality and the sovereignty of the people, embodied in the republican form of government, had been espoused by European intellectuals of the Enlightenment and provided the ideological foundations of the American and French Revolutions of 1776 and 1789, respectively. The Enlightenment's ideology of liberal democracy and representative government inspired the emerging creole bourgeoisies in the North and South American colonies in their efforts to topple the colonial empires of the European monarchies. Independence was also the assertion that the socioeconomic interests of the mother countries no longer represented, and in fact were antagonistic to, the expanding socioeconomic interests of the creoles. For the people of Latin America the successful American Revolution became a source of inspiration in their own struggle for independence, and the U.S. Constitution served as a model of political and moral virtues, and democratic rule.

Spain's position as an important European power suffered a major setback with Napoleon's invasion of 1808. A few years earlier, in 1803, Spain had sold Louisiana to the French, who in turn sold it to the United States. Then came the purchase and annexation of Florida by the United States in 1819. These two incidents served as the first indicators of U.S. intentions and future policies for territorial expansion to the west and south. Manifest Destiny was unmistakably emerging as a doctrine that guided the young U.S. nation in its conviction that it was destined to rule the entire North American continent to its natural borders.

In the Monroe Doctrine of 1823, the United States warned the imperialist-minded European nations to respect the sovereignty of the new American nations and to stay out of the Western Hemisphere. But the credo "America for the Americans" did not turn into a mere condemnation of imperialism; it became an instrument of U.S. national policy and an assertion that a new power was set to dominate the Americas. The doctrine would not prevent the United States from infringing on the sovereign rights of the new Latin American nations during the decades that followed. In the final analysis, it became a natural complement to Manifest Destiny.

By the 1830s all of the Spanish colonies in Central and South America, with the exception of the Hispanic Caribbean islands, had become independent nations. The Spanish territories to the southwest of the United States, which had constituted a part of the viceroyalty of New Spain during Spanish colonial rule, had become part of the nation of Mexico when its independence was granted by Spain in 1821. Relations between the United States and the new nation of Mexico were initially amicable, but began to deteriorate when U.S. expansionist policies continued throughout the continent, encroaching upon Mexican territory.

At the beginning of the nineteenth century, the tide of U.S. growth and expansion swelled, and Anglo settlers and merchants began to move west with irresistible force. During the early 1820s, Stephen Austin was granted permission by the Spanish government to establish a settlement of 300 Anglo families in southern Texas. Gradually, the Anglo colonists increased in population and expanded their sphere of economic and military power and influence in the area. By the 1830s some 25,000 Anglos had settled in Texas. The Anglos considered themselves superior to and more energetic than the Mexicans, and often viewed them as backward, lazy, and inferior. It has been argued that these shared Anglo images of the Mexicans, which surfaced during the disputes over Texas, provided an outline for Anglo stereotypical images of all Hispanics to date (Moore and Pachón, 1985). The U.S. government promoted a rebellion of the Anglos living in that territory that ultimately led to the declaration of Texas independence in 1836, and its annexation by the United States in 1845. Bitter images and memories of this conflict, surrounding such incidents as those related to the Alamo, remained for both sides; and relations between the two countries further deteriorated when the U.S. government attempted to annex California. The gold rush of the 1840s had brought an avalanche of adventurers to this territory that forced most of the Mexican population off their lands. As had happened in Texas, the Anglo frontier people eventually brought the demise of the original Hispanic settlers.

War between Mexico and the United States broke out in 1846, and in 1847, U.S. troops invaded and captured Mexico City. As part of the 1848 Treaty of Guadalupe Hidalgo, Mexico was forced to yield almost half of its land; all the territory north of the Río Grande was then transferred to the United States. Mexico lost what is now California, Arizona, New Mexico, and the territory from which the states of Colorado, Kansas, Nevada, Oklahoma, Utah, and Wyoming were formed.

The *hispanos,* people of Hispanic descent who remained in the new U.S. Southwest, became through the years a segregated minority with the increasing influx of Anglo citizens. Although the peace treaty between Mexico and the United States stipulated that the Hispanic population of the Southwest would have the right to continue its cultural traditons and use of Spanish, the second-class treatment of this population became common-place. Laws were often passed to drive the Hispanic population out of these territories, and legal disputes over property ownership usually found Hispanics on the losing end. Mexicans gradually became outsiders in what had been their own land.

The final stage of U.S. territorial expansionism was the Spanish-American War of 1898. During the years preceding the war, the U.S. government had recognized the strategic military importance of the Caribbean islands of Cuba and Puerto Rico, particularly if plans to construct a proposed U.S.-controlled canal through Central America, connecting the Atlantic and the Pacific as a new commercial route, became a reality. Both islands were also important sugar, coffee, and tobacco producers; thus U.S. government discussions about their annexation, as well as that of the Hawaiian islands, were commonplace in the 1890s (Foner, 1972). A mysterious explosion of the *Maine,* a U.S. Navy ship anchored in the port of Havana, gave the United States the welcomed opportunity to declare war on Spain. As a result, the United States took possession of Cuba and Puerto Rico, and the remaining Spanish overseas territories of Hawaii, Guam and the Philippines, putting an end to the once vast Spanish colonial empire. Only Cuba was granted its independence by the United States in 1902, though it remained in the U.S. political and economic sphere of influence until the 1959 revolution. Puerto Rico was governed by U.S. officials until the late 1940s, when it began to receive a larger degree of local autonomy; in 1952 it became the *Estado Libre Asociado* (Commonwealth) of Puerto Rico. This politically controversial association has not dispelled the realities of a colonial relationship, since Puerto Rico does not have national sovereignty or its own citizenship, and all monetary and military matters are controlled by the United States.

In the course of the nineteenth century, commercial contact between the Spanish colonies of Cuba and Puerto Rico, and the United States had been substantial, and island sugar, coffee, and tobacco exports had turned into some of the most desirable U.S. imports. These commercial relationships facilitated the flow of Cuban and Puerto Rican political refugees, who came primarily to New York and Florida after 1868, when both islands revolted against Spanish colonial domination. Such pioneer communities established migratory patterns of settlement for Cubans and Puerto Ricans that were to be followed by immigrants who came from these countries during the second half of the twentieth century (Poyo, 1984; Sánchez Korrol, 1983).

THE NEWCOMERS

The Hispanic settlements in the United States before the twentieth century laid significant roots for each of the three major groups: Mexicans, Puerto Ricans, and Cubans. The fact that Hispanics were not as visible then as they are in our century is due to their small relative numbers compared with the rest of the population.

For contemporary Hispanics the "discovery" of the pioneer communities has provided an ancestry, a sense of continuity and community support, and a source of ethnic identity. This is particularly important for U.S.-born Hispanics, who have fewer ties or less contact with the countries of origin of their ancestors.

The Mexicans

Mexicans constitute the largest group of Hispanics in the United States. The waves of Mexican immigrants who have come to the Southwest during this century have been highly dependent upon the fluctuations of the U.S. economy. The United States has welcomed Mexicans when in need of cheap labor, and sent them back when the need diminishes. The recruitment of Mexican labor has taken place during periods of U.S. economic expansion and labor shortages, such as the construction of the railroad system in the 1880s; the bracero (contract farm worker) program initiated in 1942, during World War II; and the more recent waves of undocumented workers during the 1980s. Systematic deportations and repatriations of Mexicans have also been common during periods of low economic activity, often in violation of the civil rights of people who were U.S.-born but could not prove their citizenship or who were not citizens but had resided in the United States for many decades. Good examples are the massive deportations during the Great Depression and during the postwar period of the 1950s, to reduce the number of people seeking employment or in need of social assistance. By 1954 nearly 4 million Mexicans had been expelled from the country, compared with about 200,000 during the 1930s. These policies clearly demonstrate how Mexicans were used during periods of pressing demand for hired hands and then abandoned to their fate. However, crackdowns on undocumented aliens such as "Operation Wetback" (*los mojados*, Mexicans who crossed the border by swimming across the Río Grande), which took place in the 1950s, and more recent efforts have not put a stop to the steady flow of undocumented workers (García, 1980; Bustamante, 1973; Bustamante and Martínez, 1979; Portes, 1978).

It has been accurately stated that some of the newest and oldest

Americans are from Mexico (Sowell, 1981). Although most Mexicans arrived in the United States after World War II, those grouped together as "Mexicans," "Mexican-Americans," or "Chicanos" represent a variety of historical experiences, ranging from the descendants of the original settlers in the Southwest; through Mexicans who migrated to the United States, became naturalized U.S. citizens, and produced subsequent generations of U.S.-born individuals of Mexican descent; to the transient Mexican population with visas or work permits; to the undocumented workers.

Documented or undocumented Mexicans who come to the United States are frequently subjected to the worst working conditions by employers, particularly in agriculture and manufacturing industries. In the early 1960s, this situation led to a crusade to organize and unionize farm workers under the leadership of César Chávez, the son of a farm worker. In 1962 the National Farm Workers Association (later the United Farm Workers Union) was founded. The union affiliated itself with the powerful AFL-CIO, and in spite of strong opposition from the Teamsters and many U.S. growers, it succeeded in getting better wages and benefits for workers through national grape and lettuce buyers' boycotts that lasted several years. It also succeeded in denouncing the exploitation of Mexican farm workers by growers, and the movement received national attention and the support of a large sector of the nonminority population.

The issue of the influx of undocumented aliens at the U.S.-Mexican border has been a pressing one for U.S. officials and politicians in recent years. The impact of the passage of the Simpson-Mazzoli bill with its amnesty program, and the new Immigration Reform and Control Act that requires documentation for U.S. employment, remains to be seen. More compelling is an understanding of the issue of "illegal" immigration as it affects Mexicans, Central Americans, and other Hispanics, within the context of an international labor migration process and world capitalism (see Chapters 9 and 10). Portes (1982) describes this process as one plagued with contradictions between its determinants and the policy measures formulated to control it. He considers the flow of undocumented workers to be a response to the economic hegemony exercised by the United States over economically peripheral countries, an influence that produces patterns of industrialization within those countries that increase rather than decrease the pressure on their working classes and maintain high levels of unemployment. Portes also indicates that there is an increasing need for cheap labor in the advanced capitalist nations, and immigrants increase the ranks of the industrial reserve army and contribute to depressing wages. Finally, he notes that undocumented labor does not pose a major threat "to middle-class nonmanual workers, to artisans and highly skilled workers, and in general to workers organized in strong unions . . ." since it does not seek or gain entry into the mainstream of the U.S. economy (1982:519). Irrespective of all the push/pull factors that influence immigration, thousands of immigrants from Latin America daily face all kinds of vicissitudes and often risk their lives to reach the prosperous *norte.*

The Puerto Ricans

It has been said that Puerto Ricans are also both old and new Americans (Sowell, 1981). This statement holds true, within the continental United States, even before Puerto Rico became a colonial territory of the United States in 1898, and Puerto Ricans U.S. citizens at birth in 1917, which allows them to travel without restrictions from the island to the U.S. mainland.

In studies of the "new" Puerto Rican community in New York City, some social scientists have failed to recognize the existence of an earlier community and its importance to the post-World War II migrations that followed (Glazer and Moynihan, 1970). More recent works have shed a light on the significance of these overlooked early settlements (Colón, 1961; Andreu Iglesias, 1977; Sánchez Korrol, 1983).

As was mentioned earlier, the roots of the Puerto Rican community in New York City were laid during the last three decades of the nineteenth century, when New York became a major center for revolutionary exiles from Cuba and Puerto Rico, who had fought for the independence of the two remaining Spanish colonies in the Americas. Freedom fighters such as the Cuban patriot José Martí, and the Puerto Ricans Ramón Emeterio Betances, Eugenio María de Hostos, Bonocio Tió, and his wife, the poet Lola Rodríguez de Tió, were among the most prominent exiles in New York City. There they garnered support for Antillean independence and participated in the city's intellectual life. Two other Puerto Rican expatriates, Francisco "Pachín" Marín and Sotero Figueroa, were particularly active in the publication of newspapers aimed at propagating their political ideals and maintaining solidarity within the community. *El Pastillón, Patria, El Porvenir,* and *La Revolución* are only a few of those publications that reflected the community's cultural and civic life.

Other early Puerto Rican migrants included merchants, students, and factory workers (Sánchez Korrol, 1983). During the early 1900s there were also migratory waves of contract sugar workers to Hawaii (Camacho Souza, 1986). The expanding U.S. cigar industry led migrants from both Puerto Rico and Cuba to settle in Key West, Tampa, and New Orleans (primarily Cubans), and Philadelphia and New York (Ojeda, 1986).

One of the most prominent nineteenth-century migrants was Arturo A. Schomburg, who arrived in New York City from Puerto Rico when he was 17. A year later he joined other Cuban and Puerto Rican exiles in the founding of the Cuban Revolutionary Party to struggle for the independence of the two Caribbean islands from Spanish colonial rule.

As a black Puerto Rican, Schomburg had profound affinities with the

New York black community and became interested in the study of black culture and history. His efforts led to the establishment in 1911 of the Negro Society for Historical Research, which gathered thousands of books and documents on the black experience and played a significant role in the *negritude* movement of those years (Ojeda, 1986). Today the Schomburg Center for Research in Black Culture stands as a tribute to the man who served two communities and two cultures.

It was not until after the United States defeated Spain and took over its colonial territories, Puerto Rico among them, that Puerto Ricans began to migrate in more significant numbers. In 1910 there were around 2000 Puerto Ricans living in the United States, but the number had increased to 53,000 by 1930, to 301,000 by 1950, and to 1,429,000 by 1970 (Wagenheim, 1975).

The small *colonia* in New York City indisputably laid the basic pattern of Puerto Rican migration for the population that came later (Sánchez Korrol, 1983). The great migrations took place after World War II, the Puerto Ricans becoming the first airborne migration. As with Mexicans, the migration flow patterns of Puerto Ricans during this century have largely depended upon the fluctuations of the U.S. economy and the peripheral economic position of their respective countries vis-à-vis the United States. Nonetheless, the fact that Puerto Ricans are U.S. citizens has facilitated their back-and-forth migration patterns, while for the Mexicans the continuous flow across the border has taken place to a substantial degree illegally.

During the late 1960s and 1970s there was a reverse migration trend of Puerto Ricans back to the island (Hernández, 1967). For the first time in many decades, more Puerto Ricans returned to the island than migrated. This is partially explained by the depressed economy of New York City during those years, and the moving out of industries, such as textiles, that employed large numbers of Puerto Ricans (Bose, 1986). For the same reasons, Puerto Ricans began to spread into other parts of the United States, to Hartford, Chicago, Newark, Boston, Philadelphia, Cleveland, and Los Angeles. The result was that by 1980 the percentage of the Puerto Rican population in New York City had decreased to 49 percent, in contrast with 64 percent the previous decade.

The reverse migration trend was, however, a temporary phenomenon. In the 1980s another new trend is developing in Puerto Rican migration. There is a higher incidence of professional Puerto Ricans who are migrating to the United States compared with the unskilled or semiskilled workers of earlier periods. If the pattern continues, it will probably have a marked effect on the U.S. Puerto Rican community.

Another situation that has caught the attention of social scientists in recent years is the large increase in Puerto Rican female-headed households, amounting to almost half of the total (Bose, 1986). But a more vital issue is the fact that most of these families live at the poverty level and are primarily dependent on welfare, maintaining a feminization of poverty pattern among Puerto Ricans.

Puerto Ricans are still the second largest group of Hispanics in the United States, with a population of more than 2 million, gradually approaching the population of the island, which stands close to 3.5 million. Ironically, Puerto Ricans, who are U.S. citizens and come from a country that is a U.S. territory, remain the Hispanic group with the lowest socioeconomic indicators (see Chapters 1, 2, and 4).

The Cubans

Before the 1959 revolution, Cuban immigration to the United States had been relatively insignificant (Portes and Bach, 1985). Nonetheless, Cuban expatriates had already left their imprint on the United States in the 1860s. About 10,000 Cubans had left the island to settle in New York City, in the areas of Key West and Tampa, Florida, and in New Orleans between 1868 and 1895, when Cuba was engaged in wars of independence against the Spanish (Poyo, 1984). Through the years they turned the area of Tampa into a major cigar manufacturing center. Taking its name from Martínez Ybor, owner of one of the most important cigar factories, Ybor City stands today as a testament to the Cuban presence in the state of Florida more than a century ago. As with the Puerto Ricans, the early Cuban communities established migratory patterns for those who came almost a century later (Poyo, 1984).

Cultural and political activity in the early Cuban community manifested itself through the proliferation of newspapers such as *El Eco de Cuba, El Cubano, La Voz de América, La Independencia, El Republicano,* and *La República,* among many others that "developed and defined separatist thinking and circulated in all centers of Cuban population in the country giving a sense of unity and commonality of purpose" (Poyo, 1984:53). These publications also became part of the annals of the Spanish-language press in the United States, a cultural tradition that has been followed by all Hispanic groups and continues to this date. From a political standpoint, the nineteenth-century publications played an important role in weakening Spanish colonial rule and in providing separatist leaders with both moral and financial support from the emigré communities.

The first sizable waves of Cuban immigration to the United States did not arrive until after the Cuban Revolution, particularly after 1961, when Castro's revolutionary government declared itself socialist and the United States decided to break diplomatic relations with Cuba. Large numbers of Cuban refugees settled in Florida, Puerto Rico, Mexico, and Spain. The U.S. government has defined the influx of Cubans into the United States as a political exodus, but it has been argued that individual determinants of immigration were frequently economic, particularly in more recent years

(Portes and Bach, 1985). The first generation of Cubans who arrived in the early years of the revolution expected to return to Cuba after the overthrow of the Castro government. This is not the case for the more recent arrivals, especially those who came in the 1980 Mariel boatlift, the second largest wave of Cuban immigrants within a single year. One out of five Cubans in the United States is now U.S.-born, and agewise they have the highest median age among Hispanic groups in the country. After almost three decades of a socialist government in Cuba that has widespread popular support, government collapse appears unlikely, and even more unlikely is the return to Cuba of the U.S.-born Cuban generation.

Many of the first wave of Cuban exiles were members of the ruling or middle classes, and contrast themselves with those who came in the Mariel boatlift. The 125,000 *marielitos* were overwhelmingly working-class Cubans; 70.9 percent were blue-collar workers. Contrary to popular belief, less than 20 percent of them were prison inmates or mental patients (Pedraza-Bailey, 1985). However, the Mariel exodus changed the image of Cubans as a professional and business-oriented middle class, and has been a cause of friction within the community itself. The exodus coincided with a sluggish U.S. economy characterized by low productivity, inflation, and high unemployment. Whether or not the volatile economic recovery of recent years will improve the lot of the *marielitos* remains an open question.

Of all the Hispanic groups, Cubans have been, in economic terms, the most conspicuous and successful. Hence, they have not been as critical as Mexicans or Puerto Ricans in their view of U.S. society. Aside from the political circumstances that brought them to a country that welcomed them as exiles, and the higher socioeconomic factors in their profile as immigrants, the prosperity they have achieved contrasts markedly with the status of the other two groups. Many of the early Cuban exiles were educated and skilled, though a large number had to retrain or be certified in their professions to be able to practice or work in the United States. They have become a controlling force in the city of Miami, and are virtually responsible for the revitalization of the city as a major center for commerce and trade with Latin America.

For many years Cuban-Americans resisted identification with other, less privileged Hispanic minorities. Now that the hopes for a return to Cuba appear to have faded, however, Cubans seem to be moving from identification as an exile group to an ethnic minority, since their leaders see this as "an opportunity to develop a wider constituency in the Latino community and to secure greater political leverage locally and nationally" (Safa, 1984: v).

The New Hispanics

Political repression and revolution in Central and South America during the late 1970s and 1980s, and the trend of international labor migration in the world capitalist economy, have brought new waves of Latin American immigrants to the United States. Varying numbers have arrived, primarily from Nicaragua, El Salvador, Guatemala, Colombia, Ecuador, Argentina, Chile, and the Dominican Republic. These "other Hispanics" number about 3 million, almost one-fourth of the total U.S. Hispanic population.

Twenty-four percent of all Hispanics in the United States (this figure includes Puerto Ricans) arrived during the decade that comprises the mid-1970s to the mid-1980s (Church, 1985). Never before has this country absorbed so many newcomers speaking the same foreign language in such a short time. There is a growing awareness in the country of "a silent invasion from the south," the latinization of Anglo culture as the Hispanic presence becomes more perceptible in sheer numbers and in all aspects of the daily lives of some major U.S. urban centers. Undoubtedly, this major shift in the ethnic composition of the United States, caused by the substantial and continuous influx of new immigrants from Latin America (and Asia)—groups that are essentially nonwhite—will probably shape and determine U.S. immigration policies in the decades to come.

The effects that these new trends will have on the United States are frequently perceived in negative terms by the majority population. Nonwhite immigrants are viewed through the traditionally racist optic that is still ingrained in the fabric of U.S. society, and that tends to favor European immigrants and facilitates their becoming an integral part of the U.S. "mainstream" culture. Recent opposition to any official bilingualism in the United States and the reduction of federal funds for bilingual education are manifestations of the country's fears of having its national unity weakened by the influence of other cultures. These prejudicial attitudes are underscored by the fact that Hispanics have a pattern of resistance to assimilation and a strong sense of ethnic consciousness (see Chapter 5).

The prevalence of these attitudes continues to undermine the value of bilingualism as an educational tool and the respect for cultural diversity (elements that are present at every stage of this country's history). There is a failure to recognize that for racial minorities, ethnic consciousness is a defense against the exploitation and discrimination they have been subjected to in U.S. society, and a way of validating themselves and improving their collective self-esteem. This process in turn helps them to become less alienated and more productive members of society. It is then understandable that Hispanics tend to favor some maintenance of a bicultural identity, but reasonable to assume that in time they will try to integrate more and more, as many other generations of Hispanics before them, into U.S. cultural and socioeconomic life and to pursue the same goals of prosperity and well-being as the average U.S. citizen.

The disparities and differences between the groups of Hispanic new-comers are considerable. There are immigrants from Chile and Argentina who are primarily white, urban, middle-class or skilled workers with formal education, and who conform more closely to the pattern of past western European immigration. Other groups, such as the Dominicans and Central Americans, do not fare so well in socioeconomic terms, and are subject to more racial discrimination (see Chapters 1, 2, 4, and 9).

The diversity among Hispanics distinguishes them from more politically unified minorities, such as blacks, Jews, and Italian-Americans. However, it has become evident in recent years that Hispanic politicians are rallying around points of commonality as their political involvement increases. Hispanics have already tried to make a significant political contribution to U.S. foreign policy in Latin America, and domestic issues such as civil rights, affirmative action, and bilingual education have often brought them together in a united front.

THE ETHNIC REVITALIZATION MOVEMENT

Being racial minorities at the bottom of the economic ladder, the status of Puerto Ricans and Mexicans in the United States is far from similar to that of the average American citizen. The consciousness-raising decade of the 1960s and the civil rights movement allowed Puerto Ricans and Chicanos to join blacks in their struggle to revitalize and reassert their ethnic identity. This process undergone by U.S. racial minorities was an attempt to rid themselves of the negative self-image and stigma internalized through years of being victimized by racism and discrimination. The search for and reconstruction of a denied positive identity led to an explosion of ethnic pride and community militancy (see Chapter 5). It also provided the ideological foundations for the emergence of black, Chicano, Puerto Rican, and Native American ethnic studies, and bilingual education programs in many U.S. universities. Furthermore, it increased political and cultural activism among nonwhite minorities.

At the community level, many organizations emerged. The Black Panther Party became the radical voice of blacks, Chicanos founded La Raza Unida, and Puerto Ricans founded the Young Lords Party. Many other less radical community advocacy organizations, such as the Mexican-American and the Puerto Rican Legal Defense and Education Funds (MALDEF; PRLDEF), counterparts of the blacks' NAACP, also emerged. Militant whites involved in the civil rights or the Vietnam antiwar movements also supported some of the minority causes. Literature, music, and art became a collective way of expressing the ideological affinities of the time, and the distinctiveness and originality of the socially oriented movement. The struggle against racism and the socioeconomic exploitation and deprivation faced by Third World peoples became a common cause, in an attempt to raise the consciousness of the divided U.S. nation. The movement received its primary support from students, intellectuals, and community leaders.

Among Hispanics, cultural activism found expression in *El Grito:*

Journal of Contemporary Chicano Thought, established in 1968, and in *The Rican: Journal of Contemporary Puerto Rican Thought,* first published in 1971. Other journals, such as *Aztlán, The Revista Chicano-Riqueña* [now *The Americas Review*], and *The Bilingual Review,* provided Hispanic scholars and artists with important vehicles of expression. While Rodolfo Gonzales published the moving verses of *I Am Joaquín* (1967), his counterpart, Puerto Rican poet Pedro Pietri, gave us *Puerto Rican Obituary* (1973). Powerful autobiographical novels, such as Oscar Z. Acosta's *The Autobiography of a Brown Buffalo* (1972) and Piri Thomas' *Down These Mean Streets* (1967), exposed the effects of U.S. racism and continued to reinforce the literary parallels and convergence between the two groups. Artistic creativity was intended to inspire social action; and the working-class origins of many of these Hispanic writers, and the nature of their literary themes, led them to assume the role of voice of the community. Luis Valdez and his *Teatro Campesino,* which emerged in support of Chávez' fledging farm worker movement and consisted solely of agricultural workers, often performed in the streets, and is perhaps one of the best examples of how this cultural movement tried to reach the masses.

At the time this ethnic revitalization was taking place, most Cubans were still recent arrivals in the United States hoping for the overthrow of the Castro government so they could return to their country. Thus, they did not have a prominent role in this particular experience, which was promoted primarily by second-generation Chicanos and Puerto Ricans.

It has been argued that "By the 1970s, the radical dreams that had inspired so many Chicano and Puerto Rican activists had evaporated" (Gann and Duignan, 1986). But despite the extreme ideological conservatism that has plagued this country since the late 1970s, and which could be considered a counterreaction to the radical liberalism of the 1960s and early 1970s, the ethnic revitalization movement gave nonwhite ethnicity a degree of visibility and acceptability it had never had before. It provided Chicano and Puerto Rican intellectuals and artists the opportunity to explore issues related to their own culture and identity, their relationship and interaction with the U.S. mainstream culture, and their place in U.S. society. It was a period of intensive search, reconstruction, questioning, and denunciation. It also allowed both groups to examine the neglected elements of their own cultures, particularly those related to the Indian or black components, often suppressed by the preponderance of the Hispanic element, and to acknowledge the subordinate role to which women have been relegated in these cultures. And, finally, it forced the U.S. government to examine and improve its policies of neglect and inequality toward racial minorities and to develop more responsive ones.

The late 1960s and the 1970s brought increased visibility to racial minorities, including Hispanics, and, more important, it fostered the emergence of new and positive symbols of ethnicity, and improved opportunities for upward mobility. The words "Chicano" and "Nuyorican," which were initially used in a derogatory way to identify second-generation Mexicans and Puerto Ricans, respectively, achieved positive meanings of cultural distinctiveness. Their cultures are not replicas of those in the "old country," but new, emerging forms born of bicultural contact and a minority experience within the larger context of a dominant white U.S. society.

HISPANIC PRESENCE IN THE ARTS, LETTERS, AND SPORTS

Any attempt to summarize the Hispanic contributions to contemporary U.S. cultural life will suffer from a compensatory tendency to focus on a handful of notable figures, and from the likely omission of many worthy names.

The film and TV industries in the United States have played a crucial role in perpetuating distorted images and stereotypes of Hispanics. Therefore, those Hispanics who made it within the ranks of mainstream distinction did not have it easy, and many saw themselves acting out some of those same stereotypes as the only way to make a living. Others were able to beat the odds and now serve as prominent role models to the Hispanic community.

Two Hispanic actors have been Academy Award winners: the Puerto Ricans José Ferrer and Rita Moreno. Actors such as the flamboyant Ricardo Montalbán, from Mexico, and Fernando Lamas, from Argentina, have also achieved distinguished careers through the years. Two Puerto Ricans, Chita Rivera and Raúl Juliá, have made their mark on Broadway, and Hispanic theater in the United States owes a great deal to the efforts of Luis Valdez with his *Teatro Campesino*, and Miriam Colón with her Puerto Rican Traveling Theater. Plays such as *Short Eyes* (1974) by Miguel Piñero and *Zoot Suit* (1977) by Luis Valdez have received critical acclaim. Many Hispanic musicians have brought the Latin beat to the United States through the tango, the rumba, the mambo, the cha-cha-chá, the bossa nova, la bamba, and salsa. The voices of Ritchie Valens, Joan Baez, Trini López, Vikki Carr, José Feliciano, Julio Iglesias, and Menudo are among the favorites on the charts of the last three decades.

Being the fourth largest Spanish-speaking country in the world, there is an expanding market in the United States for newspapers, magazines, and radio and TV shows in Spanish or dealing with Hispanics. The emergence of the now powerful Spanish International Network (SIN) and its increasing number of U.S. affiliates has played a major role in giving Hispanics increased media visibility.

Sports history has made room for Roberto Clemente, a Triple Crown baseball player and great humanitarian who died in a plane crash on his way to help earthquake victims in Nicaragua in 1972, and for many other baseball players. At least 10 percent of U.S. major league players are Hispanic. Tennis player Pancho González; golfers Lee Trevino, Chi Chi

Rodríguez, and Nancy López; jockey Angel Cordero, Jr.; and several light and middleweight boxing champions have also occupied memorable space on the sports pages.

In spite of the often conflictive and tumultuous relationship between the United States and Latin America since the mid-1800s, a persistent reciprocal interest has existed between U.S. intellectuals and writers and those from the Hispanic world. Both peninsular Spanish literature and Latin American literature have exerted their influence on American literature, and American letters have had their influence on Hispanic literatures. A few examples will illustrate the extent of this culture contact.

Friendships between Spanish and American writers have existed since the nineteenth century, and that has left a notable Spanish influence on some American writers and has inspired others to translate Spanish works into English. Washington Irving's *The Alhambra* (1832) is a collection of essays, folktales, and anecdotal or picturesque sketches that resulted from his trips to Spain and his friendship with the novelist Cecilia Böhl de Faber (known by her literary pseudonym Fernán Caballero). William Dean Howells, the father of U.S. literary realism, was a great admirer and friend of the Spanish novelist Armando Palacio Valdés, which contributed to the latter's novels gaining popularity in the United States. The poet Henry Wadsworth Longfellow did one of the best existing translations of Jorge Manríque's *Coplas*; John Dos Passos translated some of Antonio Machado's poetry; and Waldo Frank, Thornton Wilder, and Ernest Hemingway are only a few among many U.S. writers who have transferred their fascination with Hispanic culture into their own writing (Williams, 1955).

The works of U.S. Hispanists such as George Ticknor, author of *History of Spanish Literature* (1849), and William H. Prescott, author of *The History of the Conquest of Mexico* (1843) and *The History of the Conquest of Peru* (1847), have become classics in their respective fields. In 1904 Hispanist Archer M. Huntington founded the Hispanic Society of America and promoted the establishment of a Hispanic Room at the Library of Congress.

For some of the early U.S. Hispanists, their interest in Hispanic cultures was the result of a curiosity about the exotic or of intellectual elitism, and there was initially a traditional tendency to focus more on Spain than on Latin America. However, since the 1960s the impact of Latin American prose fiction writers on world literature has been immense. Many Latin American authors have provided some of the best models for U.S. writers and critics. The works of Jorge Luis Borges, Nobel Prize winner Gabriel García Márquez, Mario Vargas Llosa, Carlos Fuentes, and many others have become easily available in English translations. U.S. feminist critics have paid close attention to Third World women writers, and authors such as Luisa Valenzuela, Isabel Allende, Nancy Morejón, and Claribel Alegría are getting increased recognition. More than ever before, success for a Latin

American writer is tied to being translated into English and entering the U.S. market.

Nothing better illustrates the cultural and literary continuity of *la hispanidad* in the United States than the work done by Chicano, Puerto Rican, and Cuban-American writers and artists. Each group has its distinctive body of literature reflecting the interactions of the two cultures and languages they possess, and the contacts between the two worlds that each group shares. These bodies of literature, written primarily in English but often in Spanish or bilingual, have frequently been ignored by scholars of American and Latin American literatures alike. The language issue, compounded with the fact that these literatures tend to have a working-class character and that the books are published primarily by small ethnic presses, further limits their diffusion and marketing, and hence their possibilitics for critical acclaim.

Literature is one of the most effective ways to represent experiences, and the cultural and historical experiences of minority groups have been mediated through a literary tradition more extensive than conventional accounts allow. As the literary legacy becomes more extensive, the invisibility begins to wane. There is now a corpus of important literary works by Chicano, Puerto Rican, and Cuban-American writers that, aside from all of their artistic merit, have become major sociological sources for the study of their respective communities. Among the Chicanos the most prominent writers include José Antonio Villarreal, Oscar Z. Acosta, Rolando Hinojosa, Rudolfo Anaya, Tomás Rivera, Estela Portillo, Rodolfo Gonzales, Alurista, Tino Villanueva, and Ricardo Sánchez (Bruce-Novoa, 1980). The most prolific New York Puerto Rican writers include Piri Thomas, Nicholasa Mohr, Pedro Pietri, Miguel Piñero, Miguel Algarín, Tato Laviera, Sandra M. Estévez, Edward Rivera, and Ed Vega (Acosta-Belén, 1976; Barradas and Rodríguez, 1980; Mohr, 1982). The Cuban-American group has given us José Yglesias and, more recently, the work of Roberto Fernández. There is also a large number of first-generation Cuban exile writers who continue to publish in Spanish and whose work is generally studied within the framework of Latin American letters. Regarding the substantial number of first-generation Puerto Rican writers living in the United States who also write primarily in Spanish, it is common to see their work studied as an extension of the island's literary experience, or for them to have their work published in Puerto Rico. This situation is gradually changing as new Hispanic or bilingual publication companies continue to proliferate in the United States.

CONCLUSION

Despite the long tradition and legacy that Hispanics have generated in the United States, the Hispanic population in the early part of this century was less than 1 million. Thus, overall, Hispanics are collectively a contemporary and young immigrant group.

In spite of the persistence of ethnicity among Hispanics, many social scientists have argued that they will assimilate into U.S. society as many other immigrant groups have done before them from generation to generation. They take Hispanics' orientation toward the traditional U.S. values of consumerism and material well-being as a sign of assimilation without considering that in all capitalist societies, citizens aspire to emulate the way of life of the dominant bourgeoisie. Much has been written about how the experiences of racial minorities have invalidated to a great extent the melting pot assimilation model, since their color always represents a major barrier to total integration into U.S. society. But other significant factors that retard Hispanic assimilation are the proximity that this population has to their countries of origin and the continued back-and-forth migration patterns that characterize some of the groups. This closeness to the native countries promotes the persistence of ethnic identity within the groups themselves. Concomitantly, the larger society, unwillingly or not, continues to be impacted by the Hispanic presence, frequently tending to ignore the positive and focus on the negative. Disadvantaged minorities are viewed as "a problem" in a country that propagates the image of being the land of opportunity, equality, and justice for all. Thus, changing the "blaming the victim" perception that the majority population has about minorities is a monumental task.

Some social scientists considered the ethnic revival of the late 1960s and 1970s as just an expression of symbolic ethnicity or "a symbolic allegiance to the culture of the immigrant generation, or that of the old country; a love for and a pride in a tradition that can be felt without having to be incorporated in everyday behavior" (Gans, 1982:501). No doubt, for the third and fourth generations of most European immigrant groups that has proven to be the case; and true enough, all immigrants tend to mythicize their relationship with their native culture. However, the inevitability of assimilation is more open to argument when one looks at the continuous flow of Hispanic immigrants to the United States every year, and its end is nowhere in sight.

The average non-Hispanic American's awareness of the Hispanic contributions to U.S. society is thus far permeated with clichés about the several states and geographical locations bearing Spanish names; the accomplishments of Hispanics in TV, motion pictures, and sports; the trendy popularity of tacos, burritos, and paella in the American cuisine; or the more dubious honor of being remembered as the "bandidos of the Alamo who murdered John Wayne," or the reckless gang members in *West Side Story* singing "I like to live in America." In a country that is conditioned to react more to images than to substance, the persistent task of creating a more profound understanding of the legacy and continuous contributions of U.S.

Hispanics and constructing new nonstereotyped images is still confronting us.

Being a Hispanic in the United States entails both negative and positive experiences. Without forgetting the problems of poverty, discrimination, and economic deprivation that most Hispanics confront, there is plenty of room, as we have seen, to emphasize what Hispanics have contributed and are contributing to the growth of this country. *Tabaquero*, garment worker, taxi driver, professor, farm worker, lawyer, politician, writer, actor, baseball player, boxer, banker, physician, entrepreneur, musician, painter, privileged or disadvantaged—Hispanics are important human resources to this society and an integral part of the fabric of American life.

In 1886, when the poet Emma Lazarus, herself a descendant of Sephardic Jewish immigrants, wrote her verses of "The New Colossus" (now inscribed at the base of the Statue of Liberty), they became a symbol of the living voice of an America that welcomed the "tired, poor and huddled masses yearning to breathe free." The immigrants came, and continue to come, searching for the freedom and prosperity that this country represents. For those who are already an integral part of this society, the words of the poet of the Americas, Walt Whitman, are a good reminder of how cultural diversity has made this country what it is, and what it will be:

We Americans have yet to really learn our own antecedents, and sort them to unify them. They will be found ampler than has been supposed, and in widely different sources. . . . Many leading traits of our future personality, and some of the best ones, will certainly prove to have originated from other than British stock. . . . To that composite American identity of the future, Spanish character will supply some of the most needed parts. (1948:402-3)

REFERENCES

Acosta-Belén, Edna. 1976. "The Literature of the Puerto Rican Minority in the United States." *The Bilingual Review* 7, nos. 1-2: 107-116.

Acuña, Rodolfo. 1972. *Occupied America: The Chicanos' Struggle Toward Liberation*. San Francisco: Canfield Press.

Andreu Iglesias, César, ed. 1977. *Memorias de Bernardo Vega*. Río Piedras, P.R.: Ediciones Huracán.

Barradas, Efraín, and Rafael Rodríguez. 1980. *Herejes y mitificadores: Muestra de poesía puertorriqueña en los Estados Unidos*. Río Piedras, P.R.: Ediciones Huracán.

Bose, Christine. 1986. "Puerto Rican Women in the United States: An Overview." In Edna Acosta-Belén, ed., *The Puerto Rican Woman*. New York: Praeger.

Bruce-Novoa, J. 1980. *Chicano Authors: Inquiry by Interview*. Austin: University of Texas Press.

Bustamante, Jorge A. 1973. "The Historical Context of Undocumented Mexican Immigration to the United States." *Aztlán* 3: 257-281.

Bustamante, Jorge A., and Gerónimo G. Martínez. 1979. "Undocumented Immigration from Mexico: Beyond Borders but Within Systems." *Journal of International Affairs* 33 (Fall/Winter): 265-284.

Camacho Souza, Blase. 1986. "Boricuas Hawaiianos." In Centro de Estudios Puertorriqueños, Oral History Task Force, *Extended Roots: From Hawaii to New York, Migraciones Puertorriqueñas a los Estados Unidos,* pp. 7-18. New York: Centro de Estudios Puertorriqueños, CUNY.

Centro de Estudios Puertorriqueños, Oral History Task Force. 1979. *Labor Migration Under Capitalism.* New York: Monthly Review Press.

Church, George. 1985. "Hispanics: A Melding of Cultures." *Time* (July 8): 36-39.

Colón, Jesús. 1961. *A Puerto Rican in New York and Other Sketches.* New York: International Pubs. Co. (New edition, 1982).

Estrada, Leobardo. 1981. "Hispanic Realities of the Eighties." In *Hispanics and Grantmakers: A Special Report of Foundation News,* pp. 24-27. Washington; DC: The Foundation News.

Fitzpatrick, Joseph P. 1971. *Puerto Rican-Americans: The Meaning of Migration to the Mainland.* Englewood Cliffs, NJ: Prentice-Hall.

Foner, Philip. 1972. *The Spanish-Cuban-American War and the Birth of American Imperialism.* New York: Monthly Review Press.

Gann, L. H., and Peter J. Duignan. 1986. *Hispanics in the United States: A History.* Boulder, CO: Westview Press.

Gans, Herbert J. 1982. "Symbolic Ethnicity: The Future of Ethnic Groups and Cultures in America." In Norman R. Yetman, ed., *Majority and Minority,* pp. 495-508. Boston: Allyn and Bacon.

García, Juan R. 1980. *Operation Wetback: The Mass Deportation of Mexican Undocumented Workers in 1954.* Westport, CT: Greenwood Press.

Glazer, Nathan and Daniel Moynihan. 1970. *Beyond the Melting Pot.* Cambridge: MIT Press.

Hernández, José. 1967. *Return Migration to Puerto Rico.* Berkeley: Institute of International Studies, University of California Press.

Leonard, Irving. 1953. *Los libros del conquistador.* México, DF: Fondo de Cultura Económica.

Mohr, Eugene. 1982. *The Nuyorican Experience: Puerto Rican Minority Literature in the United States.* Westport, CT: Greenwood Press.

Moore, Joan, and Harry Pachón. 1985. *Hispanics in the United States.* Englewood Cliffs, NJ: Prentice-Hall.

Ojeda, Félix. 1986. "Early Puerto Rican Community in New York." In Centro de Estudios Puertorriqueños, Oral Task Force, *Extended Roots: From Hawaii to New York, Migraciones Puertorriqueñas a los Estados Unidos,* pp. 41-53. New York: Centro de Estudios Puertorriqueños, CUNY.

Pear, Robert. 1987. "Hispanic Population Growing 5 Times as Fast as Rest of U.S." *New York Times,* September 11, pp. 1, 22.

Pedraza-Bailey, Silvia. 1985. "Cuba's Exiles: Portrait of a Refugee Migration." *International Migration Review* 19, no. 1: 4-33.

Portes, Alejandro. 1978. "Toward a Structural Analysis of Illegal (Undocumented) Immigration." *International Migration Review* 12 (Winter): 469-484.

———. 1982. "Illegal Immigration and the International System, Lessons from Recent Legal Immigrants to the United States." In Norman R. Yetman, ed., *Majority and Minority,* pp. 509-520. Boston: Allyn and Bacon.

Portes, Alejandro and Robert L. Bach. 1985. *Latin Journey: Cuban and Mexican Immigrants in the United States.* Los Angeles: University of California Press.

Poyo, Gerald E. 1984. "Cuban Communities in the United States: Toward an Overview of the 19th Century Experience." In M. Uriarte-Gastón and J. Cañas Martínez, eds., *Cubans in the United States,* pp. 44-64. Boston: Center for the Study of the Cuban Community.

Russell, Cheryl. 1983. "The News About Hispanics." *American Demographics* 5, no. 3 (March): 15-25.

Safa, Helen I. 1984. "Foreword." In M. Uriarte-Gastón and J. Cañas Martínez, eds., *Cubans in the United States,* pp. iv-v. Boston: Center for the Study of the Cuban Community.

Sánchez Korrol, Virginia. 1983. *From Colonia to Community: A History of Puerto Ricans in New York City, 1917-1948.* Westport, CT: Greenwood Press.

Sowell, Thomas. 1981. *Ethnic America.* New York: Basic Books.

Uriarte-Gastón, Mirén, and Jorge Cañas Martínez, eds. 1984. *Cubans in the United States.* Boston: Center for the Study of the Cuban Community.

Wagenheim, Kal. 1975. *A Survey of Puerto Ricans on the U.S. Mainland in the 1970s.* New York: Praeger.

Whitman, Walt. 1948. "The Spanish Element in Our Nationality." In M. Cowley, ed., *The Works of Walt Whitman,* Vol. 2, pp. 402-403. New York: Funk and Wagnalls.

Williams, Stanley. 1955. *The Spanish Background of American Literature.* 2 vols. New Haven: Yale University Press.

4

Telling Hispanics Apart: Latino Sociocultural Diversity

J. Jorge Klor de Alva

INTRODUCTION

The recent rapid growth of the Hispanic or "Latino" population and its diffusion across the full geographical and socioeconomic spectrum of the United States has generated both controversies and opportunities among Hispanics and non-Hispanics. Many descendants of European immigrants, forgetting the early struggles of their own families as they made their way in the new country, view the rising Hispanic population as a threat to their cultural domination; along with numerous black Americans, they see them as unwelcome competitors in the work place. Some Hispanics, who have resided in the United States for a generation or more and who are unsure of their social position, fear their newly arrived compatriots not only as economic competitors but also as a challenge to the image of themselves as successfully adapted Americans and as a potential force that will bring down socioracial stigmas upon them. On the other hand, many Americans belonging to all racial and ethnic groups recognize the substantial human, cultural, and socioeconomic resources the new immigrants have brought with them.

The mass media, advertising firms, government agencies, and the non-Hispanic population attempt to simplify their response to the burgeoning Spanish-speaking population by obscuring their substantial differences through collective labels (like "Hispanic") and stereotypical assumptions concerning their supposed common cultures and socioeconomic conditions. Different Hispanic groups, generally concentrated in different regions of the country, have little knowledge of each other and are often as surprised as non-Hispanics to discover the cultural gulfs that separate them. As a consequence, useful information that addresses the differences without hiding the similarities is rare, but is daily becoming more necessary.

Over the last few years, much has been written about the socioeconomic diversity of the Hispanic population. The 1980 census and the specialized reports it spawned have focused attention on the quantitative profiles of the distinct Latino communities. However, the difficulty of studying the complex nature of culture and a sensitivity to the charge of stereotyping have made most social scientists wary of describing the diverse qualitative characteristics of the various groups. Therefore, this chapter is written against a limited background of relevant cultural sources, but it draws from the extensive socioeconomic research that is being done by both academics and practitioners. Furthermore, this chapter seeks to integrate the socioeconomic data with the cultural to present a coherent picture of the class, nationality, race, and ethnic parameters and determinants of the Hispanic subcultures of the United States. The aim is to provide the reader with a brief synthesis of the cultural dynamics that make up everyday life for the fastest-growing U.S. population segment. Serving the needs of these primarily socioeconomically limited communities is a serious challenge that must be met with intelligence and understanding. This chapter argues that such an effort cannot succeed in ignorance of what makes a Hispanic experience life as a Mexican (here also used for "Chicano" or "Mexican-American"), a Puerto Rican (or "Nuyorican" if from New York City), a Cuban, or a member of any other Latin American nationality.

MIGRATION AND CULTURE

The economic and, to a lesser extent, the political nature of migration is suggested by the different rates of immigration of the various Hispanic groups. Table 4.1 reflects statistically the migratory responses to (1) the 1950-59 increase in Puerto Rican unemployment caused by "Operation Bootstrap"; (2) the 1959 Cuban Revolution's negative effect on the economic opportunities of the middle and upper classes; (3) the turbulent political context of Central America beginning with the guerrilla wars of the 1960s; and (4) the declining economic circumstances of Mexico in the face of recent large-scale agriculture, population increases, and fiscal austerity measures provoked by its foreign debt.

The specific socioeconomic characteristics of the Hispanic subcultures of the United States are generally delimited by the central causes leading to the major migratory waves. These central causes can be broadly described as (1) directly economic, including unemployment or reduced basic economic opportunities; (2) indirectly economic, where employment opportunities at a middle-class level have been curtailed because of declining productivity or an oversupply of qualified personnel; (3) directly political, when social or physical security is directly threatened at home; and (4) indirectly political, when the political situation limits the socioeconomic opportunities. Most migrants are not social scientists and are, therefore, more likely to articulate

Table 4.1
Hispanic Immigration into the U.S. by Ethnic Group: 1950-79[1]
(including total population in 1985 by ethnic group)

Ethnic Group	1950-59		1960-69		1970-79		1985
	Number of migrants	Percent of total	Number of migrants	Percent of total	Number of migrants	Percent of total	Total pop. in U.S.[2]
Mexican	293,000	30.7	431,000	33.2	567,000	40.8	10.3
Cuban	71,000	7.4	249,000	19.2	278,000	20.0	1.0
Puerto Rican	480,000	50.2	222,000	17.1	41,000	3.0	2.6
Other Hispanic	112,000	11.7	397,000	30.6	503,000	36.2	3.1

1. Adapted from Leobardo F. Estrada, "'Understanding Demographics: The Case of Hispanics in the United States" Lester B. Brown et al., eds. *Sociocultural and Service Issues in Working with Hispanic American Clients* (Albany: Rockefeller College Press, 1985), Table 3. Total population figures from U.S. Department of Commerce, Bureau of the Census. *Persons of Spanish Origin in the United States: March 1985 (Advance Report)*, P-20, No. 403, December 1985, p. 1.

2. In millions. Central or South Americans make up 1.7 million of the Other Hispanic total. Unconfirmed estimates of Salvadoreans are 400,000 to 600,000 (*New York Times*, 15 May 1987), of Nicaraguans 200,000.

the reasons for their migration in personal terms rather than in abstract categories. Nontheless, these categories will help us to understand the relations between the causes of the migration and the resulting subcultures.

Most Mexican, Dominican, and Puerto Rican migrants, and many belonging to other Latin American nationalities, came to the United States because of direct economic factors. These migrants, who enjoyed only limited socioeconomic security at home, arrived with only agricultural or low-level, semi-industrial skills. As a consequence, their subcultures in the United States have reflected this working-class or rural context. More recently, these same national groups have suffered in their native lands from an oversupply of technical, managerial, and professional personnel and from a real decline in purchasing power. The result has been an increase in the number of indirect economic migrants who bring with them advanced skills and a middle-class cultural orientation. These relatively affluent migrants are as alienated from their poor compatriots in the United States as they were from their impoverished counterparts back home. In effect, this class division yields two widely different subcultures per nationality, which may be more distinct because of the profound class differences than the separate working-class subcultures are from each other.

On the other hand, a middle- and upper-class culture has predominated where Cubans, who left the island after the revolution of 1959 and who entered before the Mariel exodus of 1980, and Central Americans, who left their countries for indirect economic or political reasons, have concentrated. Most of these immigrants would have preferred to stay in their countries of origin, where they enjoyed the power and privileges of the ruling sector. Their communities, as a consequence of the "forced" nature of their migration, have tended to be enclave-like, that is, endogamous, enclosed, and until very recently little connected to the other Hispanic minorities. These legal refugees, who arrived with the intention of returning as soon as conditions permitted, have not acted as an American minority ethnic group. Their children, however, believe they are here to stay and thus are less prone to embed themselves in isolated, enclave, subcultural structures. As a consequence, in politics and education they are beginning to act like the other Hispanic ethnic minorities.

The 1970-85 waves of Central American Indian and peasant migrants are more difficult to categorize. Most Guatemalan Indians and peasants in the United States are both refugees (though not legally recognized as such by the Department of State) who fled solely because their lives were in immediate peril (direct political factors) and potentially direct economic migrants, who will stay because of the poor economic conditions at home. The same may be said of Salvadoran peasants and semiskilled urban workers whose lives were threatened by the government and death squads in El Salvador. The recency of their arrival makes it extremely difficult to speak about their subcultural developments in the United States. For the most part, if they lack proper documents, they have sought to blend into the dominant Hispanic groups. Nonetheless, the Mission District of San Francisco has a distinctly Central American flavor; the same can be said of the Pico-Union and west of Monterey Park areas of Los Angeles, where tens of thousands of Guatemalans and Salvadorans reside.

The varieties of causes for migration and the resulting subcultures are not exhausted by these examples. Many Mexican migrants, with or without documents, come to the United States only for short periods of employment, and return annually or eventually to their places of origin. They seek to take advantage of the best economic circumstances of both sides of the border. These migrants have the least impact on the Mexican-American subculture, but they do provide a constant "Mexicanizing" effect. Their presence, like that of first-generation migrants in general, produces a cultural counterforce to the pressure to acculturate experienced by all immigrant groups. Similarly, many first-generation Puerto Ricans who arrived during the massive migration waves of the 1950s have returned to the island or continue to contemplate doing so. Like Cubans, who also dream of returning to their homeland, these older Puerto Ricans have been a critical source of support for the culture of the old country, often in opposition to their English-speaking children or grandchildren.

The ease with which Dominicans, Puerto Ricans, and Mexicans can return to their respective countries—the former two by relatively inexpensive plane flights from the East Coast; the latter, by plane, car, or bus—permits the cultural roots of their communities to be constantly reaffirmed. Constant immigration and two-way migrations produce communities that are culturally bifurcated, even independent of class distinctions. A first-generation sector is continually at hand, providing a culturally conservative base on which second and subsequent generations create their more Americanized subcultural styles. Unlike European ethnic groups that immigrated earlier in the century, these Latinos are never very far from first-generation cultural resources or from their homeland. It is no surprise, therefore, that as a group they exhibit a significant resistance to acculturation and seem less eager to assimilate than did their European counterparts. As a final observation on the relationship between migration and culture, proximity and continual immigration maintain a constant first generation composed of all age groups, since much family migration takes place. Consequently, Hispanic residential generations cannot easily be divided into age or other cohort groups. Though the statistics on both Cubans and Puerto Ricans make clear that those over 30 are more likely to be first-generation migrants and those under 15 are more likely to be third-generation residents, substantial exceptions exist.

INITIAL SOCIOECONOMIC AND CULTURAL ADAPTATIONS

Hispanics of many nationalities have resided in the United States since the nineteenth century, but, except for the Mexicans, their numbers were relatively small until after World War II. While more than 655,000 Mexicans had immigrated by 1930 and the Puerto Rican community was already at least 53,000 strong by that date, Cubans numbered no more than 19,000, and other nationalities counted even fewer representatives.

Like many of their Puerto Rican counterparts, early Mexican migrants worked primarily in agriculture and had a rural or small town life-style. Over the years they diversified their occupations and spread from the border area to the sugar beet fields of the North and the Midwest, to the transportation and fruit industries of southern California, and to the cotton fields in Arizona. Nonagricultural employment grew as well, particularly with the onset of World War I. In Chicago and the Midwest they worked in meat-packing plants, tanneries, steel mills (especially in Ohio and Pennsylvania), and the automobile industry; in Arizona and Colorado they were employed in the mining industry; and since the nineteenth century, they have formed the bulk of railroad crews in many communities in and beyond the Southwest. This large number of Spanish-speaking laborers spawned a number of service, managerial, and supervisory positions that led to the development of a small but significant middle class.

Puerto Ricans began to replace Europeans in agriculture in the Midwest and the East when the latter practically stopped immigrating after World War I. They harvested cotton alongside the Mexicans in Arizona and sugar beets in the Midwest, and replaced them in the railroad yards in a number of localities. Contract laborers during and after World War II went to New Jersey, Utah, and the steel industries of the Midwest. Like the early Cuban migrants in the Tampa and Key West cigar manufacturing centers, Puerto Ricans made cigars in New York City; they also worked as operatives in factories and in unskilled service jobs, especially in the hotel and restaurant industries. Many Puerto Rican women worked in the garment factories.

The Mexican and the Puerto Rican communities had become predominantly urban by the end of World War II. In 1950 only 33 percent of the Mexicans resided in rural areas, and 82 percent of Puerto Ricans were concentrated in New York City. The rapid rate of urbanization continued, so that by 1970 only 15 percent of Mexicans still lived in rural communities, most of them being recent immigrants. Puerto Ricans fanned out to nearby cities and states during the 1950s and 1960s, leaving New York with only 55 percent of the mainland Puerto Ricans by 1970. There were approximately 79,000 Cubans in the United States by 1960; but, in the wake of the revolution, another 613,000 entered in three large waves, concluding with the 1980 Mariel exodus. Like the other Hispanic groups, the Cubans were thoroughly urban by 1980, with 96 percent of Cuban families residing in metropolitan areas (56 percent in Miami alone).

The stigma of being a conquered and exploited people, limited English language skills, a Roman Catholic background, a constellation of often opposed values, and the severity of the racial and ethnic discrimination faced particularly by the darker-skinned Mexicans and Puerto Ricans worked from the beginning to isolate them from the social and cultural life of Anglo America. Unlike Puerto Ricans, Mexicans confronted segregated schools and the extreme, often violent oppression not uncommon in small towns in isolated areas; both groups suffered from inferior housing, health, employment, working environments, and educational facilities, and political powerlessness. (Even in the ethnically conscious political world of New York City, Puerto Ricans were able to make few advances for themselves until recently.)

The extreme oppression and exclusion faced by these early Hispanic migrants led to the maintenance of many homeland survival strategies and the development of new adaptive maneuvers and institutions. In New Mexico in the 1880s, Mexican vigilante groups sought to protect the community from losing its land and from the violence of the Anglos. Social banditry, of the "Robin Hood" type, could also be found throughout the Southwest. Mexican union organizing stretched from the ranges of the Texas panhandle in the late nineteenth century, through the mining camps of Arizona and Colorado, and, since the beginning of this century, to the fields and orchards of southern California. The pre-Depression United States had few public welfare institutions; consequently, physical and mental health, education, and social security were primarily a family or local community self-help affair.

Herbal curers, folk and faith healers, and the strongly supportive extended kinship structures bore the brunt of health care needs; professional doctors and patent medicines were both rare and expensive. Education was almost nonexistent for the southern and midwestern rural poor. In the cities it was generally inferior in quantity and quality, and poorly geared to educate the Spanish-speaking. Of course, the type of low-skilled jobs to which the Latinos were relegated did not call for formal education; on-the-job training and pragmatic instruction substituted for a technical or literate education that could have led to professional or middle-class employment. A community network of family and friends functioned informally in a reciprocal manner to provide the bulk of "social insurance" against widowhood, old age, or disability. In addition, voluntary associations like the mutual aid (*mutualista*) societies, political clubs, hometown clubs, and trade unions provided many Mexicans and Puerto Ricans with a labor advocacy front; burial, unemployment, and disability insurance; social and political forums; and a nucleus for organizing on behalf of their many needs. Finally, the communities generally provided for their own public entertainment, with Mexican, Puerto Rican, and Latin American music, comedy, and theatrical performances common in small and big towns and in New York City.

HISPANIC LIFE IN THE UNITED STATES TODAY

Identity and Racial and Ethnic Diversity

The Hispanic subcultures, as noted above, are distinguished not only by their ethnic and national origins and the causes of their migration, but also by class, generational, and regional factors. Equally important, Latinos differ "racially" (that is, in physical characteristics) according to national group, within their own national groups, and even among members of the same family, particularly among Caribbeans. There are many Dominicans and Puerto Ricans who are considered black by Americans. The first two waves of wealthy and middle-class Cubans were composed primarily of light-skinned refugees. Black Cubans, who enjoyed fewer privileges and less prestige before the revolution, generally preferred to remain on the island rather than face the racism of the United States; many who did migrate to Florida continued their journey to the more liberal Northeast. Poor, dark-skinned Mexicans and Central Americans contrast with the white immigrants from inland Colombia, Argentina, Uruguay, and other Latin American countries. Therefore, a meeting of Mexicans *looks* racially different from a gathering of Puerto Ricans or Dominicans, or a group of Cubans.

In the extremely race-conscious environment of the United States, these different shades of humanity translate into different experiences of reality. Light-skinned Mexicans face fewer obstacles than their darker compatriots; they are less likely to be conscious of discrimination and more likely to look favorably upon American society. For those Mexicans who migrated as children or are in the second generation, problems of self-identity are focused on competing ethnic and cultural demands generated by their ambiguity concerning the degree to which they see themselves *and are seen* as Mexican, American, or "Chicano" (self-consciously Mexican-American). On the other hand, for "black" Dominicans and Puerto Ricans, like Piri Thomas in the novel *Down These Mean Streets*, problems of self-definition may triangulate around Puerto Rican, American, and black identity.

The question "Who am I?" takes on a different meaning when the choices are not just culturally delimiting (What ethnic group do I belong to?) but also socioracially constricting (What race must I belong to, and is that more important than my ethnicity, and what ethnicity is that?). Mexicans hoping to avoid discrimination presented themselves as "Spanish" or "Latin American," and light-skinned Puerto Ricans sometimes tried to pass for "Spanish," "Jewish," or, more commonly, "Italian," but black Puerto Ricans were regularly forced by American race classifications into the Afro-American community—often defending their "Puertoricanness" to no avail. Mestizo or *trigueño*-looking Puerto Ricans, who could not pass for white but lacked a predominance of black features, resisted attempts to acculturate into either community by highlighting their distinct Hispanicity. Indeed, this Hispanicity formed the collective self-reference identity of the Puerto Rican migrants until the massive migrations began in the 1950s, when the collective self-reference became more specifically Puerto Rican. Today, Dominicans, Colombians, Panamanians, and others who have congregated residentially in New York have a sufficient mass to maintain some degree of public subcultural identity, but scattered individuals or smaller national communities embedded in a sea of Cubans, Puerto Ricans, or Mexicans frequently lose their public—and at times their personal—ethnic identities. Puerto Ricans in a small California community may see themselves and be seen as "Mexicans." Very young Hondurans in New York of the first or second generation may experience their identity as Puerto Rican, especially if there are socieconomic, legal, or cultural advantages to this substitution of ethnicity.

Cultural and Socioeconomic Conditions

In the most recent census data, with some significant exceptions, most Hispanics are either in the working class or poor. They suffer from inadequate education, income, housing, health, and social and personal security. In effect, the private and public institutions of the United States do not serve the needs of Latinos successfully. The persistence of real and relative poverty in the wealthiest country in the world is the result of both structural and individual factors. Structural aspects include the Hispanics' demographic profile. They are an extremely young people, and the young not only are dependent but also suffer the highest rates of unemployment and criminal activity. Their location in the labor market is also a structural factor. Latinos are locked, through limited opportunities beyond their control, into the secondary labor market made up of dead-end jobs in highly competitive industries that are characterized by minimum wages and no promotions, benefits, status, or security. In other words, poor and working-class Hispanics, as a group, have been relegated to perform a specific role in the American economy and, therefore, have only a very limited degree of freedom to improve their specific socioeconomic condition. Other key structural problems perpetuating poverty and insecurity are racial and ethnic discrimination, the movement of jobs away from Hispanic residential areas in the inner cities, and the rise in educational requirements for the well-paying sectors of the economy.

Mainstream social scientists and practitioners, unaware of these structural problems or unwilling to face the implications of their existence, have sought to explain Hispanic socioeconomic problems as a result of individual factors alone. They have argued that the Hispanic culture (generally identified as the same for all Latinos) is deficient. Anti-intellectualism, parental indifference, an absence of future orientation (and thus an incapacity to delay gratification), and a doting child-rearing style are alleged to be responsible for the educational underachievement of most

Hispanics. A lack of commitment to the English language and a fundamental linguistic handicap resulting from nonfluent bilingualism are also blamed for the depressing educational performance. These factors, along with a noncompetitive, nonprogressive, easily satisfied psychological makeup that caters to a family-oriented, fatalistic world view, are defined as obstacles standing in the way of the development of the ambitious individualism believed to be necessary if one is to succeed socioeconomically.

A related series of dangerous stereotypes has developed around this cultural deficiency model: Hispanics are violent and dishonest, and therefore in need of punitive or restraining law enforcement procedures. They are overly dependent and, as a consequence, are prone to welfare overuse and abuse, and are easily susceptible to chemical dependency (especially alcohol and illicit drugs). Latinos are frequently irresponsible and irrational, and thus are likely to abuse their spouses and children, abandon or neglect them, and disregard family planning. In this model, Hispanics are portrayed as immature and improvident, incapable of holding a serious job or of adequately providing for themselves or their families.

To understand the connection between the structural and individual factors is to "unpack" these stereotypes and to expose them for what they are. At the personal level these are ethnocentric and, perhaps, racial prejudices; at the level of social service practice, they are justifications for doing as little as possible for Hispanics, since they are considered to be the source of their own problems; at the level of public policy and opinion, these are sophisticated rationalizations for limiting the support available and for maintaining an uneducated, powerless mass willing to perform necessary services that the privileged groups naturally shun. Without having to go as far as Oscar Lewis' "culture of poverty," with all the negative stereotypes it implies, it is evident to any serious student of modern American racial minorities that class is indeed culture. The poor inhabit a different cultural and socioeconomic world. The study of the Hispanic subcultures in the United States cannot be blind to the fact that they are composed primarily of people with limited access to resources who therefore must create cultural mechanisms different from those of their wealthier counterparts if they are to survive.

FAMILY, KINSHIP, AND GENDER ROLES

Despite much of the literature and many pervading stereotypes, there is no such thing as *the* Hispanic family. The variations among the subcultural groups are substantial; for example, in 1985 Mexican families were the largest among the Hispanics with 4.15 persons; Puerto Ricans had 3.62; Cubans, 3.13; Central and South Americans, 3.74; and families clustered together in the census data as "other Hispanic" had 3.41. The number of households headed by women also varied dramatically: 44 percent of Puerto

Rican families, compared with 18.6 percent of Mexican families, were headed by women in 1985 (compared with 16.2 for all American families with children). In 1985 the median age of Puerto Ricans was 24.3, Mexicans were close with 23.3 (the lowest among Hispanics), for Central and South Americans it was 27.1, and for "others" it was 29.6; the oldest, the Cubans, had a median age of 39.1 (the total population's median age was 31.4). Cubans are a rapidly aging group, while only 4.2 percent of Mexicans and 2.7 percent of Puerto Ricans were 65 years or older (compared with 11.5 percent for all Americans).

Most of these differences can be accounted for by studying the geographical and class context of the diverse communities. Puerto Rican families, concentrated in New York City, which experienced a severe economic depression during most of the 1970s, suffered a high rate of broken homes, which contributed to the alarming number of female-headed households. Furthermore, the substantial age differential between U.S.-born Puerto Ricans and migrants from the island (with 1970 median ages of 9.3 and 30, respectively) has led to widespread generational conflict, with children demanding more independence than is the case, for instance, in the more socially restricted rural settings inhabited by many Mexicans.

Rural and small town Hispanics, who are mainly Mexican, reflect more traditional beliefs and behavior than their urban counterparts and are more likely to live in extended family contexts. Nonetheless, extended families are rare, even among migrant Mexicans. Today, nuclear kin groups predominate, especially when the female has been married for less than a generation. Even when housing patterns permit a choice of residential location, because of a limited use of subsidized housing it is more common to see adult family members live near each other than in the same houshold. When three or more generations do reside together, it is usually for brief periods during transitional episodes, such as the arrival of newcomers, the period just prior to the departure of homeward-bound migrants, the birth and infancy of children of unmarried daughters, or changes in employment. With the exception of Cubans, few Latino groups have sizable numbers of elderly or sufficient space and economic resources for them; thus, multi-generational households are not statistically possible in large numbers and are necessarily of short duration. However, Hispanic communities have a large number of persons living as "other relatives" (other than spouse or child) of the head of the household: 8.8 percent of the total Cuban population, 5.9 percent of the Mexican, and 4.0 percent of the Puerto Rican are in this category, compared with 3.8 percent of the total U.S. population.

The importance of the family and the degree of patriarchism and matrifocality among Hispanic families are dependent not only on generational, residential, and class patterns but also on employment opportunities. First-generation immigrants bring with them a traditional family orientation whether they move into urban or rural areas, but if employment for the females is away from the family setting, modern and homeland values may conflict. The same is true if the male head of household is consistently unemployed or relegated to demeaning labor. His lowered status in the family generates increased matrifocality, even in the face of patriarchal ideals, as females take charge of domestic responsibility while the male is deprived of the prestigious role of reliable economic provider. Consequently, when the female is the consistent provider, through welfare or employment, female-based families emerge in which the central union is between mother and children, with serial monogamy (including civil, church, and consensual unions), half siblings, and nonblood-related children common in the households. This situation is particularly true among impoverished Puerto Rican and Dominican families, who often bring with them the mother-based patterns that are the result of poverty on the islands. Of course, female-based families are most common among women who have been serially monogamous or married for a substantial number of years, and who have had children by more than one man.

While research has shown that poorer Mexicans, regardless of generational status, are more affirmative about the family than are those in the middle class, it also shows that most Latinos put efficiency and economic considerations (including individual advancement) above a loyalty to family that limits employment opportunities in favor of family considerations. Nonetheless, the poor are more likely to need a family network in order to survive and, therefore, use the family as a positive economic strategy, one that undergoes modification if employment security is reached. Whether employment flexibility and upward mobility are hindered by a strong loyalty to family is a question that cannot be answered without taking into consideration the strategic role of the family and the empirically known fact that poverty *promotes* family disintegration (because of the extreme physical and emotional demands on the individual family members when critical resources like adequate space, food, clothing, security, and health are missing).

The roles of Hispanic women are varied and dynamic. Generalizations must be made with care because of the great diversity of class, generational, geographical, racial, economic, and sociocultural factors. Notwithstanding, some broad parallels exist. In the 1980 and 1985 census reports (see Table 4.2), where Hispanic women are compared with other American women, we find that most Hispanic women over the age of 15 are married and have dependent children (under 18 years), and are more than twice as likely as white women to be heads of households with no husband present. Seven out of ten in this position have dependent children. Only 4.0 percent of Mexicans and 4.2 percent of Puerto Ricans are widows, and only 5.4 percent and 8.2 percent, respectively, are divorced. Among Mexicans over 15, 31.0 percent are single, and among Puerto Ricans the figure is 37.5 percent. As a consequence, childbearing and child rearing, and accompany-

Table 4.2
Selected Socioeconomic Characteristics of Racial/Ethnic Groups in the U.S., 1980, 1984, 1985, 1986

CHARACTERISTICS	ETHNIC/RACIAL GROUPS							
	White	Black	Spanish Origin	Mex[1]	Puerto Rican[1]	Cuban[1]	C/S American[1]	Other Spanish[1]
Family Type and Marital Status (15 years and over)								
Single (never married)			31.2[1]	31.0	37.5	19.7	32.7	29.9
Married			57.9[1]	59.6	50.1	63.1	58.4	55.2
Widowed			4.7[1]	4.0	4.2	8.8	3.8	7.5
Divorced			6.2[1]	5.4	8.2	8.4	5.1	7.4
Married-couple families			71.7[1]	75.7	52.0	78.3	73.4	72.9
Families w/own children under 18 (percent)	49.4	61.0	67.8					
Female headed households, no husband	11.1	37.3	23.0[1]	18.6	44.0	16.0	21.9	21.3
Female headed households w/children under 18	56.1	68.8	72.6					
Education (25 years and over)								
Less than 5 yrs. of school (2.7% of total U.S. pop. in 1985)			13.5[1]	17.1	12.8	7.4	7.2	6.0
4 yrs. of H.S. or more			47.9[1]	41.9	46.3	51.1	62.6	66.1
4 yrs. of college or more			8.5[1]	5.5	7.0	13.7	15.5	15.3
Median school yrs. completed			11.5[1]	10.2	11.2	12.0	12.4	12.4
Less than H.S. degree	31.3	49.4	56.7					
At least a college degree	17.2	8.4	7.6					

Table 4.2 (continued)

CHARACTERISTICS	ETHNIC/RACIAL GROUPS							
	White	Black	Spanish Origin	Mex[1]	Puerto Rican[1]	Cuban[1]	C/S American[1]	Other Spanish[1]
Employment (16 yrs. or older)								
In labor force	62.2	59.2	64.2[1]	66.8	51.2	65.5	68.3	63.0
Unemployed	5.8	11.7	11.3[1]	11.9	14.3	6.8	11.0	7.1
Females in labor force	41.5	48.4	50.4[1]	51.3	39.0	56.9	55.9	53.2
Income and Wealth								
Median, 1984 (dollars)	23,647	13,476	18,833	19,184	12,371	22,587	19,785	23,470
Below poverty level	11.0[2]	31.1[2]	27.3[2]	24.1[3]	41.9	12.9[3]	23.6[3]	15.2[3]
Children under 6 yrs., below poverty	17.7[2]	45.6[2]	40.7[2]					
Median Household net worth, 1984 (dollars)	39,135	3,397	4,913					
Households w/zero or neg. net worth 1984	8.4	30.5	23.9					
Households w/net worth median over $100,000, 1984	26.2	3.9	8.2					
Home ownership, 1984	66.6	43.8	39.9					

Source: 1980 and 1979 data from U.S. Department of Commerce, Bureau of the Census. *1980 Census of Population Supplementary Reports PHC 80-S1-1 Provisional Estimates of Social, Economic and Housing Characteristics; State and Selected Standard Metropolitan Statistical Areas,* March 1982, pp. 47, 100. 1984 data, except that for median incomes and poverty levels for Hispanics, derived from 1984 census bureau data sampling of 20,000 forms. All other 1984 and 1985 data from U.S. Department of Commerce, Bureau of the Census. *Persons of Spanish Origin in the United States: March 1985 (Advance Report),* P-20, No. 403, December 1985, pp. 4, 5.

[1] The figures are from 1985.
[2] The figures are from 1986 (*New York Times,* 31 July 1987.)
[3] The figures are from 1984.

ing domestic responsibilities, are a fundamental reality for Hispanic women, who very frequently are left to perform these tasks alone.

The census data also point out that more than half of Latino women over the age of 25 lack of a high school diploma and less than 8 percent graduated from college. This means that employment in the primary labor market and access to mainstream middle-class life-styles are extremely restricted. On the other hand, in 1985 only 50.4 percent of Hispanic females over 16 were in the labor force, compared with 54.5 percent for all females. This cannot be due solely to the large number of dependent children and the shifting employment patterns, since almost the same percentage of black women heads of households have dependent children (though almost twice as many have no husband present) and black employment does not appear to be more remunerative than Hispanic employment. The difference must be due to cultural expectations concerning the appropriate roles for females. Wherever economically feasible, Hispanic female employment is restricted to what can be done at home or in the company of adult male family members, as is the case with agricultural labor or domestic piecework.

The diversity found among Hispanic women from different subcultures is best understood by studying the differences among them in race, class, education, generation, and geography. Table 2.5 in this volume underlines the extreme variations in New York City alone; across the United States the differences are even more dramatic. Puerto Rican working women, concentrated in the highly competitive industries, many of which left New York City during the 1960s and 1970s, saw their labor force participation rate plummet from 38.9 percent in 1950 to 26.3 percent in 1972. By 1980, the rate had increased to 34.8 percent, much lower than that of Mexican women (49.5 percent), who in turn have a lower rate than Cuban, Colombian, and "other" Hispanic women. By 1985, with the economic recovery of California and New York, 51.3 percent of Mexican females and 39.0 percent of Puerto Rican females over 16 years old were in the labor force.

The dissimilarities in rates of participation, with 56.9 percent of Cuban and 55.9 percent of Central and South American females in the labor force, are partly the result of wide disparities in the amount of education and the number of dependent children of each subgroup. Women with more education and fewer children, as is the case with the Cuban, Colombian, and "other" females, are more likely to work outside the home in skilled employment. Younger females, often two or more generations removed from their migrant roots, with few or no children, participate extensively in labor outside the home, but abandon it when the birth of one or more children makes it impossible to continue without expensive or nonexistent child care. However, in the late 1980s Hispanic female participation in the labor force is increasing everywhere; so is the number of female-headed households and the rate of welfare dependency, particularly among the subcultures most affected by unemployment and low wages: the Mexican, Puerto Rican, and Dominican.

Stressful role transformations among Hispanic women often result from the imposition of the socioeconomic reality of the United States on the traditional expectations of the homeland. The contradictions between the ideal of female dependence on males and the discouragement of their employment outside the home, and the very real necessity of wage labor and consequent dependence on welfare, when economic opportunities are too restricted, place great strains upon all family members.

THE LIFE CYCLE

Hispanic life cycle rituals and beliefs vary with class and subculture; but, again, some features are extensively shared. Working-class households which usually have more members than middle-class families, generally welcome babies with open arms, even those born out of wedlock (or outside a recognized consensual union) once the initial anger, hurt, and disappointment are overcome. The male-centered cultural bias dictates that fathers prefer sons, particularly in the case of the firstborn. The more acculturated the parents, the greater the probability that the first name will be in English. With each generation of U.S. residency, the number of English names increases. Many middle-class children who do not live in concentrated Hispanic neighborhoods find Spanish names embarrassing, as they do many Latino rituals. In any event, schools are quick to translate or modify Spanish names: A Jesús becomes a Jessie and an Antonio a Tony. Last names, ordinarily made up in Latin American countries of both the father's and the mother's surnames, are consistently reduced to the father's patronymic, while the mother's is sometimes transformed into a middle name, is hyphenated with the father's, or is abandoned altogether. The giving of nicknames, common among Hispanics, usually comes to an end when acculturation or self-consciousness makes the practice awkward for the name holder.

Baptism follows shortly upon birth among Hispanic Catholics, regardless of depth of religious sentiment. It is ceremony with distinct meanings: among the more acculturated parents of the second or third generations, it is a party urged by tradition, but focused on themselves and the newborn; among the less acculturated, particularly within the working class, it is an opportunity to extend their support system through the recruitment of godparents who serve as sponsors for the baby. Ritual kinship bonds are thereby established between the parents and the new *compadre* and *comadre*. These godfathers and godmothers are expected to be reliable resources in times of need, even to the point of taking care of the child in the absence of the parents, although among second or later generations of Puerto Rican and Mexican parents, the *compadrazgo* ties seem to be weakening to the point of representing little more than a public recognition of friendship.

Child rearing practices vary widely, but almost everywhere there is much physical contact between babies and both family members and close friends, particularly females. Except among middle-class and young "modern" couples, only women handle such matters as bathing and diaper changing. When the need arises, poor Puerto Rican and Dominican mothers are more likely to place the care of their children in the hands of trusted family members, friends, and *comadres* than are Mexican mothers, who usually find permanent or temporary child care outside the family unacceptable, except in truly extreme circumstances. Baby-sitters who are not members of thc family are rare. Babies and small children spend their time primarily in the company of older sisters and female adult family members. Older siblings are expected to care for their younger brothers and sisters and, particularly among Mexicans, a hierarchy of authority and respect exists, with the eldest male sibling at the top.

Boys and girls are raised very differently. The former are granted far more liberty, and their loud and aggressive behavior is more tolerated; the latter are supposed to be young ladies—demure, quiet, "feminine." Older brothers are responsible for their sisters outside the home; inside, the sisters are responsible for the domestic needs of the males. From an early age it is made clear that there is a female world centered on the home, which is the only proper place for the female, and a male world centered on the streets, where personal and family reputations are to be safeguarded and the daily bread is to be earned. For the most part, playmates are separated more by sex than by age, with each sex expected to have its own forms of amusement.

Teenagers, who are anxious to assert their independence, are the most severely affected by the many conflicts that plague the relations between the first and second generations. The seriousness of this first-second generational strife should not be underestimated. Children raised in a traditional context at home, then confront an antithetical culture at school and in the streets, are difficult for their parents to cope with and understand. The contradictions in values, demands, and expectations are added to the already stressful circumstances common to the lives of most teenagers. Difficulties at home are often resolved through imprudent peer modeling, which sometimes leads to extensive involvement in drugs and delinquent behavior, particularly among poor, urban youths. In and out of the cities, Mexican youth gangs and more informal cliques are popular, even among females. Puerto Ricans in the larger cities of the Northeast also engage in gang activities. Many of these gangs fight not only with each other but also with gangs from other ethnic or racial groups. Even so, in most areas Mexican youths mix readily with their white peers and sometimes date them if they are within the same class; but contact with blacks is limited and often hostile, particularly in urban settings where large numbers of Mexicans and blacks reside. On the other hand, darker Puerto Ricans and Dominicans, themselves often identified as black, interact extensively with black youth and often date each other, even if extensive conflicts exist when both groups struggle over the same limited resources.

Interethnic dating is less common among working-class Mexicans than among those in the middle class who do not reside in Latino neighborhoods. The high rate of intermarriage between Hispanics in New York City attests to the popularity of interethnic courtships there. Dating among Mexicans appears to be far less casual than is common among either whites or second-generation Puerto Ricans. While extremely difficult to assess objectively, the degree to which males and females feel possessive about their dates seems to be greater among Mexicans than among Puerto Ricans. The latter interchange partners at school dances with a frequency and ease that would surprise most Mexicans. This affirmation is supported by other observations, personal and in the literature, that suggest Puerto Ricans are more open, expressive, and relaxed than Dominicans, and the latter more so than Mexicans. Nonetheless, the intensity of Hispanic courtship patterns is reflected in the attitudes toward marriage, the declining age at marriage among the second generation (slowly approaching that common in the United States), and the number of children born out of wedlock to young parents.

Both old and young expect dating to be a prelude to marriage. Dating for strictly recreational purposes, as is popular with whites, is the exception among all but the more acculturated members of the middle class. Though the supervision of unmarried women is less strict than it once was, many young Cuban females, and their middle-class Central and South American counterparts, still require a chaperone if they wish to go out with a male escort; however, double-dating is the prevalent response to this conservative practice. All Latino subcultures prohibit premarital sex, although this prohibition is often disregarded in practice, particularly in the urban centers. Consequently, with dating comes intimacy, and as among all teenagers in the United States, this frequently leads to unwanted pregnancies. However, though in 1981 in the 22 states with the largest Hispanic populations, 24.5 percent of Hispanic-origin births were to unmarried women (compared with 9.8 percent of white births and 57.1 percent of black births), teenage Mexican mothers were as likely to be unmarried as their white peers. However, as they reach age 30 and over, each Hispanic group's percentage of children born out of wedlock increases in comparison with the percentage of births to white women of similar ages.

In the same 22 states the 1981 proportions of nonmarital births were 48 percent for Puerto Rican women, the highest among Latinas, and 14 percent for Cuban women, the lowest. Though the children of consensual unions are regarded as legitimate by the Puerto Rican and Dominican subcultures, that is not the case for U.S. census takers and authorities. Table 2.4 in this volume outlines the diversity of rates of illegitimacy among New York City Hispanics, including births from consensual and casual unions. Puerto Ricans, with the least resources and education, have the highest rates in every age group; the primarily middle-class Colombians have the lowest.

Interethnic dating is the necessary first step to intermarriage, and intermarriage is a critical indicator of the extent to which one community has assimilated into another. The substantial differences in rates and types of intermarriages among the Hispanic subcultures are the product of geography, degree of residential segregation, class, generation, race, size of ethnic group, and gender ratios. In general, except for the second-generation Puerto Ricans, the first generation is overwhelmingly less likely to intermarry than the second; Hispanics working in low-status occupations tend to marry almost exclusively within their group; women intermarry more frequently than men; small Latino subgroups, and those with highly skewed sex ratios (like the Puerto Ricans, who at 46.8 percent males in 1985 lacked sufficient young men for strictly in-group marriage partners) are forced to intermarry extensively. Racially distinct and/or overly segregated communities are less likely to intermarry extensively.

Given the extent of Indian and black features among Hispanics and the preponderance of low-status employment within their communities, it is not surprising that intermarriage rates among them are low in comparison with other ethnic groups (except Asians and blacks); but they have been steadily increasing since the 1960s. Among Mexicans, those in California have the highest rates (in 1974 more than 50 percent of the marriages were exogamous); Texas rates were the lowest, from 9 percent in 1971 in poor, segregated Hidalgo County, to 27 percent in 1973 in the less segregated city of San Antonio. Most of these out-group marriages took place with whites, particularly white males. (Tables 2.10 and 2.11 in this volume summarize the relevant data for New York City.) In short, intermarriage rates among Latinos in the city are relatively high for all but Puerto Ricans and first-generation Dominicans; however, unlike Mexican out-group marriages, most exogamous marriages are among members of other Hispanic subgroups.

As mentioned above, the demands that spouses make on each other are always changing. Acculturation, economic shifts, and the crises that continually confront poor families force modifications of traditional expectations. The results of poverty, including alcoholism and drug abuse, chronic illness, depression, and overcrowded and inadequate housing, all help to promote divorce and desertion. The Latino tendency toward extreme gender divisions and male superiority means that sex, the particulars of the male's employment, and female everyday culture are not ordinarily discussed between spouses, much less between parents and children, especially in working-class homes. When dialogue is overly restricted through poverty and poor education, misunderstandings, suspicion, jealousy, and intolerance, all too common in most relationships, can be more debilitating than they need to be. In effect, married life is more difficult for the poor than for their more affluent neighbors. Furthermore, the existence of welfare has made it possible for poor females to leave intolerable or abusive mates.

Non-Cuban Hispanic elderly, especially Puerto Ricans, return to their homelands in large numbers. This, along with the relatively high death rates for young Hispanics and the recency of the extensive migration waves, means that there are proportionally fewer elderly to attend to than in the white communities. Despite a growing "modern" tendency among Hispanics not to house the aged at home, research suggests that Mexicans and Puerto Ricans are more extensively integrated into the lives of their children and grandchildren, and generally enjoy more and more varied support from them, than do black or white senior citizens. However, aged Hispanics seem to suffer more from poor health than do their black or white peers; because of their migratory and occupational circumstances, they benefit less from old age pensions or Social Security and are, therefore, more dependent on family support. Fortunately, the strong commitment to family, with its deference and respect for elders, common within all Latino subcultures, helps relieve much of the alienation and loneliness that afflict many non-Hispanic elderly in the United States.

CHURCHES AND RELIGION

The overwhelming majority of Hispanics are Catholics, but each subculture has a distinct form of Catholic worship and belief that reflects the unique history of the Church in the homeland. The early colonial Church put most of its emphasis on the highly populated areas of central Mexico and the most accessible, temperate regions of Central and South America, while the Caribbean received less attention, particularly in the late colonial period, when its economic importance had declined. At the same time, the indigenous culture of Mexico and Central and South America, along with the local sociohistorical circumstances, produced national and regional forms of organization and worship. In the Caribbean, where the effective native element was destroyed within a century after contact, African religions provided the background against which the modern island churches developed. Ultimately, a lack of sufficient clergy and committed laity, and the Indians' and slaves' insistence on the maintenance of ancient faiths, resulted almost everywhere in the development of sometimes highly unorthodox folk Christianities.

The southwestern (U.S.) colonial Church was never wealthy enough in personnel or resources to tend adequately to the needs of the Mexicans in the area; this state persisted after the Mexican-American War and continued into the present century. The lack of Spanish-speaking clergy and the dominance of Protestantism in the United States served to distance the

Catholic Church from the Mexican faithful, who were neither understood nor accepted for what they were—folk Catholics. A similar separation resulted after the American takeover of Puerto Rico. The Indo-Afro-Christian folk religion of the peasants, already quite alienated from the more formal Catholicism of the urban elite, was denigrated and disregarded by the English-speaking priests sent to care for the faithful. In both cases an austere, formal orthodoxy, associated with the foreign dominators, confronted a vital, personal religiosity born out of the local needs and experiences of the people.

Hispanic religiosity has tended (and tends) to be anticlerical but all-encompassing. Consequently, the nonprivileged faithful have not been substantial voluntary contributors to church finances and have rarely had the opportunity or money to send their children to parochial schools, and working-age males usually attend Mass only on holidays; however, the poor make use of accessible church resources on a regular basis and share a spiritual orientation that seems to permeate every aspect of their everyday life. In effect, they appear to be ungrateful, superstitious, and childish to their often neglected and uninformed foreign priests, who in turn seem distant, cold, and greedy. Among the priests and hierarchy who worked with Mexicans or Puerto Ricans, the solution to this gap rested (and rests) on Americanization strategies. Historically, these projects have focused on the building of parochial schools (never enough, but quite popular even among the working class) and efforts to integrate parishioners through special Spanish-language services. However, at no time in the history of Latino migration was the creation of an ethnic Catholicism, like that popular among the Italian, Polish, or French immigrants, attempted by the Church.

In effect, unlike other Catholic immigrants, Latinos have not had the benefits of bringing with them their own priests, of founding national parishes (except a very few short-lived ones), or of establishing an adequate number of parochial schools. It was not until the 1950s that the Catholic Church seriously began to respond to the threat of Protestant conversions and initiated some programs aimed at capturing the attention of the Spanish-speaking parishioners. By the 1960s and 1970s, popular pressure forced the Church to engage in social action on behalf of poor Hispanics. Nonetheless, the relatively insignificant numbers of Latino priests (fewer than 500 in 1981) and bishops (12 in 1980), along with the conservative nature of the hierarchy, have served to limit the scope of the efforts or interest of the Church in Hispanics, despite their exploding population and the extensive inroads made by Protestant proselytizers.

Since the beginning of this century, Protestant sects have been far more active at proselytizing Hispanics, and since the 1960s they have been much more seriously involved in social action projects that support them than has the Catholic Church. These efforts have paid off; in Puerto Rico a substantial percentage of the population is Protestant, and among Mexicans in the United States the percentage is growing daily. Pentecostal churches have made a dramatic impact among both subcultures, especially among Puerto Ricans on the island and the mainland. There are various reasons for the phenomenal growth of Hispanic Protestantism, especially Pentecostalism. Most of the ministers are Hispanic, since training is minimal and recruitment focuses on the congregation. The community of worshipers is small, personal, and actively engaged in creating an everyday religious environment that addresses the actual physical, social, and emotional needs of the members. The familiarity with both cultures that the minister usually brings makes it possible for him to act as a mediator between his congregation and the dominant community; it also permits him to make use of the culture of the worshipers to help them preserve their link to the homeland and cope with life in the United States. Finally, there is room for the folk-based spiritual and healing beliefs of the congregation without challenging or ignoring them.

These folk beliefs include the Indian-Spanish herbal and faith healing practices of folk curers, or *curanderos(ras)*, which are still in use in Mexican communities. They also include the complex *santería* and *espiritismo* beliefs and rituals common among Dominicans, Puerto Ricans, and working-class Cubans. *Santería* is particularly popular among Dominicans and Cubans, who were deeply influenced by Afro-Christian religious and medical developments, and *espiritismo* is more common among Puerto Ricans. All three sets of practices blend folk religious beliefs with knowledge of curing herbs (and sometimes knowledge of patent medicines) to restore the believers to physical and mental health.

HOUSING, HEALTH, AND WELFARE

Poverty means poor housing. In 1980, while 66 percent of all families lived in their own homes, only 40 percent of Hispanics owned their home; among those with incomes under $15,000, the percentage of renters was higher than that of poor blacks. The poor pay more for their mortgages or rents. Puerto Ricans living in expensive New York or Mexicans in California pay a much higher percentage of their income for housing than do Cubans or Central and South Americans. Yet their homes are four times more likely to be overcrowded than those of all Americans, and twice as likely to be physically inadequate, lacking heat, insulation, fireproofing, upkeep, and security. Subsidized housing, common in the Northeast but rare in the Southwest, and rent control have helped to reduce the amount of income that goes for housing; however, too frequently the results of both have been to create instant slums and to make it impossible for family members to live near each other. Urban renewal and the construction of inner-city freeway systems have tended to reduce the quantity of low-cost housing while engendering isolated, insecure, dilapidated communities. The same has resulted from the systematic arson of multifamily dwellings in New York City.

Despite a lack of national documentation on the health of Hispanics, enough is known to appreciate the deplorable effects of both poverty and the few and inadequate delivery systems that exist. For instance, while Anglos are more likely to die from cancer, Mexicans and Puerto Ricans are more frequently plagued with diabetes (often fatal), and suffer disproportionately from skin and respiratory diseases. They are also subject to all the physical and mental pathologies that come with overcrowded, unsanitary environments, stressful life-styles, high fertility, and insensitive and limited health care.

Though poor Mexicans, particularly in rural areas, and working-class Puerto Ricans and Dominicans in the inner city continue to depend heavily on both traditional home remedies (grown at home or bought in neighborhood *botánicas*) and folk healers, usually older women, most Hispanics rarely draw on these resources to the exclusion of modern medicine. However, extensive underutilization of public and private mental health facilities exists. Even though studies show that the Anglo professional frequently views the poor Hispanic patient's culturally defined behavior as in itself a sign of maladjustment, leading to exaggerated claims of pathology and disproportionate findings of mental ill health, Hispanics use mental health facilities as both inpatients and outpatients at much lower rates than either blacks or whites. Yet, only since the 1960s have mental health practitioners made their services available to the Latino communities. However, the lack of Latino, Spanish-speaking personnel poses a substantial language barrier and, equally important, an unfortunate cultural barrier. Insensitivity to the Hispanic preoccupation with proper respect, discretion, modesty, and the maintenance of dignity often makes the hospital or clinic visit a traumatic experience for both patients and family members. Language, class, race, and cultural differences also combine to produce tragic results, such as diagnostic distortion through "diagnostic stereotypes," commonly applied to low-income people of color. Thus, treatment biases against extensive psychotherapy and in favor of drugs and custodial treatment are common.

Since the late 1960s mental health workers have become increasingly aware of the Mexican, Puerto Rican, and Cuban folk-curing beliefs and practices. Though their use is still rare, the importance of integrating these systems into a comprehensive community health program has been recognized and disseminated in professional journals. Etiological and treatment beliefs common to *curanderismo, santería*, and *espiritismo* have been successfully integrated with modern practices to produce sensitive and effective results, particularly in the complex field of mental health and psychosomatic illness. Respect for traditional disease classifications and treatments (whether they be the Mexican hot-cold contrasts, evil eye, evil winds, or fallen fontanel complex, or the Puerto Rican system wherein spiritualists manipulate antagonistic hierarchies of spirits through séances, holy images, and herbs) and the use of folk healers as part of the treatment team has been used to promote the kind of trust and emotional commitment needed to effect the cure of culturally defined symptoms and diseases, such as the Puerto Rican *ataque* (nervous attack) and the many other psychosomatic illnesses that plague Hispanics.

The lack of effective political and economic power reduces the alternatives most Hispanics have to resolve the causes and lessen the consequences of the precarious health, poor housing, inadequate employment, and domestic difficulties caused by poverty. One of the few options that many Latinos are being forced to exercise is participation in the local and federal social welfare programs. The numbers involved, though lower than those for blacks in almost all categories, are alarming. In 1979 the percent of poverty-level Hispanic households receiving food stamps was 53.5 percent; Medicare (for the aged), 18.0 percent; Medicaid, 52.3 percent; school lunches, 70.4 percent; and public housing, 17.6 percent. Between 1980 and 1984, when the percentage below poverty level of the total population declined from 13 percent to 11.6 percent, the percentage below poverty level of Puerto Ricans and Mexicans increased from 37.9 to 41.9 percent and from 18.1 to 24.1 percent, respectively (see Table 4.2).

Some critics argue that "welfare dependency," particularly Aid to Families with Dependent Children (AFDC), breeds promiscuity, illegitimacy, and habitual indolence. Joseph P. Fitzpatrick has answered these charges in his *Puerto Rican Americans: The Meaning of Migration to the Mainland* (1971) by arguing that domestic coping strategies among poor Puerto Ricans include keeping abandoned and out-of-wedlock babies rather than putting them up for adoption; this includes taking in the children of friends and relatives when necessary. Fitzpatrick affirms that welfare participation is primarily a product of migration and poverty stresses, declines in real wages, true unemployment, awareness of welfare rights, and welfare policies that themselves generate dependency (for instance, limitations on outside income and pressure to remove adult males from the house). To these causes could be added the effects of the depressing wealth figures noted in Table 4.2.

If Hispanics seem to use welfare disproportionately, the blame lies in the economic role they play in American society. Welfare is a public subsidy to an economic system that uses gender, color, and class as primary criteria for determining who will provide the least remunerated and most insecure labor. Latinos participate extensively in the secondary labor market and thus use welfare, especially food stamps, AFDC, and Medicaid, in the predictable proportion that their disproportionate representation in the poor and near-poor categories dictates. Furthermore, demographic particularities, made salient by the low socioeconomic position of many

Hispanics, have contributed to the disproportionate use and underutilization of some welfare services. The young median age and the large number of dependent children naturally mean greater need for AFDC and school lunches; the small number of elderly logically results in little use of Medicare; and the lack of subsidized housing in the Southwest leads to low public housing participation rates. As to the question concerning welfare aid to undocumented workers and their families, the most up-to-date and thorough studies show that in most communities the taxes paid by these people generally make up for the social services they receive.

As welfare has become a permanent fact of life for many poor Hispanics, a second generation of welfare recipients has come into existence and, along with their impoverished parents, they have started to accommodate their culture and life-style to the arrival of welfare checks, visits by social workers, performance of bureaucratic requisites, and appearances at social service offices. Many in both the first and the second generation have never had the opportunity to work for a predictable and meaningful salary; thus, no working-class ethos of respectable return for honest labor has been developed and, therefore, little hope exists for a different, more fulfilling way of life. Though in the face of urban blight and rural poverty dignified lives are still being lived by most Hispanics, hopelessness, alienation, and the constant preoccupation with survival have created a siege-and-survival mentality among the young, which reflects itself in criminal activity, drug abuse, and self-destruction.

DRUG USE AND THE ADMINISTRATION OF JUSTICE

Unlike immigrants in the past, migrants today must face the existence of a stable or declining economy and a ubiquitous drug culture. Many poor barrio Hispanics supplement welfare and low incomes with occasional or regular drug dealing, particularly in their own communities. In New York City, the highest levels of drug abuse are found where blacks and Hispanics are poorest, and Mexican drug use also is extremely high in low-income neighborhoods. Drugs form a significant part of contemporary urban and rural Latino youth culture, and much of the drug traffic is in the hands of teenage and young adult gangs.

Working-class and low-income Puerto Rican and Mexican barrio youth join gangs in large numbers. In 1982, the more than 300 Mexican gangs in Los Angeles were held responsible by police for 260 deaths, mostly resulting from barrio gang warfare. Control of territory (and the illicit opportunities within it) and the making or breaking of reputations are constant concerns of gang members, but Latino gang activity is the product of many other complex factors, particularly those related to poverty, minority status, and cultural survival. Joan W. Moore and Robert García argue in their *Homeboys: Gangs, Drugs, and Prison in the Barrios of Los Angeles* (1978) that gang membership is *not* as pathological as the literature suggests. While nonutilitarian and rebellious elements are surely present and drug use is ubiquitous, these are mixed with relevant ethnic and realistic lower-class personal and social concerns. In a barrio community, which functions like a small village, the social structure is articulated around extended families and interfamily activities. Here, age-graded gangs may provide the only context in which young males can "play a reasonably autonomous role." Nonetheless, the Mexican gangs are wholly embedded in the social matrix of the local interfamily complex, perhaps more so than Puerto Rican gangs that function in multiethnic circumstances with few family members in their proximity. As such, gang members reflect the intense concern with respect, dignity, deference, and machismo (strong preoccupation with culturally defined male responsibilities and privileges) common in their community.

Many poor Mexican and Puerto Rican youth and adults rarely encounter middle-class role models who can realistically point the way to fulfilling employment. The white middle-class expectation of a secure job with constantly increasing wages is nonexistent in a community where the lives of the elders poignantly underline the lack of connection between earnings and age. Therefore, economic survival is an equal concern among old and young. Age groups are less likely to determine the type of economic activity engaged in than is the case with the middle class.

Welfare is one alternative to the normal wage-labor market when this market has failed the community; the illegal economy is another. Besides drugs and crimes against property or persons, the illegal economy includes undocumented status, working and employing without Social Security, and circumventing the labor, administrative, and civil codes. In general, the three economies (wage-labor, welfare, and illegal) complement each other; except in the cases where adequate legal incomes exist, rarely can one suffice with the exclusion of another. Contact with law enforcement agencies, therefore, is another sad fact of life for many poor Hispanics.

Because Puerto Ricans are U.S. citizens and most Cubans are officially recognized refugees, neither group is subject to arrest by the Border Patrol or to deportation by the Immigration and Naturalization Service. However, Central American refugees, South Americans, Dominicans (many of whom have illegally remained in the United States after their tourist or student visas expired), and millions of Mexicans who have crossed or remain illegally live with a realistic fear of being discovered and apprehended. The pressure on Hispanics exerted by the immigration authorities depends on the degree to which their labor is required in the U.S. market. But even so, the hundreds of raids on Latino establishments and places of employment, and the thousands of cases of indiscriminate harassment of individuals, burden families and communities with great suffering.

The juvenile delinquency rate of Puerto Ricans in New York is twice that of Anglos, and everywhere else Hispanic rates are generally higher than those of whites. Poverty, accompanying gang activity, and the size of the population of young Latinos are the key reasons. Most crime is committed by the young, and Hispanics are primarily a young people. However, empirical experience and research confirm the fact that the judicial and criminal justice systems treat Hispanics differently from whites. The U.S. Commission on Civil Rights concluded in its 1970 report *Mexican Americans and the Administration of Justice in the Southwest* that "Law enforcement officers discriminated against Mexicans through more frequent use of excessive force against [them] than against Anglos, discriminatory treatment of juveniles, harassment, and discourteous treatment."

Little has changed since this report was written. In 1975, Latinos represented 24 percent of the people killed by Los Angeles policemen and more than 20 percent of those killed in New York; in Chicago, they suffered 13 times more casualties than whites. And between 1975 and 1980 Los Angeles County law enforcement agencies were responsible for seven Mexican deaths per year. Every relevant study points out that almost everywhere concentrations of Hispanics are found, they continue to experience law enforcement and judicial systems differently than do Anglos: they are more likely to be arrested, to be charged with narcotics offenses, and, therefore, to face mandatory jail sentences; are more likely to be incarcerated rather than placed on probation; and, once sent to prison, are the least likely to be discharged.

Fortunately, the constant movement in and out of the same prisons of Mexicans who live in the same communities creates a continuity between prison life and the outside world. Nonetheless, among Mexican youths who have spent most of their lives in institutions, the special circumstances of prison-barrio ties have promoted the development of powerful prison gangs, which have served both to protect Mexican inmates from isolation and aggression and to socialize them into the positive and negative sides of prison life. Peter Sissons asserts in his *The Hispanic Experience of Criminal Justice* (1979) that Hispanics are more readily absorbed into the prison culture than are other groups because of the existence of a Hispanic subculture that articulates familiar values like family, loyalty to neighborhood, and concern with honor, dignity, and manhood.

BUSINESS, POLITICS, AND THE FUTURE

Notwithstanding the low socioeconomic profile of Puerto Ricans and Mexicans, the economic power of Hispanics is growing. In 1982, it was estimated that the total Latino population had $60 billion in purchasing power (approximately $3000 per person). As more Hispanics join the middle class (almost 30 percent of Los Angeles Latinos are already there), they are expected not only to increase their spending but also to diversify it to include more Anglo-oriented goods than is the case today. Their special consuming patterns are dictated by both tastes and demography; for instance, they currently consume 1.5 times as much beer as the rest of the population, and 3.5 times as much baby food. Research has shown that they spend a greater proportion of their disposable income than do Anglos on food, diapers, and clothing, and they have strong "brand loyalty."

In the early 1980s some 363,000 Hispanic businesses, with sales of $18 billion, catered primarily to the Latinos' special needs. This represented a growth of 200 percent in the 1970s, compared with a 64 percent growth in the Hispanic population. At this rate as many as 611,000 Hispanic firms were expected to generate $35 billion in sales by 1987. But Hispanic businesses are not proportionately distributed across the Latino population; in California there are 30 to 35 Latino businesses for every 1000 Hispanics, while in New York State the figure is 14. This situation may point to the fact that political power, greater among Mexicans than Puerto Ricans, has much to do with the allocation of state and federal resources needed to promote the development of a Hispanic economic base.

Hispanics do not enjoy the political power that could be expected from their numbers. Nationally, there were only nine Latino congressmen in 1982 and a very small number of federal bureaucrats or administrators in key positions. Things are only slightly better at the state level. Though the governorships of at least three states were held by Mexicans in the 1980s, only three important cities—Miami, San Antonio, and Denver—had Latino mayors; and there were only slightly over 100 Hispanic state legislators. The Latino demographic explosion signals a brighter political future, but for now a number of circumstances are keeping this potential in check.

Electorally significant densities of Hispanics exist in very few places. Even though the population is highly concentrated in four key states, there are relatively few local, state, or federal voting districts with high percentages of Hispanics (only 10 congressional districts have over 50 percent Latinos). The youthfulness of the Latinos also limits the numbers of voters in each district; in 1980, almost 40 percent of Hispanics were too young to vote. This is only a temporary limitation, but the large number of recent noncitizen immigrants and the small number of naturalizations are not. In the same period in which 80 percent of Cubans are naturalized, only 12 percent of eligible Mexicans are. Yet, research shows that despite the common stereotype that Latinos do not vote, when citizenship is controlled, Hispanic voter participation is comparable with that of blacks. In Puerto Rican communities, the problem of noncitizens is also present, since these neighborhoods contain large numbers of first-generation South and Central Americans (non-Puerto Rican Hispanics make up 21 pecent and 16 percent of New York's 18th and 11th congressional districts, the city districts with the highest proportion of Latinos). Class factors like poverty and lack of education, along with recency of immigration, limit participation because potential voters are preoccupied with their homeland's politics (a very popular phenomenon among the first generation) or feel alienated from, or are ignorant of, the voting procedures, issues, or candidates. Gerrymandering, residency requirements, and, primarily in the past, poll taxes and language competence have all inhibited or made participation impossible.

Most Hispanics are Democrats (49 percent, compared with 24 percent Republicans, in 1986). Puerto Ricans have been the most loyal to the party, in part because of their concentration in liberal New York City and their belief that the Democratic Party is concerned with the welfare and economic needs of the island of Puerto Rico. However, though Puerto Ricans have about as many members in the New York state legislature as Mexicans have in California, in the late 1980s they had only one federal elected official. However, the growth of the Hispanic population and its maturity to voting age in New York, New Jersey, and Connecticut bode well for the future of their candidates. By the second generation, Colombians, Peruvians, Dominicans, Ecuadorians, and Central Americans, who are currently interested primarily in the politics of their respective countries, will be turning their attention to domestic political issues that are of concern to Hispanics in general. When this happens, the Puerto Ricans may find themselves with many new electoral allies.

Until recently and except for New Mexico, Mexicans have been very loyal to Democratic candidates (most Mexican congressmen in office are Democrats). Though the returns on this loyalty have not been commensurate with their expectations, the Mexican and Puerto Rican tendency to vote as a bloc is beginning to give them the measure of power that should be granted to "swing vote" constituencies. Even when the number of eligible voters has been small, in many important elections their "swing" capacity has been enough to give their candidate the winning edge (though rarely has this candidate been a Hispanic).

Most first-generation Cubans are staunch supporters of the Republican Party, especially since they blame President Kennedy and the Democrats for the Bay of Pigs fiasco and the 1962 U.S.-Soviet Cuban missile crisis. Their high rates of naturalization and their solid economic base in southern Florida have given them national political visibility and actual local strength that, in comparison with the large communities of Puerto Ricans and Mexicans, seem disproportionate. However, notwithstanding the support of the Cubans for the Republicans' conservative foreign policies and their avoidance of an ethnic militancy similar to that exhibited by Mexicans and Puerto Ricans, their advocacy of bilingual education, and the second generation's growing awareness of their role as an American minority, are quickly bringing domestic and ethnic issues to the forefront of their political agenda. Already Cubans are joining Puerto Rican and Mexican organizations at the national level in order to create a common front on behalf of many Hispanic causes.

In the future this united front, the continuous expansion and aging of the community, and the growing list of problems facing Latinos will surely combine to transform the nation's soon-to-be-largest minority into a powerful political force that, in alliance with the black community, will seriously challenge the socioeconomic, cultural, and political hegemony currently enjoyed by the white majority. As America's largest cities become populated primarily with those who have been relegated to the lowest rungs of the social ladder, a white minority may be tempted to renege on its democratic commitment to majority rule. The social strife and constitutional crises that could result from this can be avoided only through a genuine, even if self-serving, awareness that an understanding of the Hispanic subcultures of the United States is not so much a desirable option as a pressing social, economic, and political necessity.

BIBLIOGRAPHIC NOTE

Most of the census-generated data used in this chapter are drawn from the relevant U.S. Bureau of the Census publications noted as sources under the relevant tables. Other sources are Joan Moore and Harry Pachón, *Hispanics in the United States* (Englewood Cliffs, NJ: Prentice-Hall, 1985); Joseph P. Fitzpatrick, *Puerto Rican Americans: The Meaning of Migration to the Mainland* (Englewood Cliffs, NJ: Prentice-Hall, 1971); Douglas T. Gurak and Joseph P. Fitzpatrick, "Intermarriage Among Hispanic Ethnic Groups in New York City," in *American Journal of Sociology* 87, no. 4 (1982): 921-934; Edward Murguia and Ralph B. Cazares, "Intermarriage of Mexican Americans," in G. A. Cretser and J. J. León (eds.), *Intermarriage in the United States* (New York: Haworth, 1982); José Oscar Alers, *Puerto Ricans and Health: Findings from New York City* (New York: Hispanic Research Center, Fordham University, 1978); U.S. Commission on Civil Rights, *Mexican Americans and the Administration of Justice in the Southwest* (Washington, D.C.: U.S. Government Printing Office, 1970); Peter L. Sissons, *The Hispanic Experience of Criminal Justice* (New York: Hispanic Research Center, Fordham University, 1979); Joan W. Moore and Robert García, *Homeboys: Gangs, Drugs, and Prisons in the Barrios of Los Angeles* (Philadelphia: Temple University Press, 1978); *Hispanics in America's Defense* (Washington, D.C.: U.S. Department of Defense, n.d.); and James Jennings and Monte Rivera, *Puerto Rican Politics in Urban America* (Westport, CT: Greenwood Press, 1984).

5

Migration and Identity: A Comparison of Puerto Rican and Cuban Migrants in the United States

Helen I. Safa

Hispanics are now the second largest ethnic minority in the United States and include Mexicans (predominantly in the Southwest), and Puerto Ricans, Cubans, Dominicans, and other Hispanics (along the eastern seaboard). While there has been considerable socioeconomic analysis of this phenomenon, little attention has been paid to the possibilities of assimilation of Hispanic migrants[1] into American society and how this relates to questions of ethnic identity.[2] Many Caribbean migrants are rejecting assimilation as a goal and choosing instead to maintain their ethnic identity within a framework of ethnic pluralism. They are contributing to a movement of "ethnic revitalization" that has come to characterize much of American sociopolitical life since 1950 (Maingot, 1983) but was especially strong in the 1960s and 1970s.

This resistance to assimilation on the part of some Caribbean migrants is causing great alarm in certain circles. It has led to calls for a complete halt to such immigration, bilingual education, and resettlement programs designed to benefit these new immigrant groups. The assimilationists cannot understand why Caribbean migrants should not make every effort to become Americanized and shed their cultural identity as quickly as possible. Their resistance or inability to do so is seen as ingratitude or arrogance by some sectors of the dominant society, who view assimilation as the only possible goal not disruptive to the fabric of American life.

This chapter is an attempt to explain why many Hispanic migrants have clung to their cultural identity and why assimilation is not seen as a feasible goal. In particular, it examines the relationship among socioeconomic mobility, assimilation, and ethnic identity. Is the maintenance of a strong ethnic identity incompatible with socioeconomic mobility? Must ethnic groups shed their cultural heritage if they wish to enter the American mainstream? What are the differences among Hispanic migrants in this regard, particularly with respect to the maintenance of ethnic identity in the second generation? These are some of the questions this chapter will attempt to answer.

ASSIMILATION AND INTERNAL COLONIALISM

The theory of assimilation has been severely criticized recently, particularly in terms of its applicability to racial minorities such as Hispanics. The theory was developed primarily on the basis of empirical studies conducted among European immigrants, who did not face racial obstacles to their assimilation into American society. When applied to racial minorities, however, the theory did not work. Why?

Before answering this question, it is necessary to review briefly the theory of assimilation as applied to immigrants to the United States. Assimilation implies the gradual loss of cultural and ethnic identity, and the adoption of the values and behavior patterns of the host society. Milton Gordon (1964) has distinguished between cultural and structural assimilation. The former usually precedes the latter, since adoption of the language, norms, and values of the host society (cultural assimilation) is a necessary prerequisite to acceptance as an equal by the members of that society. It was the knowledge of the importance of cultural and structural assimilation for socioeconomic mobility that persuaded European immigrants to shed their cultural heritage and encourage their children to adopt the language, values, and behavior patterns of American society. European immigrants paid a price, but for them it was worth it.

For racial minorities, on the other hand, cultural assimilation did not guarantee structural assimilation. No matter how fervently they adopted the language, values, and behavior patterns of American society, they were still excluded from structural assimilation and socioeconomic mobility on racial grounds.

The most cogent example of the failure of assimilation is that of black Americans. Imported as slaves, forcibly separated, and deprived of much of their cultural heritage, black Americans were long thought to lack a cultural identity apart from the larger dominant white society. Differences from whites in language, family patterns, religion, and values were explained as pathological aberrations due to their marginal position in American society. It was felt they simply had not been given the opportunity to fully adopt the values and behavior patterns of the dominant society. Civil rights and equal opportunity legislation was designed to correct this and allow black Americans to integrate into the mainstream.

The failure of civil rights legislation to assist more than a minority of middle-class black Americans led to a backlash against integrationist theories and practice in the black community. In its place emerged the Black Power movement, which sought to turn the assumed inferiority of blackness into an advantage by proclaiming the unique qualities of Afro-American culture and consciously reconstituting a history and tradition that have long been denied to many black Americans. The Black Power movement sponsored a resurgence of Afro-American culture in the United States in the arts, language, religion, cuisine, and hair and dress styles.

Internal colonialism developed as the theoretical counterpart to the Black Power movement. Developed by scholars like William Tabb (1970) and Robert Blauner (1972), the theory of internal colonialism sought to explain the continued structural exclusion of black Americans on economic grounds. The maintenance of subordinate racial minorities provided the capitalist power structure with a cheap and easily exploitable reserve labor force. The weapons of internal colonialism were both economic and ideological. Racial minorities were kept subordinate economically by denying them access to such social goods as quality education, employment, and housing. Continued denial of access was justified on the grounds that they were inferior to the dominant white society and lacked the cultural capacity to assimilate into American society. Thus, many black Americans were convinced of their own cultural as well as economic inferiority to the dominant white society (Safa, 1968). Civil rights legislation addressed the economic issues, while Black Power addressed the ideological question by rejecting the cultural superiority of the dominant society and proclaiming a separate ethnic identity.

The Black Power movement led to a new racial pride that many ethnic minorities, particularly Hispanics, sought to emulate. Many rejected assimilation as a goal and strove instead to conserve their own cultural heritage as an ethnic group in American society. They tried to replace the ideology of assimilation with one of ethnic pluralism, which calls on the dominant society to respect the cultural heritage of distinct ethnic groups rather than asking them to blend into a "melting pot" (see Gordon, 1964). The change also implies a move away from an emphasis on individual mobility as a mechanism of assimilation into American society, toward a focus on collective strategies that would foster ethnic solidarity and cohesion. Groups that had been denied the possibility of structural assimilation were now also denied the validity of cultural assimilation, and consciously strove to maintain ethnic institutions that could serve as a power base in American society. The area of ethnic revitalization had arrived.

Among migrants from the Hispanic Caribbean, ethnic pride is manifested primarily in the emphasis on the retention of the Spanish language along with other cultural items, such as music, dance, and food. The ideological value of the struggle is most clearly evident in the intense debate over bilingual education. Hispanics fought for bilingual education so that their Spanish-speaking children would not be placed at a disadvantage, and could learn and appreciate their native language. Opposition to bilingual education came chiefly from sectors of American society who continued to believe that ethnic groups must shed their cultural heritage and adopt the language and customs of the dominant culture. They won a major battle through President Reagan's cut in the budget for bilingual education programs. The assimilationist group is again in the ascendancy.

How can we explain the resurgence of ethnic identity among Hispanics in the United States? Is it simply due to slower rates of socioeconomic mobility, compared with European migrants? Portes (1984) notes that there are two opposing hypotheses to explain the maintenance of ethnic identity. The one he terms "ethnic enclosure" explains ethnic identity through confinement to low-status residential and occupational settings. In other words, ethnic identity will be greater among groups failing to assimilate because of their socioeconomic and cultural differences from the larger society. The ethnic enclosure hypothesis, as Portes notes, does not really challenge assimilation theory, but merely emphasizes the reverse: that failure to assimilate can be explained by socioeconomic barriers such as education, occupation, residence, and cultural differences such as language, race, and religion. Portes contrasts the ethnic enclosure hypothesis with the ethnic competition hypothesis. The latter poses a direct challenge to the assimilation model, since it argues that ethnic consciousness arises primarily out of competition with other groups through entry into mainstream occupations and other roles in the larger society. Thus the very features that assimilation models use as predictors of success, such as language competency, and higher educational levels and occupational status, may actually lead to increased levels of ethnic awareness and competition.

I propose to test the validity of these three competing modes of incorporation into American society (assimilation, ethnic enclosure, and ethnic competition) through a comparison of ethnic identity in two contrasting Hispanic ethnic groups: Puerto Ricans and Cubans. Several factors distinguish Hispanic migration from the earlier European models that proponents of the classic assimilation model describe. These factors include the volume of Hispanic migration in the post-World War II decade, their generally low social status, the high percentage of undocumented migrants, and, above all, their racial differences from the dominant white society. Do these differences explain the persistence of ethnic identity among Hispanic migrants? In other words, can ethnic consciousness be explained in terms of barriers to assimilation, or does it arise out of entry into the mainstream society and competition with other groups? We shall examine the evidence below.

ETHNIC IDENTITY AND THE PUERTO RICAN COMMUNITY

Though sharing a similar historical and cultural heritage, Puerto Ricans and Cubans differ markedly in socioeconomic status, due in part to their reasons for migrating. Cubans are political refugees, while Puerto Ricans are classic labor migrants seeking employment and economic opportunities. In comparison with Cubans, Puerto Ricans in the United States have a much lower level of income and education, lower rates of labor force participation and employment, and a higher percentage of households headed by women (Gurak and Kritz, 1985). How has this affected their degree of structural assimilation into American society and their level of ethnic identity?

In a comparison of Hispanic migrants to the Northeast in the 1970s, Gurak and Kritz note that Puerto Ricans show less tendency toward acculturation or assimilation in the second generation than do other Hispanic immigrants. In particular, Puerto Ricans show a marked degree of endogamy and residential segregation, which Gurak and Kritz attribute to the large size of the Puerto Rican community in New York and its low socioeconomic status. They also suggest a bifurcation of the Puerto Rican population between those who are in the labor force and those who are not, the latter reaching 34 percent of the New York Puerto Rican population. This latter population probably includes a large percentage of female householders (43.5 percent of the New York Puerto Rican population) who are dependent on welfare and other forms of transfer payments. Higher levels of socioeconomic status and rates of intermarriage are found among Puerto Ricans living outside New York, providing additional evidence for the bifurcation of the Puerto Rican community in the United States. (cf. Safa, 1984).

According to Gurak and Kritz, then, among Puerto Ricans, low socio-economic status, coupled with geographic concentration, has led to a lack of structural assimilation, while other Hispanic migrants in New York are following the classic assimilation model. In particular, they cite the high degree of out-group marriage among other Hispanics, many of whom marry other Hispanics but an increasing number of whom marry non-Hispanics, especially in the second generation. For example, in 1975 over 90 percent of second-generation Cubans in New York married non-Cubans, of whom 19 percent were non-Hispanics (Gurak and Kritz, 1985:11).

Gurak and Kritz thus follow the classic assimilation model, though in their attempt to explain the lack of structural assimilation among Puerto Ricans in New York they come close to the ethnic enclosure hypothesis. A study, by Rogler et al. (1980), of intergenerational change in ethnic identity in the Puerto Rican family also is based on the ethnic enclosure model. They start with the postulate "that ethnic identity is influenced by receptivity to external influences stemming from the host society and by length of exposure to the new host environment" (p. 208) which is measured in terms of generation, education, age at arrival, length of residence on the mainland, sex, Puerto Rican composition of the neighborhood, and family cohesion. They compare Puerto Rican first-generation families and their children living in New York City.

As we would expect, the children do not face their parents' barriers to assimilation, such as low educational levels and lack of ability to speak English, but, contrary to assimilation theory, their ethnic identity is not significantly less. While 45 percent of the children consider themselves to be exclusively Puerto Rican, the remaining children consider themselves to be part Puerto Rican and part American. Not even one of the Puerto Rican children considers himself or herself to be exclusively American, and the strength of ethnic identity remains stable even in those with postsecondary education (Rogler et al., 1980:212). Rogler et al. attribute the strength of ethnic identity in the Puerto Rican community to a movement toward biculturalism (as opposed to complete assimilation). Their data tend to support the ethnic competition hypothesis, since ethnic identity does not diminish greatly in the second generation, despite significant socioeconomic gains.

It would seem that the reasons for the persistence of ethnic identity may differ between the first and second generations. First-generation Puerto Rican migrants tend to take their cultural identity for granted and are more likely to subscribe to traditional values in terms of religion, language, and family life. Like other first-generation migrants, they tend to think of their stay as temporary, and dream of returning home someday. Second-generation migrants do not have this kind of escape. They have to come to terms with inequality in U.S. society and to confront subordination in all its forms. Even those who are able to advance socioeconomically may feel discrimination from the larger society and reject total assimilation in favor of a bicultural identity, which maintains their ethnic heritage. Ethnic consciousness is thus a defense against the exploitation and discrimination of the larger society.

However, the culture that emerges from such a process is not a mere replica of the older island culture brought by the first generation. The circulatory nature of Puerto Rican migration certainly leads to constant merging and blurring of distinctions between the island and mainland cultures. Yet it is clear that with the passage of the generations, there is emerging on the mainland a distinct "Nuyorican" subculture that borrows heavily from black Americans in both language and behavior patterns. Much of the literature and other Nuyorican forms of artistic expression exhibit an increased awareness of African culture, in opposition to both Spanish and Anglo traditions, and stresses the need for racial unity among peoples of Afro-American descent. Tato Laviera, a Nuyorican poet, writes:

> a blackness in spanish
> a blackness in english
> mixture-met on jam sessions in central park
> there were no differences in
> the sounds emerging from inside. (Flores et al., 1981:205)

For this generation of Puerto Rican writers, the island "remains a key source of reference and collective identity, a wellspring of resistance to the arrogant workings of pervasive cultural subordination'' (Flores et al., 1981: 209). But they recognize that Puerto Rico is no longer a refuge, as it was for the first generation, and that they must forge a new cultural identity based on life in the United States. For the Nuyorican, this new cultural identity shares a strong element of racial pride, ethnic consciousness, and rejection of conventional American middle-class norms. It seeks to promote socioeconomic mobility through ethnic solidarity and collective struggle rather than through individual achievement. Ethnic consciousness is thus more than seeking roots in the native culture. It is a struggle to forge a new identity based on shared elements from both the United States and Puerto Rico.

Not all second-generation Puerto Ricans on the mainland share in this new ethnic identity. Undoubtedly, many of the upwardly mobile Puerto Ricans have assimilated, or retain a bicultural perspective, as Rogler suggests. Some Puerto Rican scholars reject Nuyorican writings and other forms of cultural expression as a type of deculturation and loss of traditional values. This split is evident in the intense debate over bilingualism that continues to divide the Puerto Rican community. The debate is less over the need for bilingual education (on which most agree) than over the nature of bilingualism in the New York Puerto Rican community. Is code switching (using Spanish and English interchangeably) evidence of deculturation or of a failure to learn either Spanish or English adequately, or does it represent an "expansion of communication of expressive potential" (Flores et al., 1981:200). In larger terms, this debate asks whether migration leads inevitably to moral and cultural degradation, as the Puerto Rican writer René Marqués suggests in *La Carreta*, a well-known play about Puerto Rican migration; or can migration lead to a new form of cultural identity, rooted in the native culture but not merely a transplant? Thus, the validity of the Nuyorican subculture is questioned not only by writers from the dominant American culture but also by island Puerto Ricans who decry the loss of traditional values and language (Seda-Bonilla, 1972).

Cultural identity has long been a subject of intense debate in Puerto Rico itself, due to the island's colonial relationship to the United States. The U.S. presence in Puerto Rico since 1898 has imposed a strong American cultural impact on the island and has led to extensive proletarianization of the population (History Task Force, 1979; Safa, 1974). The massive migrations occurring since the 1950s, which nearly doubled the Puerto Rican population on the mainland in each decade, have reinforced this process and have led to an even greater need to establish a separate cultural identity. This helps explain why ethnic consciousness does not appear to have diminished significantly in the second generation, despite advances in education, occupation, and English-language competency, which should have facilitated assimilation. While a good part of the Puerto Rican community in the United States did not share in these advances, it would appear that ethnic consciousness in this community is less a product of isolation and deprivation than of increased awareness of ethnic and class inequality in American society, produced by entry into the mainstream, chiefly by the second generation. We will find additional support for this hypothesis as we examine ethnic identity in the U.S. Cuban community.

CULTURAL IDENTITY AND THE CUBAN COMMUNITY

Cuban migrants differ from other Hispanics, particularly Puerto Ricans, in several important ways: (1) Cubans entered the United States primarily as political refugees rather than for economic reasons; (2) until the Mariel migration in 1980, Cubans were largely white and middle-class in origin, and brought with them capital, skills, and other assets that aided in their socioeconomic mobility; (3) they are more concentrated geographically than other migrant groups, with over half of the entire Cuban-origin population in the Miami-Fort Lauderdale area. The 1980 census reveals a trend toward accelerated concentration in this area, compared with a tendency toward dispersion among Puerto Ricans and Mexicans (Pérez, 1984:4).

Their status as political refugees and their white, middle-class origins tended to favor the rapid and relatively easy assimilation of Cubans into American society. Their flight from the Communist regime of Fidel Castro led to much greater receptivity on the part of the American government, which took full advantage of their exodus to try to discredit and delegitimize the Castro regime. As political refugees, they were given considerable state assistance not extended to economic migrants, such as resettlement and cash assistance, special educational programs (including retraining for professionals), college tuition loans, and relaxed citizenship requirements. Bilingual education programs for Cubans were instituted in Florida as early as 1960 and served as prototypes for programs in other areas of the country (Pedraza-Bailey, 1982:88). The importance of these various forms of state assistance in the economic success story of the Cuban refugees has been well documented.

Wilson and Portes (1980) have argued that the mode of incorporation of the Cuban community into the United States differs from both assimilation and internal colonialism, and is best characterized as an "economic enclave" similar to that developed by the Jews, the Japanese, and, more recently, the Chinese and Koreans. While other immigrant groups, both European and racial minorities, serve primarily as a source of cheap labor, economic enclaves tend to be characterized by a strong entrepreneurial element, beginning in the first generation (connoting an obvious class difference). These entrepreneurs build up small enterprises that tend to employ fellow migrants and serve primarily the needs of the ethnic community. This economic advance is followed by consolidation and growing political influence in successive generations. Economic mobility in this case does not necessarily presuppose cultural integration, since the enclave tends to develop a whole gamut of institutions to preserve and defend cultural identity against external pressure. The enclave resists assimilation because it recognizes that the loss of cultural identity and geographic dispersion would weaken the resources and the economic viability of the ethnic community in a hostile society bent on reducing it to a source of cheap labor (Portes, 1980:13).

In a sense, then, ethnic consciousness in the U.S. Cuban community has followed a very different trajectory from that of other Hispanic minorities. As an enclave, Cubans started with a high degree of national or cultural identity, based both on their geographical concentration and on their status as political refugees. Many of their initial efforts were directed at the overthrow of the Castro government, and exile organizations were set up to persuade U.S. public opinion and pressure the U.S. government toward this goal (Boswell and Curtis, 1984: Ch. 10). Government support of their political goals reinforced the generally favorable opinion Cuban refugees had of the United States. As time passed and support waned, however, Cuban opinions of the U.S. government became less favorable, and many were forced to realize that their stay was no longer temporary. This change has resulted in a decline in membership in exile organizations and an increase in Cubans applying for U.S. citizenship (ibid).

The realization that they must remain in the United States has not led to a decline in ethnic consciousness in the U.S. Cuban community but, as in the case of second-generation Puerto Ricans, the form and basis of ethnic identity have changed. Cubans in the United States no longer focus exclusively on a common political struggle, but are beginning to see themselves as an ethnic minority subject to discrimination and subordination by the dominant society. Initially favorable attitudes, which partly grew out of government support for their political goals, have been replaced by greater awareness of inequality and discrimination. A longitudinal study conducted by Portes and Bach demonstrated that perceptions of discrimination increased from almost zero in 1973 to over 25 percent of the sample three years later, while by 1979 half of the respondents indicated that Anglos saw themselves as superior (Portes, 1984:386-87).

However, what is most interesting about Portes' results is that perceptions of social distance and discrimination are all positively correlated with factors that should lead to greater possibilities for assimilation. That is, these perceptions are found principally among Cubans with higher levels of education and occupational status, and more knowledge of English and information about U.S. society. Ethnic awareness is not tied to residence in a predominantly Cuban neighborhood, but is higher among employees working in the Miami Cuban enclave, which tends to support the ethnic enclosure hypothesis. However, upon further analysis, ethnic awareness is found primarily among employees in the enclave who had previously worked in non-Cuban firms and returned to the ethnic economy. If exposure to the outside economy leads to greater ethnic awareness, as these data suggest, this supports the argument that it is contact and competition with outside groups rather than confinement in ethnic communities that leads to heightened ethnic awareness (Portes, 1984:392).

Portes (1984:394-95) indicates that ethnic awareness in the Miami Cuban community increased still further after 1980 due to the 125,000 new Cuban refugees from Mariel, and to the passage of the Dade County referendum prohibiting the use of public monies to support bilingual education and other cultural activities. Both events convinced the Cuban community in Miami of the hostility of the dominant Anglo society, and of their status as an ethnic minority. The negative reaction to the Mariel Cubans was reinforced by the severe unemployment then existing in Miami, which increased competition with domestic minorities and contributed to the black Liberty City riots; by the undue attention given the small number of criminals, mental patients, and other deviants in the Mariel population; and by the high percentage of blacks among Mariel entrants compared with earlier Cuban refugees. In addition, the federal government's refusal to grant political asylum to either Cuban or Haitian refugees (who also arrived in 1980) deprived them of benefits that earlier cohorts had enjoyed and to which they were entitled under the 1980 Refugee Act. This has resulted in high rates of unemployment and low household incomes among the Mariel Cubans (Portes and Stepick, 1985), further consolidating the status of Cubans as an ethnic minority. In response there have emerged several important Cuban organizations explicitly oriented to the defense of Cubans as an ethnic minority (Portes, 1984:395). These events tend to confirm the hypothesis that ethnic awareness in the Cuban community is the result of increased ethnic competition and discrimination rather than ethnic isolation. They certainly do not point to assimilation.

Portes' results contradict other studies of the U.S. Cuban community which maintain that Cubans are rapidly assimilating into American society. Boswell and Curtis (1984:190-191), for example, point to five key indicators of rapid assimilation: residential patterns; changing occupational structure (which is becoming more similar to Anglos'); family patterns such as low fertility rates, high labor force participation rates for women, and the high rate of intermarriage with non-Hispanic whites in the second generation; changing language patterns, particularly greater use of English among the second generation; and increasing desire to remain and become U.S. citizens. In other words, the more closely Cubans approximate U.S. middle-class norms, the more they must be assimilated. But Boswell and Curtis fail to measure subjective indices of ethnic identity, as Portes and Rogler have done. They simply assume, in line with traditional assimilation theory, that higher levels of socioeconomic mobility inevitably lead to increased assimilation.

Rogg and Cooney's (1980) restudy of the Cuban community in West New York, New Jersey, the second largest Cuban community after Miami, tends to dispute Boswell and Curtis' claim. Though Rogg's earlier study pointed toward assimilation, in their restudy Rogg and Cooney found a low level of cultural assimilation and English-language ability, except for those Cubans who were young and better educated when they arrived. Occupational achievement shows no relationship to cultural assimilation, supporting Portes' finding that mobility is not a deterrent to retention of ethnic identity. Most important, they found that integration into the Cuban community of West New York (another measure of ethnic identity) does not hinder assimilation or English-language competency; on the contrary, community integration is associated with better adjustment and greater political assimilation, measured in terms of acquisition of U.S. citizenship.

Rogg and Cooney (1980:65-66) note the high increase in actual and potential naturalized citizens among the West New York residents compared with the previous study in 1968, as well as the high level of voter registration and voting. However, this high level of political participation may be less indicative of assimilation, as they assume, than of the need to build an effective voting bloc to pursue their political and ethnic goals. In short, instead of forming exile organizations bent on the overthrow of the Castro government, Cubans are now constituting themselves into a legitimate political constituency capable both of lobbying for anti-Castro activities and of defending their status as an ethnic minority. As Portes (1984) indicates, in Miami, Cuban candidates in local elections, infrequent before 1980, have started to proliferate, with several elected to the Florida state legislature, to the Metro-Dade Board of Commissioners, and other positions. In 1985 a Cuban was elected mayor of Miami, and in 1986 a man of Hispanic origin was elected governor of Florida. Maingot (1983) claims that for Cubans, U.S. citizenship is "a matter of strategic choice not primordial attachment" and implies no loss of ethnic identity. On the contrary, Cubans, like other Hispanic migrants but more effectively, have used political participation to pursue their own ethnic goals.

CONCLUSION

The transformation of the U.S. Cuban community raises interesting questions regarding the relationships among ethnic identity, the process of assimilation, and socioeconomic mobility. Resistance to assimilation through the maintenance of a strong ethnic identity was assumed to constitute a barrier to socioeconomic mobility. In fact, it was assumed that only those who lacked the socioeconomic qualifications for mobility and assimilation retained a strong ethnic identity, as a defense against a hostile dominant society. This is because mobility was thought to depend upon adoption of the values and behavior patterns of mainstream American society. Mobility was assumed to be equated with loss of ethnic identity.

The data presented in this chapter on ethnic identity among Puerto Ricans and Cubans in the United States do not support these earlier assumptions. On the contrary, we have seen that ethnic identity does not necessarily weaken with upward mobility or movement of the second generation into the mainstream of American society. The second generation is more likely to be aware of discrimination by the dominant society than is the first generation, which is more isolated by language, residence, and occupation. Thus ethnic awareness grows out of ethnic competition rather than enclosure in an ethnic community, as earlier theories suggested. The nature of ethnic identity in the two generations may also be different, with the first generation, which is more isolated by language, residence, and generation forms a new identity based on its status as an ethnic minority. Portes and Bach (1985:333) describe the process well:

Early adaptation . . . is not a matter of simply moving from the ethnic community into the broader society. It is instead a simultaneous and complementary process whereby close ethnic ties are emphasized precisely as individuals attempt to gain entry into institutions of the host society and move up its different social hierarchies. Rather than abandoning personal relationships within their own groups, immigrants who have moved farthest into the outside world would seem to rely more heavily on such bonds. Ethnic resilience, not assimilation, is the theoretical perspective more congruent with his interpretation. This resilience is not, however, a force leading to collective withdrawal, but rather a moral resource, an integral part of establishing and defining a place in a new society.

Critics like Maingot (1983) fear that ethnic revitalization threatens to increase divisiveness in American society and to produce a backlash in the form of cuts in bilingual education, greater restrictions on immigration, and calls for the adoption of English as the only official and legal language. Even proponents of cultural pluralism such as Lawrence Fuchs, who served for two years as executive director of the Select Commission on Immigration and Refugee Policy, argue that bilingual education programs may threaten the maintenance of civil unity in the United States. He questions government sponsorship of bilingual education programs and other services "that help to maintain ethnic segregation and retard the acquisition of a common language," and argues that "to be against such programs is not to be against cultural diversity" (Fuchs, 1983:308). Here we see how strongly even liberal thinkers like Fuchs and Maingot feel that ethnic consciousness may threaten the civic unity of American society and how acquisition of the English language is taken as a sign of belonging and commitment to the nation. Fuchs makes an eloquent case for American respect for cultural diversity in the history of incorporation of European immigrant groups, but notes that U.S. society has seldom confronted the maintenance of large ethnic, non-English-speaking enclaves for more than one generation (Fuchs, 1983:307), as is now occurring among Hispanic migrants. In short, cultural diversity could be accommodated, as long as it did not persist into the second generation.

However, as Portes and Bach (1985) point out, ethnic consciousness may constitute a resource rather than a force leading to withdrawal or separatism. It may encourage Americans to regard Hispanics as equals, not only because of their socioeconomic achievements but out of respect for the rich cultural heritage they are striving to maintain.

NOTES

1. The term "migrant" used in this chapter is intended to cover "immigrant," "refugee," "entrant," "undocumented alien," and other more specific terms applied to Hispanic persons entering the United States. "Migrant" if preferred to "immigrant" because Puerto Ricans, as U.S. citizens, are not immigrants, nor are undocumented aliens and refugees.

2. In this chapter the term "ethnic identity" is used interchangeably with other terms such as "ethnic consciousness" and "ethnic revitalization," although the latter refers to more dynamic processes of building ethnic identity.

REFERENCES

Blauner, Robert. 1972. *Racial Oppression in America*. New York: Harper and Row.

Boswell, Thomas D., and James R. Curtis. 1984. *The Cuban-American Experience: Culture, Images, and Perspectives*. Totowa, NJ: Rowman and Allanheld.

Centro de Estudios Puertorriqueños, Oral History Task Force. 1979. *Labor Migration Under Capitalism: The Puerto Rican Experience*. New York: Monthly Review Press.

Flores, Juan, John Attinasi, and Pedro Pedraza, Jr. 1981. "La Carreta Made a U-Turn: Puerto Rican Language and Culture in the United States." *Daedalus* 110, no. 2: 193-217.

Fuchs, Lawrence H. 1983. "Immigration, Pluralism and Public Policy: The Challenge of the Pluribus to the Unum." In *United States Immigration and Refugee Policy: Global and Domestic Issues,* edited by Mary M. Kritz, pp. 289-316. Lexington, MA: Lexington Books.

Gordon, Milton. 1964. *Assimilation in American Life*. New York: Oxford University Press.

Gurak, Douglas, and Mary M. Kritz. 1985. "The Caribbean Communities in the United States." *Migration Today* 12, no. 2: 6-12.

Maingot, Anthony P. 1983. "Immigrants, Refugees and Ethnic Bargaining in an Era of Ethnic Revitalization." In *United States Immigration and Refugee Policy: Global and Domestic Issues,* edited by Mary M. Kritz. Lexington, MA: Lexington Books.

Pedraza-Bailey, Silvia. 1982. "Cubans and Mexicans in the United States: The

Functions of Political and Economic Migration." *Cuban Studies* 12, no. 1: 79-98.

Pérez, Lisandro. 1984. "The Cuban Population of the United States: The Results of the 1980 U.S. Census of Population." Occasional Papers Series, Dialogue no. 40. Miami: Latin American and Caribbean Center, Florida International University.

Portes, Alejandro. 1980. "Emigración, Etnicidad y el Caso Cubano: Problemas de un Exilio en Transición." Paper prepared at the Center for Advanced Study in the Behavioral Sciences, Palo Alto, California, and later published in revised form in the *Miami Herald* (Spanish edition), 31 May and 7 June, 1981.

_____. 1984. "The Rise of Ethnicity: Determinants of Ethnic Perceptions Among Cuban Exiles in Miami." *American Sociological Review* 49: 383-397.

Portes, Alejandro, and Robert L. Bach. 1985. *Latin Journey: Cuban and Mexican Immigrants in the United States.* Berkeley: University of California Press.

Portes, Alejandro, and Alex Stepick. 1985. "Unwelcome Immigrants: The Labor Market Experiences of 1980 (Mariel) Cuban and Haitian Refugees in South Florida." *American Sociological Review* 50: 493-514.

Rogg, Eleanor Meyer, and Rosemary Santana Cooney. 1980. *Adaptation and Adjustment of Cubans: West New York, New Jersey.* New York: Hispanic Research Center, Fordham University.

Rogler, Lloyd H., Rosemary Santana Cooney, and Vilma Ortiz. 1980. "Intergenerational Change in Ethnic Identity in the Puerto Rican Family." *International Migration Review* 14, no. 2: 193-214.

Safa, Helen Icken. 1968. "The Case for Negro Separatism: The Crisis of Identity in the Black Community." *Urban Affairs Quarterly* 4, no. 1: 45-63.

_____. 1974. *The Urban Poor of Puerto Rico: A Study in Development and Inequality.* New York: Holt, Rinehart and Winston.

_____. 1984. "The Differential Incorporation of Hispanic Women Migrants in the United States Labor Force." In *Women on the Move,* edited by S. Timur. Paris: UNESCO.

Seda-Bonilla, Eduardo. 1972. *Requiem por una cultura.* Río Piedras, PR: Ediciones Bayoán.

Tabb, William. 1970. *The Political Economy of the Black Ghetto.* New York: Norton.

Wilson, Kenneth L. and Alejandro Portes. 1980. "Immigrant Enclaves: An Analysis of the Labor Market Experiences of Cubans in Miami." *American Journal of Sociology* 86 (September): 295-319.

6

Latinismo among Early Puerto Rican Migrants in New York City: A Sociohistoric Interpretation

Virginia Sánchez Korrol

Since the turn of the century, Puerto Ricans residing in New York City have identified themselves as *latinos* or *hispanos*, sharing this preference with other Spanish-speaking inhabitants of their community. This sense of ethnic consciousness, based on common cultural traditions, heritage, language, and a colonial past, has resulted in feelings of solidarity basic to the cultural survival of all the groups. In 1950 Mills et al. pointed to a growth of Spanish consciousness among Puerto Ricans that could evolve into "the adoption of lifeways and social values somewhat different . . . from those of the generalized (middle-class) American."[1] This projection of a *latino* identity, *latinismo,* rested firmly on a common language and manifestations of Spanish culture in the development of the community. The same phenomenon was noted by Elena Padilla. In her study of "East-ville," the word *hispanos* was cited as the preferred manner by which Puerto Ricans addressed themselves. They lived in the *barrio latino* and identified with other Spanish-speaking individuals as *hispanos.*[2]

Yet the issue of ethnic identity among Puerto Ricans has also been controversial. While scholars like Mills, Padilla, and more recently Felix Padilla in his study of Puerto Ricans in Chicago, have identified a collective Latino image, others have discounted its existence.[3] The latter support the theory that during the late 1940s, Puerto Ricans were provincial and that the inability to achieve socioeconomic stability today stems from the ethnic divisions among Hispanics.[4] Given the historical limitations of many of the studies on Puerto Ricans in the United States, the specific factors that led Mills, Padilla, and others to their conclusions are unclear. However, current research on the Puerto Rican experience, before and immediately after World War II, confirms the presence of a collective ethnic image and suggests its roots were far more extensive than previously imagined.

THE EARLY PUERTO RICAN COMMUNITY IN NEW YORK CITY

The Puerto Rican community that existed in New York prior to World War II was conditioned to cushion the impact of the migration experience and to perpetuate essential characteristics designed to maintain intact settlements similar to those the migrants had known in Puerto Rico.[5] Overwhelmingly working-class, survival for the majority of the migrant population was subject to the fluctuations of the mainland economy. Despite their basic struggles, many articulated support for a Puerto Rican life-style, customs, and traditions, coupled with a sense of affiliation to a broader, equally oppressed Spanish-speaking community. For some, these formed priorities in more ways than one. Efforts were especially focused on the preservation of Spanish as the preferred language of communication and the institutionalization of organizations prepared to nurture, insulate, isolate, and advocate for the nascent community. One migrant aptly identified the locus of this activity: "In New York City, the *colonia hispana* was called Harlem and is still Harlem today . . . the Puerto Rican colony . . . Harlem . . . was composed predominantly of Puerto Ricans and it has grown enormously throughout the decades." Puerto Ricans indeed formed the bulk of the city's Spanish-speaking population, according to the calculations of the New York Mission Society and community estimates, but Cubans, Venezuelans, Colombians, Mexicans, Dominicans, and Spaniards were also represented.[6]

The use of Spanish as the language of communication served as a bond that not only welded intercommunity relationships but also secured connections with the island and Spanish America. New York *hispanos* read Spanish-language newspapers, saw Mexican and Argentine films, listened to Spanish-language radio stations, formed associations that promoted language, culture, and civic concerns, and danced and listened to Latin music. To a lesser extent, Spanish was the language for worship and Christian ritual.[7] Puerto Ricans readily identified with the ideas, life-cycle events, and circumstances experienced by other Spanish-speaking groups, accepting without question their unique position within this network. More specifically, although they had been American citizens since 1917, many Puerto Ricans in New York viewed themselves as part and parcel of the collective Latino experience. Less provincial in attitudes and background, community leaders like Jesús Colón, Bernardo Vega, and Carlos Tapia articulated the importance of a unified Puerto Rican/Latino identity in the local presses and in the associations of the day.[8] Above all others, it was precisely in the arena of communications and mass media that a Latino/Hispano alliance was forged and sustained.

An abundant supply of foreign or domestically published newspapers and periodicals inundated the Hispanic *colonia* on a daily basis. Among them were *El Buscapié* (founded in 1877); *El Avisador Cubano* (1888); *El Economista Americano* (1887); *Revista de Literatura, Ciencias y Artes*

(1887); *América* (1883); *El Latino-Americano* (1885); *Las Novedades* (1887); and *La Juventud* (1889). They were augmented in the twentieth century by *Cultura Proletaria; El Heraldo*, a bilingual publication published by Muñoz Rivera; and *La Prensa*.[9] The latter began publishing in 1913 on a weekly basis, appearing as a daily by 1918. This newspaper was destined to become one of the most significant journalistic enterprises of the community. Responsive to the concerns of the city's Hispanics, its motto was "Único diario español e hispanoamericano en los E.E.U.U." (the only Spanish and Hispano-American newspaper in the United States).

Direct community involvement centered on the sponsorship of projects or activities appealing to a diverse Spanish-speaking public. In 1919, for example, *La Prensa* cosponsored a gala ball in conjunction with several community groups, the proceeds of which were slated for building a Hispanic sanitorium. Another example was the participation of the paper's director, José Camprubi, in the inauguration of a newly federated association composed of representatives of numerous neighborhood groups. Finally, *La Prensa* frequently collaborated in fund raising for important community projects, concerts, contests, beauty pageants, and *juegos florales*, which consisted of competitive poetry recitations. The latter was significant because it was one of the many cultural activities that perpetuated Spanish traditions in the New York *colonias*.[10]

Journals and magazines also appealed to a collective Hispanic image. One example was *Gráfico*. Its motto was "Semanario defensor de la raza hispana" (weekly defender of the Hispanic race). While it focused predominantly on the concerns of the Puerto Rican working class, it viewed its subject through the lens of an all-encompassing Latino community. *Gráfico* printed announcements, an advice column, organizational news, literary reviews and essays, fiction, and editorials. One representative issue contained an editorial, a novella, a brief biography of the educator-philosopher José Vasconcelos, an autobiographical article by the historian Cayetano Coll y Toste, an article on sports, a movie review of *The Jazz Singer*, and social and cultural news of Puerto Rico, Spanish America, and the New York *colonias*.[11]

The editorial, in particular, was the vehicle for grappling with pivotal concerns such as the relative status of Puerto Ricans in the city. One specifically compared Puerto Ricans with other Hispanics in the United States, underscoring the precarious position in which they found themselves:

The most vulnerable group of those who comprise the large family of Ibero-Americans in New York City is the Puerto Ricans. Truly it seems a paradox that, being American citizens, they should be the most defenseless. . . . For these reasons it is here that Puerto Ricans require a knowledgeable individual authorized to represent and advise them in those relationships which, by virtue of the environment in which we, as aliens, find ourselves, must be maintained with other social groups.[12]

Undoubtedly, those involved with this publication were sensitive to Puerto Rican issues and aware of social relationships among Latinos and non-Hispanics in the city. Their choice of words was quite deliberate. Puerto Ricans could perceive themselves as "aliens" because, in spite of their American citizenship, they failed to enjoy the more obvious protection afforded other Latinos through the intercession of their embassies. On numerous occasions Puerto Rican civil rights were put to a test when individuals were forced to "prove" their citizenship. From time to time the local press reported incidents of harassment and confinement on Ellis Island for failure to show such proof. In these cases, Puerto Ricans could not seek redress through a consulate.

On yet another occasion, *Gráfico* denounced discrimination and injustice inflicted upon the "large Hispano-American family" by the dominant society: "Not a day goes by that we do not hear of some maltreatment directed against individuals of our race."[13] The editorial repudiated the physical and mental abuse suffered by "yesterday, a Venezuelan, today, a Mexican, tomorrow, a Cuban, and later on, a Puerto Rican." The solution proposed by the editor, Ramón del Valle, was to intensify Hispanic political representation in the city, utilize diplomatic channels, and educate Hispanics on their basic civil rights.

From 1933 to 1945, a less militant publication that continued to focus on issues of *hispanidad* was *Revista de Artes y Letras*. Founded and edited by a Puerto Rican woman, Josefina Silva de Cintrón, it staunchly supported the preservation of the Spanish language, and the continuous development and dissemination of Hispanic culture.[14] Like its predecessors, it centered on matters affecting the city's Spanish-speaking inhabitants and printed the news and cultural events of their countries of origin as well. In addition, editorials highlighted the federal, state, or municipal policies that most affected the Hispanic community.

The unique structure of the journal's editorial board ensured both feminine input and international representation. The board consisted of eleven members, six of whom were female, each from a different Latin country. The majority of these individuals were well-educated and accomplished, and related easily to their peer groups in the United States as well as in their native countries.

The journal's preoccupation with the language issue was clearly demonstrated in the March 1936 issue. In its editorial, *Artes y Letras* launched a crusade against the testing of Harlem school children, many of whom were Puerto Rican, by the city's Chamber of Commerce. Denouncing the Chamber's findings as inconclusive, the journal alerted the community to the situation and organized a mass meeting to plan its response. Significantly, while the children involved were mostly Puerto Rican, the plea for justice was not limited to this group. All Hispanics were critically affected, and the journal's response reflected community solidarity on a highly sensitive issue.[15]

While some of the reading material of the interwar *colonia* molded, refined, and underscored a Hispanic consciousness and a Latino ethnic image, the bonding inherent in a common language became apparent in other ways as well. One was in the area of entertainment; another, through musical and artistic expression. Movies and screen stars generated a subculture that offered escapism in a pre-television era. During the golden age of the Spanish cinema, Argentina and Mexico were the chief exporters of comedies, melodramas, tragedies, musicals, and westerns.

Latin filmgoers responded to live and celluloid entertainment, enthusiastically promoting the popularity of such multinational personalities as María Félix, Mapi Cortés, Libertad Lamarque, Carlos Gardel, and Pedro Infante. Thrilled by the exploits of superheroes like Jorge Negrete and Pedro Armendáriz in Mexican westerns or historical melodramas, audiences also applauded the comic antics of Cantinflas and Tin Tan. Viewed by Hispanic audiences of various national origins throughout the country, the films set forth a collective life-style, value system, and historical legacy that stressed the similarities and respected the differences among Latinos, and at the same time inculcated a common experience not shared by non-Hispanics.

In addition to films, vaudeville appealed greatly to the Puerto Rican audiences of the 1930s and 1940s. Stand-up comedians, singers, dancers, and musical groups alternated their performances with the films projected on the screens in theaters across the country. Individually or in groups, Puerto Ricans shared directly in the creative process by staging or acting in neighborhood pageants, contests, and other extravaganzas. Community sentiments regarding the entertainment world were expressed in the local press as well as at the box office. On one occasion the inauguration of a new theater on Forty-second Street between Seventh and Eighth Avenues elicited the good wishes of the public, while on another the increasing numbers of English-speaking actors in movies billed as Spanish were severely criticized.[16]

Music also played a vital role in uniting Hispanics in New York and in the United States. Two decades into the twentieth century, *danzas, danzones, plenas,* and *aguinaldos* had already been recorded by Columbia and RCA Victor Record companies, finding a lucrative market in the city.[17] By the 1930s, Latin bands played to packed houses in the Teatro Hispano and the Campoamor in the heart of the *barrio latino.* Dance halls like Hunts Point Palace, Tropicana, Park Palace, and the Audubon Ballroom hired popular Latin bands to attract ethnically mixed audiences. Neighborhood music stores blared the latest hits and filled the melodic void for those unable to attend public dance halls. Organizations raised funds, celebrated holidays, and rewarded their members with dances held at local halls and hotels.[18]

The small music stores spread quickly throughout the *colonia hispana* and grew to symbolize the Latino settlements in much the same way that "Mom and Pop" candy stores characterized previous immigrant neighborhoods. But while the family businesses served primarily as local hangouts for social exchange, the music store's role was more emphatic. By playing the popular tunes of Spanish America, the Caribbean, and the New York settlements, migrant feelings and attitudes, particularly toward the new environment and the absent homeland, were communicated. Songs were nostalgic, focusing on country, unrequited love, or the impoverished conditions of the migrants. They expressed feelings of patriotism, protest, and alienation. Day and night, the rhythms of *el son* and the *guaracha* combined with the more romantic *boleros* and *danzas* to serenade the streets of Harlem, Brooklyn, or the South Bronx, nurturing a wide range of vital cultural expressions.

The preservation of a shared language and heritage represented one process in defining a Hispanic or Latino ethnic image; the formation of neighborhood organizations was another. Groups based on common goals and interests appeared and disappeared in accordance with the developmental agenda of the community. Some cultivated social, cultural, or educational concerns, while others dealt with the labor issues or political aspirations of the day. Still others served as buffers between the Spanish-speaking groups and the larger, non-Hispanic society.

The earliest Puerto Rican organizations to appear in New York were mutual-aid societies patterned on island counterparts.[19] These were followed by regional or hometown clubs and social/cultural units that incorporated some of the practices and operational modes of the earlier associations. In time, the dispersal of Spanish-speaking individuals throughout the city spurred the growth of more organizations, especially in response to urgent conditions and the changing concerns of their constituents. These included social clubs pledged to provide the migrants with the music, language, and socialization necessary for survival or, more significantly, the insulation for resisting the hostile environment. Others catered to more collective national interests. La Liga Puertorriqueña e Hispana, as a case in point, was a group whose officers and founding members were active in other community organizations.[20] This federation labored to protect the civil rights of all Hispanics, fostered educational goals, and in general spoke for the entire community.

Political clubs, in particular, encompassed a wider Hispanic image for two reasons. First, membership in organizations that became political was not limited to Puerto Rican Latinos.[21] Other Hispanics were welcome as well. Second, the issues central to the clubs' membership ranged from concern for the immediate community to the nation and to the country of origin. For example, although the turn-of-the-century Puerto Rican political associations were formed primarily in support of Antillean independence, by the late 1920s and early 1930s, such organizations were broadening their bases and aligning themselves with the Democratic, Republican, or Socialist Party. For the most part, these clubs were formed independently of the regular assembly district units, but often sought and received the recognition of the county, borough, and local bosses. Nationality clubs, as they were known, were not technically part of the regular party organization, but they participated in general electoral activities, especially when votes were needed.[22]

These groups combined many of the features of both the regional or hometown clubs and the mutual-aid societies. They sponsored baseball teams, provided jobs and entertainment for their followers, celebrated Puerto Rican holidays, and observed patriotic events.

Evidence suggests the Puerto Ricans of the interwar years were far more politicized than previously assumed. One estimate is that over 7000 registered Puerto Rican voters participated in the 1918 election of Governor Alfred E. Smith. By 1926, one community organization calculated that "two thousand Porto Rican voters were credited to the 19th Congressional District while the entire registration for the city was over five thousand."[23]

Latin American politics and issues were of equal interest and importance to these organizations. In New York, Puerto Ricans and other Caribbean Hispanics took a stand opposing the dictatorships of Gerardo Machado in Cuba and Juan Vicente Gómez in Venezuela. They protested the rise of fascism in Spain and denounced the Puerto Rican Ponce Massacre by taking to the streets of *el barrio latino* by the thousands, under the banners of community associations. They closely observed political changes in Puerto Rico and in the rest of the hemisphere. Through the creation of neighborhood relief and emergency units, they actively supported the Sandinistas in Nicaragua.

LATINO CONSCIOUSNESS OUTSIDE NEW YORK

Did the size and political, economic, and cultural vulnerability of the interwar settlements necessitate the formation and continuous renewal of a Latino ethnic consciousness? Was it, as Mills stated, the "core of resistance to assimilation"? Apparently the juxtaposition of the Spanish-speaking community and the numerically larger, more discriminating, and impenetrable non-Hispanic society did motivate alliances across national boundaries, but this factor was merely one of many. According to some of the early leaders of the Puerto Rican community, a sense of *latinismo* already existed among the migrants during the first decades of the migration. In part, this stemmed from an acute awareness of their historical place within the Ibero-American family.[24]

Throughout Latin America and the Spanish Caribbean, the early decades of this century witnessed a reaction against U.S. policies that resulted, among other things, in a renewed commitment to Pan Americanism, coupled with a rise in nationalism. Cultural and literary movements fanned the fires of solidarity by stressing national consciousness, heritage, and the colonial past. By the 1930s, the Civil War in Spain stimulated dormant sentiments among Latin Americans for the spiritual mother country. Many expressed these feelings through direct military involvement in the International Brigades, while others lent moral support through their writings. In all, national consciousness, as well as international bonds, were reinforced.

Similar sentiments had already been voiced by prominent *pensadores* of each nation. Writers and essayists, such as José Martí, Eugenio María de Hostos, and Lola Rodríguez de Tió, had applauded unity and solidarity among Latins regardless of where they resided. Others, particularly the essayists who honed the genre as a vehicle of protest, noted and articulated the irreconcilable differences between North and South America. José Enrique Rodó, Uruguayan born and one of the most outspoken critics of U.S. policies, underscored its crude materialism by comparing it with the idealism and superior cultural values of Spanish-America in *Ariel*. Rubén Darío warned against U.S. penetration, while José Martí, among the first to denounce imperialism, observed and rejected capitalism firsthand, during his years in New York. Like Martí, many of the *pensadores* visited the New York *colonias*. Their words and those of their Latin compatriots were known and internalized within the migrant community.

The 1920s, characterized in Puerto Rico by a period of search and indecision, gave way to the dissemination of a new consciousness throughout Latin America. In the wake of the Mexican Revolution, the philosopher José Vasconcelos postulated his theory of the "new man" in his *Cosmic Race*. An affirmation of *mestizaje* formed the crux of his lectures at the University of Puerto Rico, where he was a visiting lecturer.[25] The desire to stimulate national awareness and the continual search for a Latin American identity, as well as an openness toward the rest of the Spanish-speaking world, structured the literary focus of Juan Carlos Mariátegui, a Peruvian; Juan Marinello, a Cuban; Manuel Ugarte, an Argentinian; Pedro Henríquez Ureña, a Dominican; and Gabriela Mistral, a Chilean. In Puerto Rico the publication of Antonio S. Pedreira's *Insularismo* and the *Prontuario Histórico de Puerto Rico* of Tomás Blanco set the stage for explaining the Puerto Rican experience on the island and within a hemispheric perspective. At the same time, the rise of the Nationalist Party under Pedro Albizu Campos, in direct response to North American colonialism, expressed the movement on the political front.

The 1930s witnessed a further strengthening of the cultural bonds between Puerto Rico and Latin American when such writers as Mariano Picón Salas, Germán Arciniegas, and Fernando Ortiz lived, lectured, taught, and traveled on the island. Along with native writers, they collaborated on the journals *Asomante, La Torre,* and *Sin Nombre,* which were read on both sides of the ocean. These conveyed the message of common roots, brotherhood, nationhood, and unity. As one scholar stated:

I do not share the thesis of the cultural isolation of Puerto Rico. Sporadic separations, yes, but never a total disjuncture. Alienation might exist on an international level, on official planes. . . . But here there have always been people preoccupied with stretching the bonds with the Spanish American and Antillean countries. And you cannot attempt to study [Puerto Rican] letters, thought, theater, music, and art, history or even the ideas that shake up the modern university without taking into account the multiple contacts established.[26]

CONCLUSIONS

Undoubtedly the ties between Puerto Rico and the rest of the Spanish-speaking world were repeated to some extent in the New York *colonias.* In their attempts to cope with the difficult U.S. racial, class, and economic reality, Puerto Ricans created communities that reflected those they knew on the island. Our brief overview of the early Puerto Rican community in New York indicates that it encompassed formal and informal institutions that, more often than not, included Hispanics of other countries. Solidarity, particularly on political or cultural issues, was openly demonstrated by the advocacy and organizational positions taken by community groups.

By the 1950s, when the largest migration of Puerto Ricans left the island for continental shores, the U.S. presence in Puerto Rico was well entrenched. For those born, educated, and drafted under the American flag, affiliations with other Latinos were somewhat obscured and less understood. This turn of events was further qualified by the social significance placed on race and class in the United States, which motivated some Puerto Ricans to align along racial rather than cultural classifications. The consequence, in part, was reflected among New York Hispanics by a limited historical memory, a decline in organizational interaction, and a lack of appreciation for the benefits of solidarity.

More recently, university-based programs have begun to emphasize commonalities in the U.S. experience of Spanish-speaking people. Their history has formed the focus of numerous studies. Support for bilingual education programs and an awareness of Hispanics as a potentially dynamic force in U.S. politics have motivated collaborative efforts. Productive political coalitions have already surfaced in major urban centers. Clearly, the collective ethnic image of U.S. Latinos has not totally disappeared: it has merely entered another historical phase.

NOTES

1. C. Wright Mills, Clarence Senior, and Rose K. Goldsen, *The Puerto Rican Journey* (New York: Harper and Bros., 1950).
2. Elena Padilla, *Up from Puerto Rico* (New York: Columbia University Press, 1958).

3. Félix M. Padilla, "The Theoretical and Practical Sides of Latino Ethnic Conscious Behavior in Chicago, 1970-1974" (DeKalb, IL: Northern Illinois University, Latin American Studies Program, 1985). Unpublished manuscript.

4. Included among these are Sidney W. Mintz, *Worker in the Cane* (New Haven: Yale University Press, 1967); and Julian Steward et al., *The People of Puerto Rico: A Study in Social Anthropology* (Urbana: University of Illinois, 1956).

5. Several studies have focused on the history and development of the Puerto Rican community in New York. Among the most recent is César Andreu Iglesias (ed.), *Memorias de Bernardo Vega* (Río Piedras, PR: Ediciones Huracán, 1977), translated by Juan Flores as *Memoirs of Bernardo Vega* (New York: Monthly Review Press, 1984). See also Virginia Sánchez-Korrol, *From Colonia to Community: The History of Puerto Ricans in New York City, 1917-1948* (Westport, CT: Greenwood Press, 1983); and Centro de Estudios Puertorriqueños, Oral History Task Force, *Labor Migration Under Capitalism* (New York: Monthly Review Press, 1979).

6. A report issued by the New York Mission Society in 1927 estimated a Hispanic count of between 100,000 and 150,000 individuals. Approximately 85,000 were believed to be Puerto Ricans. In 1926, the annual report of the Porto Rican Brotherhood of America, a fraternal organization based in New York City, estimated Puerto Ricans numbered about 100,000. These figures are not substantiated by census and other indicators, which estimate Puerto Ricans numbered about 45,000 during the 1930s. Undercounting was probably as problematic then as it is today.

7. The Catholic Church was not overly responsive to Puerto Ricans as a group and established few programs for the Spanish-speaking before midcentury. By contrast, Protestant churches, especially the Pentecostal, were highly visible and receptive. See Virginia Sánchez Korrol, "In Search of Non-traditional Puerto Rican Women: Histories of Preachers in N.Y. Before Mid-century," paper presented at the American Historical Association Conference, New York City, December 1985. See also Ana María Díaz Ramírez, "The Roman Catholic Archdiocese of New York and the Puerto Rican Migration, 1950-1973: A Sociological and Historical Analysis" (Ph.D. diss., Fordham University, 1983). A classic analysis of religion and the Puerto Ricans is still Joseph P. Fitzpatrick, *Puerto Rican-Americans: The Meaning of Migration to the Mainland* (Englewood Cliffs, NJ: Prentice-Hall, 1971, 2nd ed., 1987).

8. Jesús Colón, *A Puerto Rican in New York and Other Sketches* (New York: International Publishers, 1982). See also Ramón Colón, *Carlos Tapia: A Puerto Rican Hero in New York* (New York: Vantage Press, 1976); and Andreu Iglesias, ed., *Memorias de Bernardo Vega.*

9. Sánchez Korrol, *From Colonia to Community,* Ch. 2. See also Iris Zavala and Rafael Rodríguez, eds., *Intellectual Roots of Independence* (New York: Monthly Review Press, 1980), Introduction.

10. *La Prensa,* July 21, 1919, p. 2. Also Sánchez Korrol, *From Colonia to Community,* p. 71.

11. *Gráfico,* July 1, 1928.

12. *Gráfico,* March 27, 1927.

13. Ibid.

14. For an interesting overview of these early pioneers and their community

activity, see Rosa Estades, "Patterns of Political Participation of Puerto Ricans in New York City" (Ph.D. diss., New School for Social Research, 1974). Much of this information on Josefina Silva de Cintrón is taken from a telephone interview conducted by Sánchez Korrol in 1977.

15. *Revista de Artes y Letras,* March 1936.

16. *Nuestro,* May 1980, pp. 26-27; *Gráfico,* July 8, 1928; *Revista de Artes y Letras,* January 1936; *Gráfico,* April 12, 1930, p. 10.

17. Max Salazar, "Latin Music: The Perseverance of a Culture," in Clara E. Rodríguez, Virginia Sánchez Korrol, and José Oscar Alers, eds., *The Puerto Rican Struggle: Essays on Survival in the U.S.* (Maplewood, NJ: Waterfront Press, 1985).

18. Sánchez Korrol, *From Colonia to Community,* pp. 80-81.

19. Andreu Iglesias, ed., *Memorias de Bernardo Vega,* p. 123.

20. Liga Puertorriqueña e Hispana, certificate of incorporation, File no. 056-59-27C (March 1928), County Clerk's Office, Municipal Building, New York City.

21. For an excellent account of Puerto Rican politics in New York, see James Jennings, *Puerto Rican Politics in New York City* (Washington, DC: University Press of America, 1977). See also Andreu Iglesias, ed., *Memorias de Bernardo Vega.*

22. Reference to Puerto Rican nationality clubs appears in Roy V. Peel, *The Political Clubs of New York City* (New York: G. P. Putnam & Sons, 1935). See also Sánchez Korrol, *From Colonia to Community,* Ch. 6.

23. Adalberto López, "Vito Marcantonio," in *Caribbean Review* 8, no. 1 (January-March 1979): 16-21.

24. Among the community leaders who articulated such attitudes were Jesús Colón, Bernardo Vega, and Carlos Tapia.

25. Arturo Morales Carrión, "Puerto Rico en el Caribe," in *El Nuevo Día,* July 8, 1984, pp. 12-15.

26. Ibid.

7

Culture Contact and Value Orientations: The Puerto Rican Experience

Barbara R. Sjostrom

INTRODUCTION

This chapter is based on an exploratory study conducted to ascertain, describe, and analyze the dominant value orientation profile for a group of Puerto Rican college students born and reared in the continental United States in comparison with their island and Anglo counterparts. A secondary aim was to study the extent to which the mainland Puerto Rican sample approximated the value orientation patterns of the island or Anglo samples.

Evidence of congruence between mainland[1] and island Puerto Rican respondents served as an indicator of the maintenance of Hispanic cultural values among those born and reared on the mainland. Conversely, evidence of a match between the mainland Puerto Rican and Anglo study participants suggested the impact of acculturation on the value orientations of second-generation Puerto Ricans on the mainland. An analysis of which group's value orientations the mainland Puerto Rican orientation resembled more closely was contingent upon obtained differences in value orientation patterns between the Anglo and island samples.

The methodology utilized in the present study consisted of administering the Kluckhohn Value Orientation Schedule (KVOS), an instrument designed to elicit rank-order preference on 4 value orientation categories— time, relational, man/nature and activity—to the 3 samples of 30 participants each. This instrument presents hypothetical everyday problems that occur cross-culturally and expects participants to select and rank-order from the 3 solutions offered for each category across 22 items. The responses to these items generate a profile for each group and indicate between-group similarities and differences in value orientation patterns.

The underlying theoretical assumptions of this study dealt with acculturation processes and the maintenance or persistence of values from the culture of origin for second-generation mainland Puerto Ricans. Literature on culture contact, acculturation/assimilation, and dominant value orientation profiles for Anglos and for Hispanics in general, and Puerto Ricans in particular, guided the interpretation of study findings.

Considerable research interest has centered on cross-cultural analyses using values and value orientations as a means of exploring the variations that occur across groups. Such an analysis is of particular interest in culture contact situations like those representative of societies with large immigrant populations. The United States is an excellent example of such a society, since its development has been due largely to the continuous influx of immigrant populations (with the exception of the Native Americans who inhabited this territory at the time of colonization). Dinnerstein and Reimers illustrate this unique phenomenon as follows: "Never before—and in no other country—have so many varied ethnic groups congregated and amalgamated as they have in the United States" (1975:1). It is estimated that more than 45 million people have come to the Americas during the past 350 years, a number constituting the largest human migration in recorded history.

According to the U.S. Census Report for 1980, one of the most rapidly growing groups within the country is the Hispanics, who represented close to 17 million (7.2 percent) of the total U.S. population. The three largest subgroups among Hispanics were Mexican-Americans (60 percent), Puerto Ricans (15 percent), and Cubans (7 percent), while Central Americans, South Americans, and Spaniards accounted for the remaining 18 percent.

A closer look at the Puerto Ricans, the focal point of the present study, reveals that the majority are located in the New York City area. The figures for New York State alone in the 1980 Census Report indicate that 1.6 million people (9.5 percent) identified themselves as Hispanic, and 60 percent of these were of Puerto Rican ancestry. Furthermore, projections from *The Hispanic Almanac* suggest that by 1990, the Hispanic population of New York State will approximate 21 percent of the total population if demographic patterns continue as expected (1984:101).

Given the large concentration of Puerto Ricans who currently reside on the U.S. mainland, particularly in New York City, coupled with the sizable second-generation population represented in the urban areas, there is a striking need to explore and analyze the value orientations of this group within the context of its Hispanic heritage and ethos components. Hence, a comparison of Hispanic and Anglo value orientation patterns served as a point of departure in studying this group.

In the 1950s several social scientists studied the importance and nature of values in contemporary U.S. society (Parsons, 1951; C. Kluckhohn, 1953; Dukes, 1955). They viewed values primarily as part of a stable system of beliefs representative of the world view of any given society. Florence

Kluckhohn (1953, 1961), in building upon the work of the aforementioned theorists, added another dimension to the study of values in her seminal work on value orientations. Her major premise was that while there is stability or continuity in values within a society, there are *variations* within a particular group and between different cultural, ethnic, and linguistic groups. Nevertheless, she suggested that one dominant value orientation profile emerges within a given society. Kluckhohn's unique contribution to the field was her emphasis on value orientations within a cross-cultural perspective that allowed for an exploration of the impact of culture contact in the context of the mainland United States.

In establishing categories for ascertaining the particular orientations for a group or society, Kluckhohn departed from the premise that there are certain universal questions guiding the desirable behavior within cultures or societies. These general questions revolve around people's relationship to nature, to the temporal focus of life, to human activities, and to others, thus generating the *man/nature, time, activity* and *relational* orientations, respectively. Furthermore, according to Kluckhohn, the alternatives for value orientation patterns based on these categories are finite, and have been present or common to all peoples through history. However, they are differentially preferred across diversified groups (Kluckhohn and Strodtbeck, 1961:10). Table 7.1 presents the value orientations and range of variation for each as utilized by Kluckhohn in the KVOS.

Utilizing these four categories, Kluckhohn developed the KVOS for measuring value orientation patterns cross-culturally. The schedule presents 22 hypothetical situations considered representative of everyday life in contemporary urban settings. Respondents rank-order their choices for each item, thus providing a pattern for each of the four categories.

The first category (Man/Nature) deals with how people view their place in the natural order of the universe. Do they feel that they are controlled by nature (whatever will be, will be," "may God's will be done"), live in harmony with nature by understanding and respecting processes through observation and interaction with nature, or have certain control over natural forces through technology, science, and other advances. An example from the KVOS instrument illustrates this dimension:

Hypothetical situation

Three people were talking one day about the changes which science has brought about in the way people live. They mentioned all such things as changes in farming methods, in transportation, in the field of medicine, in types of food and housing. All agreed some changes had come, but each one of them had quite different ideas about what the long run effects would be. Here is what each one said.

Responses

The first person felt that although there had been advances in science and technology, overall, luck was the most important factor guiding life [Subjugated to Nature

Table 7.1
The Value of Orientations and the Range of Variations Postulated for Each Category in the KVOS

ORIENTATION	POSTULATED RANGE OF VARIATIONS		
MAN-NATURE	Subjugation to nature	Harmony with nature	Mastery over nature
TIME	Past	Present	Future
ACTIVITY	Being	Being in Becoming (BIB)	Doing
RELATIONAL	Lineality	Collateralism	Indvidualism

Source: Compiled by the author from Kluckhohn and Strodtbeck, 1961.

orientation]. In contrast, the second individual felt that people can control and overcome most problems presented by nature [Mastery over Nature]. The third claimed that people must keep a balance between themselves and the forces of nature [Harmony with Nature].

Category 2 emphasizes the temporal dimension of human life and reflects past, present, and future foci: whether people attribute more importance to tradition and the way things were done in former days, live each moment or day as it happens, or look to the future in planning their lives. Following is an example of this dimension:

Hypothetical situation

Some people in a community like yours were discussing religion and how religious ceremonies were changing from what they used to be.

Solutions

The first individual liked the changes and considered them progressive [Future Orientation] whereas another one felt that by changing, old traditions were lost and much of the meaning of religion with them [Past]. The third individual believed that there should be changes reflecting contemporary society [Present].

The activity pattern centers on how people view their work or livelihood. The alternatives represent a continuum of task orientation, and achievement to one of being, flowing with what comes, and integrating leisure as part of one's activities. The following situation is exemplary of this category:

Hypothetical situation

Three young married men were discussing notions about the ideal job for them.

Solutions

The first individual stressed the need for a job which allows for flexibility and leisure rather than one that was highly competitive [Being orientation]. The second chose a highly competitive job with opportunities for advancement and showing one's expertise [Doing orientation]. The last respondent thought of the ideal job as one which allowed an expansion of horizons [Being in Becoming orientation].

Last, the relational pattern centers on how people relate to significant others in their lives. From this pattern, one can infer the child-rearing patterns and preferred family structure. The alternatives suggest a focus on nuclear or extended family structures and deal with how authority is perceived in relating to family members. The following example illustrates this dimension:

Hypothetical situation

Three parents were talking about the kind of character they wanted their young children to have. Here are three different opinions that were expressed:

Solutions

The first response focused on the need for children to become independent and accountable for their actions [Individual orientation]. The second person felt that the primary goal in child rearing was respect for elders because of their wisdom [Lineal orientation] whereas another one felt that by changing, old traditions were lost and ties with close relatives and having lots of family surrounding one [Collateral orientation].

Responses to these four situations from the KVOS indicate people's preferences regarding the best way of interacting within their own societal contexts. Kluckhohn applied these categories in analyzing variations in value orientations occurring between and among various ethnic, religious, and linguistic groups on the U.S. mainland. Subsequently, the study of value orientations has been based on the replication of her study and other methods of measuring value orientations cross-culturally for diversified ethnic groups, including Ukrainians, Italians, Hispanics, and Japanese (Born, 1970; Calhoun, 1975; Caudill and Scarr, 1962; Dempsey, 1973; Feather & Rudzitis, 1974; Rokeach, 1968a, 1973).

The literature on value orientations suggests that they can be used as indicators of stability or change in the cultural fabric of both host (United States) and immigrant groups within the United States. Several empirical studies have indicated that the greater the value alignment between the immigrant and host value orientation profiles, the smoother the adjustment and the more rapid the acculturation into the value structure of the United States (Kluckhohn and Strodtbeck, 1961; O'Flannery, 1972; Portes et al., 1980; Schermerhorn, 1970).

There is a consensus among immigration theorists that the evidence of change in value orientations or transition to a value orientation profile consonant with that of the host society is prevalent among the second-generation offspring of most immigrant groups. This generation is considered to be the one to experience greater marginalization, since acceptance of the cultural mores of the United States frequently means rejection of those of the culture of origin. Therefore, members of the second generation are frequently caught between the two cultures and experience marginalization or alienation from both.

In focusing on the impact of culture contact on immigrant groups in general, and on their offspring in particular, there are divergent views regarding the outcome of the contact situation. One view, referred to as the "melting pot" or assimilationist perspective, contends that immigrant groups lose the value orientations of their native culture and integrate or assimilate into those of the host society by the second or third generation (Fitzpatrick, 1971; Gordon, 1964; Greeley, 1971; Schermerhorn, 1970). While these studies emphasize the acculturation process as impinging primarily on the immigrant groups, they acknowledge that, extrinsically, the host society is also changed in the process. However, at the level of value structures, the host society profile tends to prevail. Schermerhorn exemplifies this position as follows: "Integration is a process whereby units or elements of a society are brought into action and coordinated in compliance with the ongoing activities and objectives of the dominant group" (1970:66).

A different position is that of a pluralistic model, whereby systems in general and cultures in particular are constantly undergoing change, thus having a constant impact on each other. Inherent in this model is the acceptance of cultural diversity (Femminella, 1973; Glazer and Moynihan, 1975; Tirayakian, 1967). Femminella illustrates this position through his claim that both the host and the immigrant (ethnic) groups, through contact, conflict, and resolution of conflict, affect each other, thus constantly changing U.S. culture.

In terms of empirical studies supporting these theoretical positions, the vast majority support to varying degrees the assimilationist perspective and explain the phenomenon on the basis of variables such as schooling, mass media, and other institutions reflective of American society (Blu, 1977; Colleran, 1984; Feather, 1972; Glasser, 1958; Kluckhohn and Strodtbeck, 1961; Nahirny and Fishman, 1965). Upon reviewing the empirical works related to Hispanic value orientations in particular, the results indicated that this culture's value orientation profiles were markedly different from those of the cultures of origin and more closely approximated those of the host society (Baldassini, 1980 [Colombians]; Calhoun, 1975 [Mexicans]; Colleran, 1984; Rogler and Santana Cooney, 1984; Segalman, 1966; Sjostrom, 1983 [Puerto Ricans]; and Szapocznik and Curtines, 1979 [Cubans]).

In order to place the Hispanic experience within the context of cross-cultural value orientations, an analysis of the impact of culture contact on immigrant groups within the United States becomes pertinent. The next section presents a review of the literature on culture contact as well as the results of empirical studies related to this area of inquiry.

CULTURE CONTACT AND IMMIGRANT GROUPS

The effects of culture contact on immigrants and their offspring have been researched extensively. Central to an understanding of the adaptation process is an analysis of what the first generation of the immigrants experience as a result of the move from one culture or society to another, and how their offspring, the second generation, respond to the impact of the two cultures. One way of achieving such an analysis is to treat the two groups separately and explore how the process affects each generation differentially.

e literature written about first-generation immigrants deals
shock or the immigrant's confrontation with values and
ferent from those he/she was enculturated into. This places
in a situation of having to make choices that ultimately guide
tho... tation to the new environment. According to Greeley (1974:59),
there are six steps in the acculturation process for immigrant groups: (1)
culture shock; (2) organization and emergent self-consciousness about their
ethnicity; (3) assimilation of the elite values from the core or dominant
culture; (4) militancy toward the maintenance of an ethnic identification;
(5) self-hatred and antimilitancy in an attempt to eliminate the remnants of
the culture of origin; (6) emerging adjustment or adaptation into the host
society.

A salient variable in the acculturation of immigrants appears to be a
shared past in another culture, which gives them a point of reference to pass
on to their offspring in the form of an often idealized view of the native
country. Blu stresses the importance of this connection for the first-
generation immigrants in their adaptation to the new host society: "For
members of an ethnic group, their shared past as they perceive it provides a
bond between them, an image of their former behavior and experience, and
often one or more guides for present activities" (1977:266). Feather points
out that for the new immigrants, change is abrupt and dramatic, since they
must not only deal with the unfamiliar but also face the anguish of having
left behind those who had been important in their own socialization, such as
parents, friends, and relatives. The culture they enter may be very different,
thus exposing them to a new language and value system, which creates a
constant need for adaptation (Feather, 1973). As Handlin put it: "The
newcomers were on their way toward America almost before they stepped
off the boat because their own experience of displacement had already
introduced them to what was essential" (1963:55).

Another variable that appears throughout the immigration literature
deals with the rate of acculturation as something dependent upon the
closeness of fit or the degree of value congruence that exists between the
receiving and the immigrant cultures (Kluckhohn and Strodtbeck, 1961;
Portes et al., 1980; Schermerhorn, 1970). Schermerhorn summarizes this
aspect as follows: "When the ethos of the subordinates has values common
to those of the superordinates, integration (coordination of objectives) will
be facilitated; when the values are contrasting or contradictory, integration
will be obstructed" (1970:72). Freedle and Hall (1975:4) concur in their discussion of two divergent types of subcultures that serve as models for integration of immigrant groups into the host society. These are the embedded
subculture, which functions as if it were an integral part of the larger culture
but with fewer rights and privileges (for instance, black Americans and
Hispanic Americans), and the encapsulated subculture, which is allowed to
maintain its cultural practices as long as its impact on the prevailing culture

is minimal or nonexistent (for example, Chinese-Americans and Native Americans).

The vast majority of empirical studies conducted on value orientations between cultural groups have addressed this issue of congruence of values between the host and immigrant cultures. Their findings support the hypothesis that there is a positive correlation between congruence in value orientation profiles and the rate of acculturation for an immigrant group (Feather and Wasyluk, 1973; Kitano, 1972; Kluckhohn and Strodtbeck, 1961; Pido, 1977). A few studies indicate that variables such as racism, discrimination, and socioeconomic status influence the rate of acculturation (Calhoun, 1975; Isser, 1976; Ogawa, 1975; Rokeach, 1973). In their study, Kluckhohn and Strodtbeck concluded that "The rate or degree of assimilation of any ethnic group to dominant American culture will depend in large part upon the degree of goodness of fit of the group's own rank-ordering of value orientations with that of the dominant culture" (1961:26).

The second generation of an immigrant group, in contrast with the first, has had no firsthand experience or socialization in the societal norms of the culture of origin. Therefore, culturally transmitted customs have been selectively passed on by parents and relatives, and filtered through the immigrants' perceptions of their children's functioning within the context of the new society. Kluckhohn and Strodtbeck describe the dynamics of this process for the second generation: "It is the child of the immigrant family who within the family structure is socialized in accord with the dominant values of traditionalism and who, outside the family—in schools, play groups, and other associations—comes to know and feel the impact of ways of behaving which express the dominant American values" (1961:32).

In order to appreciate the predicament in which the immigrants' offspring find themselves in dealing with the two cultures simultaneously, Nahirny and Fishman suggest that the more intensely the children reject and despise their ethnic heritage, the more aware they become of their ethnic identity; and by suppressing their ethnicity, they rebel against parts of themselves (1965:318). Glasser contends: "In situations where a subject has prolonged interaction with persons of different ethnic identity and identification patterns, investment [in the new society] encourages marginality in his ethnic identification patterns" (1968:39).

There is general agreement among immigration theorists that the offspring of the immigrant groups usually experience greater marginality than their parents because of their constantly being placed in situations of choosing between the two cultures. This is a painful predicament, since acceptance of the cultural mores of the United States often forces them to reject their own parents and family structure. Also, acceptance of the value orientation patterns of the host society does not necessarily assure equal access to benefits or acceptance by members of that society. This is illustrated by the experience of several racially mixed groups of immigrants in the United States, such as the Afro-Americans and Asian-Americans.

Having analyzed the culture-contact situation inherent in a racially and ethnically diversified society like the United States, a comparative study of the specific value orientations attributed to Hispanics and Anglos guided the present study. Furthermore, a closer look was taken at the value orientations of Puerto Ricans and the extent to which these fit within the context of traditional Hispanic ethos components or within the dominant U.S. value orientation patterns.

U.S. VALUE ORIENTATION PROFILE

Within the United States, the white Anglo-Saxon Protestants who settled this country during the colonial times are credited with having made the main contribution to the formation of an American value orientation profile as it is known today. The salient features of this profile are (1) an emphasis on the individual and his/her responsibility in taking the initiative toward success; (2) active mastery in controlling the forces of nature through scientific discovery; (3) a time orientation with a strong focus on the future; and (4) a concentration on the external, material aspects of things and events rather than on the inner experience of meaning and effect (DuBois, 1955; Fitzpatrick, 1971; Kluckhohn and Strodtbeck, 1961; Mason, 1955; Williams, 1960).

Examples of these patterns are exhibited in the concern for social mobility and process, medical technology, and space programs, as well as in the socialization of children toward achieving early independence. Benjamin Franklin's pragmatic adages such as "A penny saved is a penny earned" and "The early bird gets the worm" are exemplary of value orientations attributed to the North American people since the formation of the colonies.

HISPANIC VALUE ORIENTATION PROFILE

In contrast with the value orientation patterns dominant in the United States, the components of the Hispanic cultural ethos historically have been oriented toward the past or present rather than the future. As a group, they have emphasized the value of the extended family and the individual within the context of the collectivity, and have tended to accept destiny or nature's control over humankind. Finally, there is more emphasis on the internal aspects of life rather than on events or external ones (Gillin, 1955; Leavitt, 1974; Wagley, 1968). Examples of these patterns are Spanish expressions such as "Que será, será" (What will be, will be) and "Si Dios quiere" (God willing). Also, in terms of the socialization of children, there is a focus on cooperation rather than competition.

Latin Americans, like other Catholics, believe that every individual has a soul, and that the soul has intrinsic worth and is unique (Leavitt, 1974). Personal relationships are very important, and they are established on the basis of kinship, ceremonial kinship (such as *compadrazgo*), and friendship between individuals. According to Gillin, "Friendship is the essential element of interpersonal relations in the Latin American culture" (1955:494).

PUERTO RICAN VALUE ORIENTATION PROFILE

In discussing specific Puerto Rican value orientation patterns, one must view the group within the context of Hispanic cultural heritage, and consider the impact of industrialization and urbanization on the island during the late 1940s and 1950s, as well as the cultural influence of the United States since its acquisition of Puerto Rico in 1898 as a result of the Spanish-American War. Steward states:

It is necessary to view the processes of industrialization against the background of the cultural tradition of the island. For four centuries, the culture has been essentially Hispanic, both in its national institutions and its folk aspects. . . . The Hispanic heritage, however, was the basis of Puerto Rican culture and subcultures, and, despite the effects of industrial trends, many features of the tradition survive today: the Spanish language, certain familial patterns, religious practices, forms of recreation, food, habits and others. (1972:120-121)

It should be pointed out that in addition to the Spanish influence on Puerto Rican society, two other cultures—African and indigenous—have left their mark on Puerto Rican society. However, the dominant cultural ethos of Puerto Rico is considered to be deeply rooted in the Spanish legacy, which dates back to the conquest and colonization of the New World. Within this context, the literature on Puerto Rican values attests to the presence of a Hispanic ethos in Puerto Rican culture. Hispanic value orientations are based on an extended family structure, a past-to-present time line, an emphasis on personalism (the individual within the larger context of the collectivity), and the individual controlled by destiny/nature (Brameld, 1958; Cooper, 1972; Fitzpatrick, 1971; Maldonado-Denis, 1976, Steward, 1972).

According to Fitzpatrick, four major influences have contributed to the structure of family life, kinship patterns, and the patterns of family living in Puerto Rico: the culture of the Taino Indians, natives of the island when Columbus arrived; the influence of the Spanish colonial culture; the existence of slavery on the island; and the influence of the United States, and subsequent economic development and modernization (1971:77). While it is difficult to assess the degree of impact of any or all of these factors on modern Puerto Rican society since World War II, the industrialization of Puerto Rico has probably been the major feature in the formation of its sociocultural and political value system. In an article in *Portrait of a Society* (Méndez, 1972), Steward states, in support of this hypothesis:

All segments of the Puerto Rican population have been influenced by industrialization, but the town and urban centers have responded most uniformly. While these new urban functions tend to create greater similarity between towns, they also differentiate the population within each town into special segments, classes, or sociocultural groups: wealthy commercial and professional personnel; civil servants, transportation workers, and services and building trade groups; and skilled and unskilled laborers. Most characteristic of these are the new middle classes of varied occupations and income. They represent a new trend, a new set of values which ascribes major importance to the symbols of personal achievement and wealth. Upward mobility in the socio-economic hierarchy becomes a crucial goal; and individual effort, thrift, education, and utilization of governmental services and opportunities become means to the goal. (p. 119)

Regardless of the extent of the U.S. influence on the island, the cultural norms in Puerto Rico continue to reflect predominant Hispanic value orientation patterns rather than those of the American profile. This statement is supported by several social scientists. Maldonado-Denis states: "Afirmamos anteriormente que Puerto Rico es una sociedad de cultura nacional vinculada historica, étnica y lingüísticamente al universo cultural latinoamericano y más específicamente al ámbito del Caribe hispanoparlante" (1976:123). [As has been stated on previous occasions, Puerto Rico is a society representing a national culture placed historically, ethnically, and linguistically within the framework of a Latin American cultural universe in general and of the Spanish-speaking Caribbean in particular] (author's translation).

The prevalence of a Hispanic value orientation profile for Puerto Ricans born and reared on the island, in spite of the urbanization and industrialization and the American sociocultural influences over several decades, is still confirmed by much of the literature dealing with this group.

The value orientation profile predicted in this study for mainland Puerto Ricans was expected to differ from Kluckhohn's findings regarding the Latin American value orientation profile. One of the five groups used by Kluckhohn for the first testing of cross-cultural value orientation theory was Mexican-Americans from a rural village in the Southwest, which she named Atrisco. The dominant orientations of this group in 1951, during the preliminary use of the KVOS, were found to be Lineality, Present Time, Subjugation to Nature, and Being. Kluckhohn predicted changes in these values as small villages such as Atrisco disappeared and the inhabitants moved to urban centers. This change was expected to appear in the island sample of this study due to the transformation of Puerto Rico from a fundamentally agrarian society to an industrial one during the 1950s and 1960s. This study attempted to ascertain whether such a transformation in value orientations has, in fact, taken place on the island, and if so, to what extent.

THE STUDY

Purpose of the Study

In light of the aforementioned discussion, the present study sought to explore the value orientation patterns for Puerto Ricans born and reared on the U.S. mainland in comparison with their island and Anglo counterparts. In accomplishing this objective, the main research question that emerged was, What are the dominant value orientations of second-generation mainland Puerto Ricans and their island and Anglo counterparts? The KVOS was utilized in determining the patterns on the four value orientations (Time, Relational, Man/Nature, and Activity).

An analysis of the between-group similarities and differences on the value orientation series led to a secondary question: To what extent does the mainland Puerto Rican profile approximate either the Anglo or the island profile? Results from the latter question were then interpreted as indicators of the acculturation processes impinging on the mainland Puerto Rican group, or of the continuity of values from the culture of origin.

Three sample groups of 30 individuals were drawn from a population of college undergraduates at public institutions in New York State and Puerto Rico. The institutions were selected on the basis of the type of student body and course offerings. The sampling frame was derived from a process of serially numbering course offerings at both institutions and then taking a random sample of 20 classes for each sample. Once permission was obtained from the professors teaching these courses, a preliminary questionnaire designed to ascertain ethnicity and place of birth and rearing was administered to those students volunteering to participate.

From the questionnaires meeting the criteria for inclusion, the three random samples were drawn, and individuals were contacted by telephone and invited to participate. Those who agreed were sent a formal letter requesting them to sign a release form and arrange a 45-minute meeting with the researcher to complete the KVOS. Each of the 3 samples included 30 college students identified as (1) mainland Puerto Ricans (individuals born of Puerto Rican parents and reared in the mainland United States); (2) island Puerto Ricans (persons born and reared in Puerto Rico); and (3) Anglos (U.S. citizens born and reared in the continental United States and native speakers of English).

Data for this study were collected utilizing the KVOS. This instrument consists of 22 items delineating hypothetical life situations considered common to most present-day urban societies. The items elicit value orientation patterns for the Time, Relational, Man-Nature and Activity categories, and the respondents are asked to rank each item in terms of a first and second choice. Topics addressed in the four series consist of universal themes that appear in all cultures, such as child-rearing practices, rules for social interaction, and ways of handling crises.

The KVOS was individually administered to the participants. All of the subjects were provided with a copy of the schedule and asked to follow along as the researcher read each item. Each respondent was then asked to select his or her first and second choice for each of the 22 items; these were then recorded on a coding sheet by the researcher.

Data Analysis

The data from the KVOS were analyzed to determine within-group consensus on all items and between-group similarities and differences in the rank-ordering of these items, thus generating total orientation patterns for each series. The statistical measures utilized were the Kendall S, t test, binomial analysis, and Kruskal-Wallis One Way Analysis of Variance (ANOVA). The level of statistical significance was established at .05 for each measure.

The first test for determining within-group consensus or total item patterning for each of the three groups was the Kendall S statistic. It tested the null hypothesis that there were no preferences among respondents for each sample in ranking the three alternatives for each of the 22 items. The Kendall S was computed for each item by group, for a total of 66 separate tests.

The second statistical test was the binomial analysis, which measured intra-item patterning to test the null hypothesis that there were no preferences between the alternatives in a given pair.

In testing the total orientation patterning or the general tendency toward consensus within each group on preferences between any two value orientation positions, the two-tailed t test was used on all pairs of alternatives in each of the four orientation categories. The null hypothesis tested was that there are no preferences among respondents from each sample for alternatives in the series representing one particular value orientation position over those of a second particular position.

The last statistical test, the Kruskal-Wallis One Way ANOVA, measured between-group differences and tested the null hypothesis that the respondents from the groups did not differentially prefer the alternatives in a specific orientation position to those representing a second particular position. The results of the ANOVA form the foundation for addressing the research questions posed in this study, since the results present a comparative analysis of between-group similarities and differences across the three samples for the four value orientation categories.

Findings

The results of this exploratory study on the value orientation patterns of mainland Puerto Rican college students compared with island and Anglo cohorts indicated consensus in the rank-ordering of preferences for the Time and Activity categories. All three groups chose Present as their first preference, Future as their second, and Past as their third for the Time category, and Being-in-Becoming as their first, Doing as their second, and Being as their third for the Activity category. Regarding the Man/Nature category, the mainland Puerto Rican sample selected Subjugated to Nature as their first preference, Harmony with Nature as their second, and Mastery over Nature as their third choice. This rank ordering differed from the island and Anglo samples, who chose the pattern of Harmony, Subjugated, Mastery.

In the Relational category, the mainland Puerto Ricans matched their island counterparts with a rank-order preference of Collateral over Individual over Lineal. The Anglo sample, in contrast, chose a ranking of Individual over Collateral over Lineal.

In summarizing the findings, it is evident that the answer to the first research questions regarding the dominant value orientation patterns for mainland Puerto Ricans in comparison with the other groups is that for two of the four categories—Time and Activity—there were no differences in value orientation patterns across the three groups. The dominant value orientation patterns that emerged for all three samples were Present to Future to Past for the Time Category, and Being-in-Becoming to Doing to Being for the Activity category.

Mainland Puerto Ricans matched the island sample on the Relational category with a preference pattern of Collateral to Individual to Lineal, whereas the Anglo sample differed from both Puerto Rican groups. Finally, mainland Puerto Ricans were alone in choosing a preference pattern of Subjugated to Harmony to Mastery on the Man/Nature category, in contrast to the Harmony-Subjugated-Mastery selected by the other two samples.

Table 7.2 presents the rank-ordering of choices for all three samples across the four value orientation categories.

It should be noted that although the above rank-ordering patterns for each orientation series were strongly preferred by the groups as indicated, statistically significant differences at the established .05 level were reached on the ANOVA solely for the following dimensions or pairs of items: (1) Past/Present and Past/Future for the Time category for mainland Puerto Ricans and island Puerto Ricans; (2) Individual/Lineal preference of the Relational category for the mainland and Anglo samples; (3) Mastery/Subjugated preference for the Man/Nature category for the mainland and Anglo groups; and (4) Being/Doing preference of the Activity category for the mainland and Anglo samples.

The second question of this study centered on the extent to which the mainland Puerto Rican value orientation profile approximated the Anglo profile, thus suggesting acculturation, or the island profile, implying continuity of Hispanic value orientations.

In answering the second question, the research task was more complex, given the homogeneity of choices across the three groups. In order to make

Table 7.2
Value Orientation Patterns by Group

ORIENTATION	ISLAND PR	MAINLAND PR	ANGLO
Time	Pres>Fut>Past	Pres>Fut>Past	Pres>Fut>Past
Relational	Coll>Ind>Lin	Coll>Ind>Lin	Ind>Coll>Lin
Man/Nature	With>Subj>Over	Subj>With>Over	With>Subj>Over
Activity	BIB>Doing>Being*	BIB>Doing>Being	BIB>Doing>Being

> indicates preferred over
* indicates statistical significance at the .05 level

a definitive statement regarding the impact of acculturation or the persistence of values from the culture of origin, the underlying assumption was that the island and Anglo samples would differ markedly in their value orientations, and that the mainland Puerto Rican sample would be more like one or the other. The results, however, indicated that the Anglo and island samples were congruent in value orientations on all but the Relational category. The mainland Puerto Rican sample matched the other two groups for the Time and Activity categories.

The most significant finding of the study, and the only one indicating the presence of value orientation patterns derived from the culture of origin, was in the Relational category. In this series, mainland Puerto Ricans matched the island sample and the Anglo profile was different from both Puerto Rican groups. Only one anomalous case in the mainland Puerto Rican sample surfaced: the Man/Nature category, where a pattern different from both the Anglo and the island profiles was chosen.

The above findings indicate that the value orientation patterns for the Anglo and island Puerto Rican cultures are more congruent than different except in the Relational category, the area that covers interpersonal relations. Furthermore, mainland Puerto Ricans' value orientations appear to differ little from those of the other two groups, except for the differences found in the Relational category.

Discussion of Findings

The framework for analyzing the findings of this study is supported by three major theoretical positions. The first one refers to the presence and continuity of a primarily Hispanic value orientation pattern among Puerto Ricans. Supporting this view is the work of a number of scholars who contend that there are clearly distinguishable and dominant cultural ethos components that define Puerto Rican culture as part of the Hispanic cultural heritage (DuBois, 1955; Gillin, 1955; Leavitt, 1974; Mason, 1955; Mintz, 1960; Wagley, 1968). In relating the study findings to this theoretical position, the value orientation patterns of the island and mainland Puerto Ricans are considered as they fit within Hispanic value orientations.

Study results pertaining to the Relational category, how island and mainland Puerto Ricans perceive their relation to family and others, provide evidence that the Hispanic cultural values are still dominant in Puerto Rico. Furthermore, they appear to have been maintained by second-generation mainland Puerto Ricans, since both groups chose the same pattern of Collateral over Individual over Lineal orientation within the Relational category. The significance of this finding takes on added importance in that it is the only example in which a match between the value orientations of island and mainland Puerto Ricans differed from the Anglo preferred pattern of Individual over Collateral over Lineal. It is a well-documented fact that the extended family structure is a salient feature of Hispanic culture (Brameld, 1958; Cooper, 1972; Fitzpatrick, 1971; Maldonado-Denis, 1976; Steward, 1972; Stycos, 1955). Stycos exemplifies this feature as follows:

The unusually high degree of interpersonal relationships [in Puerto Rico] plus the wide range within the family toward whom these relations may be directed, may result in greater identification within the family, with the group, than upon the mother or father, as characteristic of the small, privacy-conscious nuclear family typical of industrial Western society. (1955:89)

It is not surprising, therefore, to find evidence of the Collateral (extended interpersonal relations) preference among island Puerto Ricans. However, the existence of the same pattern among second-generation mainland Puerto Ricans is more striking because it challenges the assimilationist perspective that by the second generation, immigrant groups will adhere to a value orientation structure approximating that of the host society.

One other emergent value orientation pattern lends credence to the persistence of Hispanic cultural ethos components among mainland Puerto Ricans in this study: the Man/Nature category. This particular group preferred Subjugated to Harmony to Mastery, in contrast with the island and Anglo samples, who preferred Harmony to Subjugated to Mastery. The ranking for the mainland Puerto Rican sample reflects the maintenance of Hispanic cultural traditions, since they refer to one's place in nature in terms of God's will determining one's fate. The problem with interpreting this particular finding is that the island sample showed no evidence of a preference for the Subjugated choice. Therefore, a case for the continuity of value orientations from the culture of origin is tenuous.

One plausible interpretation of the presence of the Subjugated preference among mainland Puerto Ricans may be the idealization of Hispanic traditions, including religious views. These, in turn, may be transmitted by parents to the second-generation Puerto Ricans on the mainland as a way of maintaining a link with Puerto Rican culture. Studies cited previously suggest that since the only connections immigrant offspring have with the culture of origin are through secondary sources, they tend to have idealized visions of the customs and values of that culture. A second explanation for the appearance of the Subjugated preference may have to do with the mainland Puerto Ricans' subordinate position within the U.S. social structure, influenced by variables such as socioeconomic status, race, ethnicity, and language.

A second theoretical position regarding the dominant value orientations of the Puerto Rican people relates to a body of literature posing the counterargument that Americanization, industrialization, urbanization, economic dependence, and reverse migration have been variables impinging upon changing cultural values among island Puerto Ricans. Proponents of this view further contend that these factors have had a marked influence not only on the Hispanic culture but also on the language (Negrón de Montilla, 1971; Nieves-Falcón, 1975; Seda-Bonilla, 1972; Silén, 1973).

The findings of this study support this particular perspective for two reasons. First, one can infer from the similarity of value orientation patterns for the Anglo and island samples on three of the four categories—Activity, Time, and Man/Nature—that the U.S. influence has had an impact on island Puerto Rican culture. This influence has been exerted through economic domination and capitalist expansion. Second, the fact that mainland Puerto Ricans manifested the same value orientation profile as the island and Anglo samples on the Activity and Time categories is further evidence of the impact of capitalist development on value orientations. It is apparent that the value orientation profiles indicating some Anglo influences can be acquired through enculturation on the island itself or through acculturation as a minority/immigrant group within the context of the U.S. mainland.

What is evident from the findings of this study is that no clearly distinguishable Hispanic cultural ethos components emerged from the KVOS regarding Time, Man/Nature, or Activity orientation patterns. The reason for this may be the impact of acculturation processes occurring in Puerto Rico and within the mainland Puerto Rican population. If this is the case, the present study strongly indicates changes in value orientations due, in part, to the superordinate/subordinate relationship between the United States and Puerto Rico and, further, within the mainland Puerto Rican population in the U.S. society.

Another position regarding Puerto Rican value orientations represents the convergence of the first two arguments. It concurs with the assumption that Americanization and industrialization have had a direct impact on the socioeconomic, political, and cultural realities of contemporary Puerto Rican society. It diverges from the second position, however, in that it claims that the influence of those processes has not impeded the preservation of the basic cultural aspects of the Puerto Rican value orientation structure on the island (Steward, 1956; Maldonado-Denis, 1972, 1976).

The only significant finding in this study that adds support to this position is that there was a match between the mainland Puerto Rican and island samples on the Relational category, which suggests the maintenance of Hispanic values regarding familial patterns. Furthermore, the lack of between-group differences for the three samples on the Activity and Time categories indicates the impact of industrialization upon contemporary Puerto Rican society.

Summary

The present study was primarily exploratory, given the uniqueness of the target population within the framework of culture contact in the United

States. Some of the variables making mainland Puerto Ricans a particularly interesting group to study were (1) their recent migration to the mainland; (2) their demographic patterns, which show more than one-third of the Puerto Rican population living in the United States, and high fertility rates, given the low median age; (3) the proximity of the island to the mainland, which encourages back-and-forth migration patterns; and (4) the socio-political and economic status of the island as a colonial territory of the United States.

An analysis of the findings went beyond the initial scope of inquiry because of several unexpected outcomes. For example, the homogeneity in value orientations between the island and Anglo samples on three of the four value orientation categories drew attention to the cultural contact between the mainland and Puerto Rico as a point of reference, rather than between the immigrant/migrant and host groups. The findings from this study further suggested that worldwide industrialization and multiple acculturations of groups are major variables that impinge upon the study of contemporary value orientations, particularly of groups with a superordinate/subordinate relationship to each other (colonies, territories, and such).

The results of this study indicate that the island of Puerto Rico is undergoing changes in value orientations, given the influence of the United States, the fact that Puerto Ricans are U.S. citizens, and the strategic geographical location and economic dependence of the island. While the U.S. influence in Puerto Rico in these areas has been extensively documented for decades, there has been little empirical investigation of the extent of acculturation on the specific value orientations prevalent on the island.

The most significant finding of this study centers on the alignment of value orientations between the island and mainland Puerto Rican samples on the Relational category. This was the one category out of four for which there was no match between the island and Anglo rank-ordering of choices. This suggests a resistance to acculturation processes regarding family relations. Furthermore, it is the only category for which the mainland Puerto Rican sample matched its island counterpart, and differed from the Anglo sample, thus signaling the continuation of the extended family structure and interpersonal relations typical of the Hispanic cultural ethos for second-generation mainland Puerto Ricans.

Those who adhere to the view that there is a continuity or persistence of value orientation patterns intergenerationally from one's culture of origin will find evidence of such in this study for the Relational category. On the other hand, those who contend that acculturation processes are a fact of life for all immigrant groups in the United States will view the homogeneity in value orientations manifested by the three groups in this study as evidence supporting their position. In this context, mainland Puerto Ricans will be considered dually susceptible to acculturation because of the U.S. influence on Puerto Rico itself as well as because of the minority status of Puerto Ricans within the United States.

Regardless of how this study's findings are interpreted or utilized, it is important to note that further research, including a cross-sectional sample of island Puerto Ricans, Anglos, and particularly third-generation mainland Puerto Ricans, is essential. Such a study should go beyond the exploratory nature, and the scope and limitations, of the present analysis.

Given the size of the school-age population of Puerto Ricans on the mainland, their high dropout rate within the public school system, and the linguistic diversity found in the classroom, the need for understanding value orientations becomes especially important for educators. By the year 2000, it is projected that Hispanics will represent the largest minority group in the United States, and a large proportion of this group will be of school age.

The need for a major shift in the preparation of teachers and other professionals, focusing on the multicultural composition of the United States, is becoming more urgent. If such training and initiative are not forthcoming, in terms of curriculum and of cultural awareness, the educational system in large urban centers of the United States will be unprepared to educate its youth in the next century. The comparative study of value orientations is an approach that facilitates the understanding of cultural diversity and the awareness needed for functioning more effectively in our contemporary global community.

NOTE

1. Several terms have been used to identify second-generation Puerto Ricans born and/or reared on the U.S. mainland. Fitzpatrick (1971) was the first to use the term "Puerto Rican Americans," but it was widely rejected by members of this group, who felt they were not "American"; others considered it redundant, since Puerto Ricans are U.S. citizens by birth. Therefore, "mainland Puerto Rican" became the more acceptable term, especially among scholars of the Hispanic experience in the United States (Senior, 1961; Fitzpatrick, 1971; Wagenheim, 1975). Glazer and Moynihan (1970) refer to the second generation as "Puerto Ricans," as do a number of Puerto Rican scholars when referring to anyone of Puerto Rica ancestry or national origin (Maldonado-Denis, 1972; Nieves-Falcón, 1975). The term "Nuyorican" has also been used (Seda-Bonilla, 1972), originating from the fact that the largest concentration of second-generation Puerto Ricans is in New York City. However, this term has been used primarily to differentiate second-generation Puerto Ricans born and/or reared in the United States from those born and/or reared on the island. It used to carry a negative connotation, although it is now more acceptable and more commonly used.

The term "mainland Puerto Rican" is generally used throughout the literature but has also been rejected, mainly by scholars who view Puerto Rico not as a territorial extension of the United States but as a separate nation, given its cultural heritage within the Latin American and Caribbean traditions. In spite of the limitations of any given term to describe the second generation of Puerto Ricans in the United States, the present study utilizes "mainland Puerto Rican" to mean a person born and/or reared on the U.S. mainland.

REFERENCES

Baldassini, J. G. 1980. "Acculturation Process of Colombian Immigrants into American Culture." Ph.D. diss., Rutgers University.

Blu, K. I. 1977. "Varieties of Ethnic Identity: Anglo-Saxons, Blacks, Indians, and Jews in Southern County." *Ethnicity* 4:263-286.

Born, D. O. 1970. "Value Orientations and Immigrant Assimilation in a Southern Illinois Community." Ph.D. diss., Southern Illinois University.

Brameld, T. 1958. "Explicit and Implicit Culture in Puerto Rico: A Case Study in Educational Anthropology." *Harvard Educational Review* 28:197-213.

Calhoun, E. E. 1975. "Value Orientations of Mexican-American and Anglo-American Ninth Grade Students." Ph.D. diss., New Mexico State University.

Caudill, W., and H. Scarr. 1962. "Japanese Value Orientations and Culture Change." *Ethnology* 1:53-91.

Colleran, K. J. 1984. "Acculturation in Puerto Rican Families in New York City." *Hispanic Research Bulletin* 7 (3-4):2-6.

Cooper, P. (ed.). 1972. *Growing up Puerto Rican.* New York: New American Library.

Dempsey, T. M. 1973. "Variations in Value Orientations Among Four Ethnic Sub-groups of Migratory Agricultural Workers." Ph.D. diss., University of Miami.

Dinnerstein, L., and D. Reimers. 1975. *Ethnic Americans: A History of Immigration and Assimilation.* New York: Harper & Row.

DuBois, C. 1955. "The Dominant Value Profile of American Culture." *American Anthropologist* 57(6):1232-1239.

Dukes, W. E. 1955. "Psychological Studies of Values." *Psychological Bulletin* 52(1):24-50.

Feather, N. T. 1972. "Value Systems and Education: The Flinders Programme of Research." *Australian Journal of Education* 16:136-149.

Feather, N. T. 1973. "Value Change Among University Students." *Australian Journal of Psychology* 25:57-70.

Feather, N. T., and A. Rudzitis. 1974. "Subjective Assimilation Among Latvian Adolescents: Effects of Ethnic Schools and Perceptions of Value System." *International Migration Review* 12:17-87.

Feather, N. T. and G. Wasyluk. 1973. "Subjective Assimilation Among Ukrainian Migrants: Value Similarity and Parent-Child Differences." *Australian and New Zealand Journal of Sociology* 9(11):16-31.

Femminella, F. X. 1973. The Immigrant and the Melting Pot. In M. Vrofsky (ed.), *Perspectives on Urban America.* New York: Doubleday.

Fitzpatrick, J. P. 1971. *Puerto Rican-Americans: The Meaning of Migration to the Mainland.* Englewood Cliffs, NJ: Prentice-Hall.

Freedle, R. O., and W. S. Hall. 1975. *Culture and Language: The Black American Experience.* New York: Hemisphere Publishing Company.

Gillin, J. 1955. "Ethos Components in Modern Latin-American Culture." *American Anthropologist* 57:488-500.

Glasser, D. 1958. "Dynamics of Ethnic Identification." *American Sociological Review* 23:31-40.

Glazer, N., and D. P. Moynihan. 1970. Second edition. *Beyond the Melting Pot.* Cambridge: MIT Press.

Glazer, N., and D. P. Moynihan. 1975. *Ethnicity: Theory and Experience*. Cambridge: Harvard University Press.

Gordon, M. 1964. *Assimilation in American Life*. New York: Oxford University Press.

Greeley, A. M. 1971. *Why Can't They Be like Us?* New York: E. P. Dutton.

Greeley, A. M. 1974. *Ethnicity in the United States: A Preliminary Reconnaissance*. New York: John Wiley and Sons.

Handlin, O. 1963. *The Americans*. Boston: Little, Brown.

The Hispanic Almanac. 1984. New York: Hispanic Policy Development Project.

Isser, N. 1976. *Asian-Americans: Then, Now and Tomorrow*. Washington, D.C.: ERIC Document Reproduction Service no. ED130984.

Kitano, H. H. 1972. "Japanese-Americans: The Evolution of a Sub-Culture." Washington, D.C.: ERIC Document Reproduction Service no. ED061393.

Kluckhohn, C. 1953. "Universal Categories of Culture." In A. Kroeber (ed.), *Anthropology Today*. Chicago: University of Chicago Press.

Kluckhohn, F. 1953. "Dominant and Variant Value Orientations." In C. Kluckhohn et al. (eds.), *Personality in Nature, Society and Cultures*. 2nd edition. New York: Alfred A. Knopf.

Kluckhohn, F., and R. Strodtbeck. 1961. *Variations in Value Orientations*. New York: Row, Peterson & Co.

Leavitt, R. R. 1974. *The Puerto Ricans: Culture, Change and Language Deviance*. Tucson: University of Arizona Press.

Maldonado-Denis, M. 1972. *Puerto Rico: A Socio-historic Interpretation*. New York: Random House.

Maldonado-Denis, M. 1976. *Puerto Rico y Estados Unidos: Emigración y colonialismo*. Mexico, DF: Siglo XXI.

Mason, L. 1955. "The Characterization of American Culture in Studies of Acculturation." *American Anthropologist* 57(6):1264-1279.

Méndez, F. E. (ed.). 1972. *Portrait of a Society: Readings on Puerto Rican Sociology*. Río Piedras: University of Puerto Rico Press.

Mintz, S. 1960. *Worker in the Cane: A Puerto Rican Life History*. New Haven: Yale University Press.

Nahirny, V. C., and J. Fishman. 1965. "American Immigrant Groups: Ethnic Identification and the Problem of Generations." *Sociological Review* 13:311-326.

Negrón de Montilla, A. 1971. *Americanization in Puerto Rico and the Public School System: 1900-1930*. Río Piedras, PR: Editorial Edil.

New York State Hispanics: A Challenging Minority. 1984. Albany: Governor's Advisory Committee for Hispanic Affairs.

Nieves-Falcón, L. 1975. *El Emigrante puertorriqueño*. Río Piedras, PR: Editorial Edil.

O'Flannery, E. 1972. "Social and Cultural Assimilation." In F. Cordasco and E. Bucchioni (eds.), *The Puerto Rican Community and Its Children*. Metuchen, NJ: Scarecrow Press.

Ogawa, D. M. 1975. "Communication Characteristics of Asians in American Urban Settings: The Case of Honolulu Japanese." Washington, D.C.: ERIC Document no. ED124462.

Parsons, T. 1951. *The Social System*. Glencoe, IL: The Free Press.

Pido, A. J. 1977. "Social Structure and the Immigration Process as Factors in the Analysis of a Non-white Immigrant Minority: The Case of the Filipinos in Midwest City, U.S.A." Ph.D. diss., Michigan State University.

Portes, A., R. N. Parker, and J. A. Cobas. 1980. "Assimilation or Consciousness: Perceptions of U.S. Society Among Recent Latin-American Immigrants to the United States." *Social Forces* 59(1):200-224.

Rogler, L. H., and R. Santana Cooney. 1984. *Puerto Rican Families in New York City: Intergenerational Processes.* Maplewood, NJ: Waterfront Press.

Rokeach, M. 1968a. *Beliefs, Attitudes and Values: A Theory of Organization and Change.* San Francisco: Jossey-Bass.

Rokeach, M. 1968b. "A Theory of Organization and Change Within Value-Attitude Systems." *Journal of Social Issues* 24:13-33.

Rokeach, M. 1973. *The Nature of Human Values.* New York: The Free Press.

Schermerhorn, R. A. 1970. *Comparative Ethnic Relations: A Framework for Theory and Research.* New York: Random House.

Seda-Bonilla, E. 1972. *Requiem por una cultura.* Río Piedras, PR: Ediciones Bayoán.

Segalman, R. 1966. "The Immigrant Poor and the Residual Poor." Paper presented at the Southern Sociological Association Meeting.

Senior, C. 1961. *The Puerto Ricans: Strangers—Then Neighbors.* Chicago: Quadrangle Books.

Silén, J. A. 1973. *Historia de la nación puertorriqueña.* Río Piedras, PR: Editorial Edil.

Sjostrom, B. 1983. "An Analysis of Value Orientations of Mainland and Island Puerto Ricans and non-Puerto Rican College Students." Ph.D. diss., State University of New York at Albany.

Steward, J. H. (ed.). 1956. *The People of Puerto Rico: A Study in Social Anthropology.* Urbana: University of Illinois Press.

Steward, J. H. 1972. "Culture Patterns of Puerto Rico." In E. Fernández Méndez (ed.). *Portrait of a Society* (Río Piedras: University of Puerto Rico Press, 1972), pp. 119-129.

Stewart, E. C. 1972. *American Culture Patterns: A Cross-cultural Perspective.* LaGrange Park, IL: Intercultural Network.

Stycos, J. M. 1955. *Family and Fertility in Puerto Rico.* New York: Columbia University Press.

Szapocznik, J., and W. Kurtines. 1979. "Acculturation, Biculturalism and Adjustment Among Cuban-Americans." Paper presented at the American Association for the Advancement of Science Annual Meeting, Houston.

Tirayakian, E. A. 1967. *Sociological Theory, Values and Sociocultural Behaviors.* New York: The Free Press of Glencoe.

U.S. Bureau of the Census. 1981. "Persons of Spanish Origin in the United States." *Current Population Reports*, Series P-20, no. 361. Washington, D.C.: U.S. Government Printing Office.

Wagenheim, Kal. 1975. *A Survey of Puerto Ricans on the U.S. Mainland.* New York: Praeger.

Wagley, C. 1968. *The Latin-American Tradition: Essays on the Unity and Diversity of Latin-American Culture.* New York: Columbia University Press.

Williams, R. M., Jr. 1960. *American Society: A Sociological Interpretation.* New York: Knopf.

8

Spanish in the United States

Arnulfo G. Ramírez

Spanish has been spoken in what is now the United States since the sixteenth century. Juan Ponce de León, while searching for the legendary Fountain of Youth, landed in Florida in 1513, and by 1565 a permanent colony was established at St. Augustine. In the Southwest, Francisco Vásquez de Coronado had explored by 1540 what is now Arizona, Texas, Colorado, and New Mexico. In 1598 Juan de Oñate founded San Gabriel de los Españoles, today called Chamita, known as the oldest continuous Spanish settlement in the Southwest. The city of Santa Fe, New Mexico, was established in 1609, and other settlements in present-day Arizona, western Texas, and southern Colorado soon followed.

During the early eighteenth century, Spanish settlements were established in central and eastern Texas. Father Margil founded the Mission of Our Lady of Guadalupe of Nacogdoches in 1716. Two years later, a Franciscan mission, San Antonio de Valero (that later became known as the Alamo) and a presidio were established in 1718 along the San Antonio River. Between 1769 and the early 1800s, Father Junípero Serra and other missionary friars founded missions along the California coast, extending from present-day San Francisco in the north to San Diego in the south. Many of these mission-presidial settlements continued to serve as linguistic and cultural centers, ensuring the persistence of the Spanish language and culture. According to Conklin and Lourie (1983:15-16) at least two factors have helped to maintain the Hispanic presence in the early settlement regions: (1) Hispanics, as members of the oldest European culture in these areas, were more resistant to Anglo assimilation than were members of other cultural groups who arrived later, and (2) the proximity of the southwestern United States to Mexico and of the southeastern United States to the Spanish-speaking Caribbean (Puerto Rico, Cuba, and Santo Domingo) has reinforced the language and provided a new cultural vitality.

DEMOGRAPHIC CONSIDERATIONS

According to the 1980 census, 11.5 million people reported that they spoke Spanish at home. This statistic makes the United States the sixth-largest Spanish-speaking country in the world. As can be seen in Table 8.1, the people claiming to speak Spanish at home are concentrated in four states (California, Texas, New York, and Florida). In terms of percentage of the population using Spanish, New Mexico registers nearly 30 percent (29.4%), Texas includes almost 20 percent (19.2%), California and Arizona have close to 15 percent (14.5% and 13.3% respectively), and New York and Florida report almost 9 percent each (8.6%).

LEVELS OF SPANISH PROFICIENCY

Many speakers of Spanish can be classified as bilingual. Some have speaking skills in both English and Spanish and literacy skills (reading and writing proficiency) primarily in one language, often English if they have attended a traditional, monolingual school. Others are both bilingual and bi-literate, able to comprehend, speak, read, and write both languages. Some children of Hispanic bilingual parents become only passive bilinguals, able to understand Spanish but not use it productively in communication situations.

Table 8.1
Estimated Numbers and Percentages of Home Speakers of Spanish, Aged 3 and Older, by State: United States, 1980

STATE	NUMBER	% OF TOTAL POPULATION	% OF SPANISH SPEAKERS BY STATE	CUMULATIVE
All States	11,559,000	5.3 %	100.0 %	100.0 %
California	3,270,000	14.5	28.3	28.3
Texas	2,595,000	19.2	22.5	50.7
New York	1,453,000	8.6	7.0	70.3
Florida	807,000	8.6	12.6	63.3
Illinois	524,000	4.8	4.5	74.8
New Jersey	431,000	6.1	3.7	78.6
New Mexico	362,000	29.4	3.1	81.7
Arizona	343,000	13.3	3.0	84.7
Colorado	184,000	6.7	1.6	86.3
Pennsylvania	140,000	1.2	1.2	87.5
Massachusetts	114,000	2.1	1.0	89.4
Connecticut	108,000	3.6	0.9	89.4
Michigan	107,000	1.2	0.9	90.3
Ohio	101,000	1.0	0.9	91.2

Source: 1980 census, as presented in testimony by D. Waggoner (1983).

The specific language abilities of Hispanic groups, particularly with respect to Spanish proficiency, have not been addressed in large-scale studies. Census reports tend to focus on language "traits" (English-only households, Spanish as usual language, English-Spanish bilingual, and Spanish monolingual). Macias (1985) conducted a survey among 199 Mexican-American parents having children in Head Start programs in East Los Angeles in 1973 and found that a larger percentage reported more facility in Spanish verbal skills ("can speak," 88.4% and "do speak," 81.4%) than Spanish literacy skills ("can read," 78.4%; "do read," 67.8%; "can write," 73.9%). Persons who could read in both languages included 34.7 percent of the respondents; 16.6 percent were able to read in English only; and 39.7 percent could read only in Spanish. A somewhat similar pattern was observed in the area of writing skills. The high degree of Spanish literacy skills was due to the fact that the majority of those surveyed had been born and had received some schooling in Mexico (53.3%).

In a survey conducted in South Bend, Indiana, in 1974 among persons of Spanish origin randomly selected and including 135 households, the percentage of persons who reported greater oral proficiency was higher in Spanish (understand, 89.6%; speak, 87.4%) than in English (understand, 69.5%; speak, 61.9%). Some of the results appear skewed, since more people report that they can *speak* English (31.8%) or Spanish (11.9%) than say they can *understand* "some" English (25.2%) or Spanish (9.6%). A greater number of the respondents had no literacy skills in Spanish (reading, 20.7%; writing, 25.2%) than in English (reading, 12.9%; writing, 21.2%).

In a study of Mexican-American high school students from Texas (N = 50) and California (N = 80), Ramírez, Milk, and Sapiens (1985) found that most pupils rated their ability to use Spanish within the range of "well" to "extremely well": 96 percent (well = 28%, very well = 46%, and extremely well = 22%) in understanding; 85 percent (well = 34%, very well = 33%, and extremely well = 18%) in speaking; 72 percent (well = 25%, very well = 32%, and extremely well = 15%) in reading; 67 percent (well = 25%, very well = 32%, and extremely well = 10%) in writing. In the "not at all" category, relative frequency increased from 1.5 percent for understanding to 22 percent for writing, while in the "extremely well" category the pattern is the reverse—fewer students read and write Spanish as well as they understand it, suggesting that indeed these students are bilingual, but literate primarily in English.

The surveys reported above ask the respondents to evaluate their relative proficiency in Spanish with respect to four language skills (listening, speaking, reading, and writing). With this approach it is not clear whether the participants confuse *language proficiency* (what the speaker can do) with *language use* (what the speaker actually does). At the same time, each language skill can include a range of familiar/unfamiliar topics (family, sports, food, health, education, and science), different sociolinguistic situations (home, neighborhood, school, and work), and various discourse styles (narration, exposition, and argumentation).

VARIETIES OF SPANISH

Four major varieties of Spanish are spoken in the United States. These include Mexican Spanish, particularly in the Southwest and large urban centers of the Midwest (Detroit, Cleveland, and Chicago); Puerto Rican Spanish, principally in the eastern states (New York, New Jersey, Pennsylvania, and Connecticut); Cuban Spanish, in Miami, Boston, and New Orleans (Cárdenas, 1970). Peninsular Spanish can be heard in New York City, and *islens*, a dialect from the Canary Islands, still survives in Bayou Lafourche, Louisiana (Craddock, 1981). Within the Southwest, four dialectal zones with some degree of overlapping are noticeable: (1) Texas Spanish, with considerable influence due to Mexican migration; (2) New Mexican and Southern Coloradan Spanish, which includes a number of archaisms due to its relative isolation until recently; (3) Arizonan Spanish, with a number of linguistic features in common with New Mexican Spanish but with a significant influence of northern Mexican Spanish due to its proximity to Sonora; and (4) Californian Spanish, an extension of Arizonan Spanish greatly influenced by borrowing from English (Cárdenas, 1970).

The Spanish spoken in the Southwest has more recently been described in terms of an English-Spanish continuum ranging from Standard (formal) Mexican Spanish to Standard (formal) English with several dialects or speech styles blending into each other between the two standard varieties (Elías-Olivares and Valdés, 1982:155-156). The continuum is illustrated in Figure 8.1

Differences among the varieties are established on the basis of linguistic criteria. Popular Spanish contains a number of nonstandard features with respect to vowel and consonant changes, verb tenses and conjugations, and gender/number agreement rules. Mixed Spanish and Caló (Pachuco) contain elements of both English and Spanish while maintaining basic Spanish word order and pronunciation of English borrowings (*londri* for "laundry," *escrín* for "screen," and *esquiplar* for "skip"). Mixed Spanish can serve for informal speaking and sometimes is used by children who have

Figure 8.1
Language Varieties Among Hispanics in the Southwest

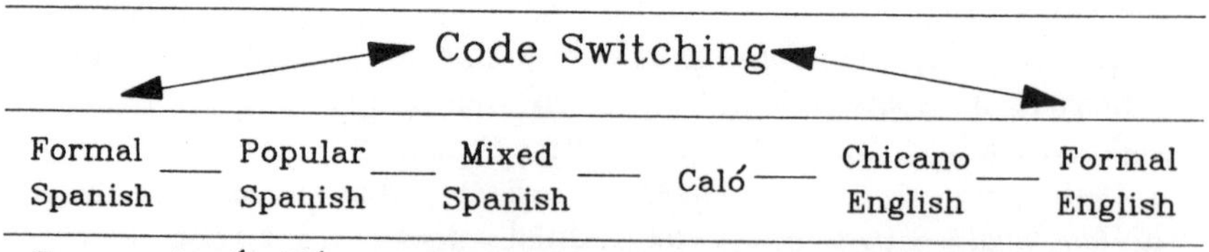

Formal Spanish	Popular Spanish	Mixed Spanish	Caló	Chicano English	Formal English

with Code Switching indicated by arrows spanning the range.

Source: Lucía Elías—Olivares and Guadalupe Valdés, 1982, p.155.

Reprinted by permission of the publisher. © 1982 by Teachers College, Columbia University.

not been exposed to either English or Spanish as a separate code. Code switching involves the alternating use of the two languages on the word, phrase, clause, or sentence level. For example, while speaking Spanish, a speaker may say:

1. No voy a ir al gym.
   (I'm not going to the gym.)
2. Estoy muy cansado, so I'm going to bed.
   (I'm very tired, so I'm going to bed.)

In the case of code switching at the word level (1) and code switching at the clause level (2), both English pronunciation and word form are maintained with no attempt to "adapt" to Spanish, as in the case of Mixed Spanish or Caló, a colloquial variety containing delinquent jargon, slang expressions, and gypsy argot.

Sánchez (1983) argues that there are basically two principal varieties of Spanish in the Southwest. One is the standard and the other the popular, which can be further subdivided into urban and rural codes in many cases. Within each subcode there are special varieties such as Caló, which is an urban subcode. Differences among the three major varieties occur primarily at the morphosyntactic level (the formation of word within sentence construction), although variation can exist at the level of words in the case of archaic terms, English loanwords, or rural vocabulary. Contrasts among the three varieties can be observed in Table 8.2.

More than at the code level, speakers often shift speaking styles (formal, informal, and intimate) to "accommodate" a change in topic (food, family, religion, sports), addressee (relative, stranger, friend), context (home, church, work, street), and language function (apology, reprimand, suggestion, advice). Table 8.3 illustrates some lexical and phonological differences among four speech styles identified by Sánchez.

Some of the linguistic processes affecting Spanish in the Southwest can also be seen in the language behavior of Puerto Ricans living in New York City. The adaptation of English words into Spanish has often been cited as the proof that some Puerto Ricans speak "Spanglish," presumably a new language variety (a pidgin created from a mixture of English and Spanish without a complete grammatical system). Of course, many of the English loan words in question are used because of the necessity to communicate in an environment different from that of the island. In New York one has lunch (*lonchar*), washes clothes in a laundry (*el londri*), lives in a block (*el bloque*), works in a factory (*la factoría*), and talks to the superintendent (*el super*). According to Milán (1982), the phenomenon of borrowing English words can be explained in terms of three basic processes:

1. Semantic reassignment—a Spanish word takes a new meaning because of its similarity to an English word (for instance, *carpeta* [folder] is used to mean "carpet").

Table 8.2
Contrast Between Standard and Popular Urban and Rural Codes

Standard	Urban popular	Rural popular
1. Fuiste. ¿Qué hiciste?	1. Fuistes. ¿Qué hicistes?	1. Juites/Fuites. ¿Qué hicites?
2. Salimos a las tres. Decimos.	2. Salimos/Salemos. Decimos/Dicemos.	2. Salemos a las tres. Dicemos.
3. No traía nada.	3. No traía nada.	3. No traiba nada.
4. No traje nada. No vi nada. Somos la nueva . . .	4. No traje nada. No vi nada. Somos la nueva . . .	4. No truje nada. No vide nada. Semos la nueva generación.
5. Ibamos todos.	5. Ibamos todos.	5. Ibanos todos.
6. Cuando volvamos . . .	6. Cuando vuélvamos	6. Cuando vuélvanos . . .
7. muchos padres muchos papás	7. muchos papás	7. muchos papases munchos papases
8. ¿El libro? Se lo di a ellos.	8. ¿El libro? Se los di a ellos.	8. ¿El libro? Se los di a ellos.
9. Nos lo dio . . .	9. No los dio . . .	9. No los dio . . .
10. Nos trajo a nosotros.	10. Los trajo a nosotros. Nos trajo a nosotros.	10. Los trujo a nosotros.

Source: Sánchez, 1983, 135.

2. Large-scale word borrowings (for instance, block/*bloque*, elevator/*elevador*, boiler/*boila*).
3. Loan translations and literal translations from English to Spanish (for instance, to take advantage of, *tomar ventaja de* instead of *aprovecharse de*).

In addition there are a number of syntactic readjustments (for instance, the pronoun is placed before the verb instead of after as in questions: ¿Qué Ud. piensa? for ¿Qué piensa Ud.? ("What do you think?"). Nevertheless, Pousada and Poplack (1982) note that in the verb system of mainland Puerto Rican Spanish, there is overwhelming empirical evidence suggesting that tense, mood, and aspect differ little from standard Puerto Rican Spanish. Moreover, there is a great degree of similarity between vernacular Puerto Rican and Andalusian Spanish, a dialect from Spain that has not had extended contact with English.

SPANISH/ENGLISH BILINGUAL PUPILS

The Spanish and English the bilingual child brings to school may not be the "standard" languages used in the school's textbooks or by the teacher. A child acquires the particular form of a language he or she hears at home. The variety of Spanish, marked regionally and socially, spoken at home is

Table 8.3
Some Examples of Style in Chicano Spanish

Formal	Informal	Intimate	Familiar
1. Usted es	1. Usté es		
2. Todo el día	2. To'o el día	2. to'o el día	
3. No he tomado	3. No he tomao		
4. Y luego	4. Y luego luego	4. Y lo' luego; Y lo' lo'	
5. Mi padre	5. Mi papá	5. Mi 'apá	5. Mi jefito~mi apá
6. Está bien	6. Está bien	6. 'Tá weno	
7. ¿Qué hora es?	7. ¿Qué hora es?	7. [Kjorés?] [Kjorasón?]	
8. Está cerca . . .	8. Está cerca . . .	8. 'Tá cerquita . . .	
9. ¿Dónde estaba?	9. ¿Dónde estabas?	9. ¿'On 'tabas?	9. 'Ontablas?
10. Se fué al trabajo	10. Se fué al trabajo.	10. Se fué a chambear	10. Le talonió pal jale
11.	11. Metí la pata	11. La regué	
12. ¿Qué pasó?	12. ¿Qué pasó?	12. ¿Quiubo?	12. ¿Qué pasión? ¿Qué ondas?
13. ¡Está fenomenal!	13. ¡Está fenomenal!	13. ¡'Tá a todo dar!	13. 'Tá de aquellas!
14. la policía		14. la ley	14. la jura
		la chota	la placa

Source: Sanchez, 1983, 137.

the one the child will learn. If the family also uses English at home and the variety of English is strongly influenced by Spanish pronunciation or grammar, the child acquires that particular variety of English.

Some children can switch from one language to another when speaking. This ability, known as code switching, may occur in certain domains only, and is not an example of a speaker confusing his or her two languages or speaking a random mixture of words with no grammatical base. Code switching is a common phenomenon among Spanish/English bilinguals. It has a significant influence on teachers' expectations and, therefore, on the learning environment. The teacher in a culturally diverse classroom should understand that code switching is not a random mixing of English and Spanish words and that it may not reflect lack of vocabulary in either language. Code switching is a complex process that carries meaning. Recent research suggests that subtle social and psychological factors may be involved. The following sentences are cases in point: "On Sunday voy a ir a rezar"; "Don't be a dummy así no se hace" (Valdés Fallis, 1978; Poplack, 1982; Sánchez, 1983).

Code switching may be used to convey important social information, such as personal feeling, confidentiality, and emphasis: "I would like to eat it, pero es que me hace daño"; "No, hombre, I got real sick y me llevaron al hospital." Some things are more readily recalled in one language than in the other, perhaps because that language was used in the situation being discussed. Sentences like "Dile a José that we need a ride" and "Estoy con Mónica y Lupe en el drugstore" are examples of this phenomenon. Occasionally there is a slip of the tongue or unfamiliarity with a particular word or expression: "No me dijo, she was desperate, you know"; "Cuando van shopping se visten muy bien"; "You have to realize que no me gusta llegar tarde."

One must remember that words carry culturally specific associations, attitudes, and values, and teachers should appreciate the divergence in their pupils' communicative strategies. Code switching does not mean a child's language is "degenerate" or "structurally underdeveloped." Some form of code switching occurs whenever different language groups come in close, sustained contact.

Table 8.4 presents the principal code switching patterns identified by Valdés-Fallis.

In describing the speech of Spanish/English bilingual pupils with reference to the "standard," one might analyze the differences in terms of the various elements that constitute a language: (1) phonology—the sound system of a language; (2) morphology—the study of the structure of words and their formation; (3) lexicon—the vocabulary or words of a language; and (4) syntax—the way words are related to each other in a sentence or the way they are arranged. Differences or deviations from the "standard" can occur at any one of these four levels, and may be attributable to one or more of three sources: dialect, interference, or developmental errors:

Table 8.4
Principal Code Switching

Patterns	Definitions	Examples
Switching Patterns that Occur in Response to External Factors		
Situational Switches	Related to the social role of speakers	Mother uses English to chat with daughters but switches to Spanish to reprimand son.
Contextual switches	Situation, topic, setting, etc., linked to the other language	Students switch to English to discuss details of a math exam.
Identity markers	In-group membership stressed	*Ese bato, órale, ándale pues* used in English conversations, regardless of actual Spanish fluency.
Quotations and paraphrases	Contextual: related to language used by the original speaker	Y lo (luego) me dijo el Mr. Johnson que *I have to study.* (Remark was actually made in English.)
Switching Patterns that Occur in Response to Internal Factors		
Random switches of high frequency items	Unpredictable; do not relate to topic, situation, setting, or language dominance; occur *only* on word level	Very common words, such as days of the week or cclors. Function like English synonyms: gal—girl, guy—fellow, etc. Fuimos al *party* ayer y estuvo tan suave la fiesta.
Switches that reflect lexical need	Related to language dominance, memory, and spontaneous versus automatic speech	Include the "tip of the tongue" phenomenon; item may be momentarily forgotten.

Table 8.4 (continued)

Patterns	Definitions	Examples
Triggered switches	Due to preceding or following items	Yo lo vi, you know, *but I didn't speak to him*. (Switch is triggered by the preformulation.)
Preformulations	Include linguistic routines and automatic speech	*You know, glad to meet you, thanks for calling, no te molestes, que hay de nuevo*, etc.
Discourse markers	*But, and, of course,* etc.	*Este . . este . . yo si quería ir*.
Quotations and paraphrases	Non-contextual: not related to language used by original speaker	He insisted *que no me fuera*. But I did anyway. (Remark was originally made in English.)
Stylistic switches	Obvious stylistic devices used for emphasis or contrast	Me tomé toda la cafetera, *the whole coffee pot*.
Sequential switches	Involve using the last language used by the preceding speaker	Certain speakers will always follow the language switches of other speakers; others will not.

Source: Valdés-Fallis, 1978, 16.

1. Dialect—a "nonstandard" dialect intrudes on the "standard" dialect (of either English or Spanish)
2. Interference—one language intrudes upon the second (the English upon the Spanish, the Spanish upon the English)
3. Developmental errors—Children learning a second language may go through developmental stages resembling those characteristic of children learning their first language.

Pinpointing the cause of a deviation inevitably involves guesswork. Deviations may have multiple causes. "They won't have no fun" looks like a double negative common in some "nonstandard" English dialects, but it may also reflect the influence of the "standard" Spanish negative (no-nada, no-ningún). It may also be a developmental error, for with respect to negative quantifiers such as "nothing" or "nobody," the multiple negative can be a simplification occurring in a child's language. Furthermore, what appears to be interference may actually be a dialectical variation: "Mi hermana hizo un cake" (my sister made a cake).

The following is a conversation at home involving children bilingual in Spanish and English with a subsequent analysis of the "deviations" from "standard" Spanish (see Figure 8.2). The dialogue is *not* an actual conversation, but it serves to illustrate the interplay of various linguistic phenomena. The numbers in parentheses refer to aspects included in a chart followed by an explanation (Ramírez et al., 1976: 20-24).

Madre: ¿Qué pasa, hijo, no tienes hambre?	What's the matter, son, aren't you hungry?
Ricky: No muncho (2), 'ama (2), me duele el est*ógamo* (2).	Not very much, Mom, I have stomach ache.
Abuelita: Ricardo, se dice estómago, no est*ógamo* (2).	Ricky, one says "estómago," not "est*ógamo*."
Ricky: Nada más la carne, ¿O.K., 'buelita (2)?	Only the meat, O.K., Grandma?
Abuelita: Cristina, el niño quiere la tetera.	Cristina, the baby wants his bottle.
Cristina: Hey, Ricky, ¿qué te dió la Patterson para *E*nglish (5)?	Hey, Ricky, what did Mrs. Patterson give you in English?
Madre: ¿Les dieron los report cards ahora?	Did they give you your report cards today?
Cristina: Yeah, y Ricky flonqueó (7) dos cursos. Por eso no *tenés* (1) hambre, ¿verdad?	Yeah, and Ricky flunked two subjects. That's why you're not hungry, right?
Ricky: Nobody asked you, so keep out of it mechuda. It's just that esa vieja Patterson hates me.	Nobody asked you, so keep out of it, nosy. It's just that old Patterson hates me.

Figure 8.2
Deviations from "Standard" Spanish

Linguistic Level

	Phonological	Morphological	Lexical	Syntactic
Dialectal	1 mayestra l'oficina	2 'amá estógamo 'horita cencia 'buelita muncho	3 agarraste	4
Interference	5 English teas<u>h</u>er	6	7 saineabas marcas flonqueó	8
Developmental	9	10 tenes	11	12

Source: Compiled by author.

Abuelita: Nunca maldigas a tu maestra. A la maestra se le da el mismo respeto que a los padres. Eso es muy importante, y no estén peleando en la mesa.

Never curse your teacher. It is very important that you respect your teachers as you do your parents. And don't fight at the table.

Padre: Ah, pues eso sí que *agarraste* (3) buenas *marcas* (7) en deport-ment, ¿pero qué pasó con tu English (5) y cencia (27)?

Well, you did get good grades in deportment, but what happened with your English and science?

Ricky: She speaks English (5) too fast, y no la entiendo.

She speaks English too fast, and I don't understand her.

Padre: Bueno, parece que también necesitas más estudio. Ve ponte a hacer tu homework 'horita (2) mismo. Voy a ir a l'oficina (1) a hablar con tu tea*sh*er (5) mañana. ¿Por qué no me dijo tu ma*y*estra (1) que tenías trouble con tu English (5) y cencia (2)?

Well, it seems you also need to study more. Go do your homework right now. Tomorrow I'm going to go to the office to talk to your teacher. Why didn't your teacher tell me you were having trouble with English and science?

Ricky: She did, esas eran las notas en English (5) que *saineabas* (7).

She did, those were the notes in English that you signed.

Explanation of Deviations

1. Epenthesis—the addition of the sound "y" between two vowels: *maestre/ mayestra*.

   The article *la* elides to *l'* before singular nouns that begin with strong vowels: *la oficina/l'oficina*.

2. Aphaeresis—the omission of an initial sound or syllable: *mamá/'amá, ahorita/ 'horita, abuelita/'buelita*.

   Metathesis—transposition of two sounds in a word: *estómago/estógamo*.

   Archaism—the use of archaic words, phrases, or expressions in present-day Spanish: *mucho/muncho*.

3. Semantic shift of the verb. The meaning of *agarrar* has been extended beyond its general usage: use of *agarrar* instead of *recibir*.

5. The lack of differentiation in Spanish between the sounds /i/ as in "meet" and /I/ as in "bit"; English/Inglish. Spanish interference in the production of the sound "ch": teacher/teasher.

7. English word integrated into the lexical system of Spanish with the same mean-ing in English extended into Spanish: signed/*saineabas*, marks/*marcas*, flunked/*flonqueó*.

10. Overgeneralization of a rule—a stage in language acquisition. In this case, the child treats *tener* as a regular verb without making the necessary alteration in the stem *ten* to *tien: tienes/tenes*.

LANGUAGE USE AND ATTITUDES

The relative use of Spanish with respect to English can be examined in terms of sociolinguistic domains, broad institutional and functional categories that are congruent combinations of a particular kind of speaker, topic(s), and place, each of which calls for a particular type of language use. Thus, "home," "neighborhood," "church," "work," and "recreation" may be considered domains. English may be the language of school, government, and work, while Spanish may be employed in the home, church, and neighborhood. In some domains, both languages may be used, depending on the participants, topics, and/or speech acts (advice, compliment, warning, greetings). The relative use of the two languages may be characterized through the following illustration (Figure 8.3), which can be representative of a particularly Hispanic community.

If the two languages are separated functionally, a stable form of bilingualism may be the result. In other cases, the situation may resemble transitional bilingualism, where the two languages assume overlapping functions (English *or* Spanish for home, neighborhood, church, and recreation), resulting in the displacement of one language (Spanish) by the more dominant one (English).

A number of studies have examined the use of Spanish with respect to English in various contexts. Aguirre (1982), for example, investigated language usage patterns among adolescent Mexican-American students (N = 75) in a border town in California, focusing on such aspects as different social situations (school, neighborhood, and home) and type of speaker (English

Figure 8.3
Relative Use of Spanish and English According to Sociolinguistic Domain

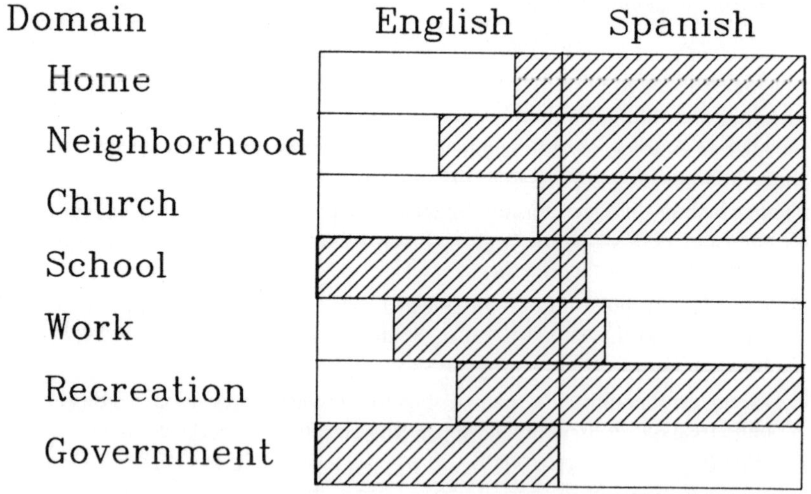

dominant, Spanish dominant, and "balanced" bilingual). He noted that in all three social situations, *both* languages were reported to be used for various purposes. Solé (1982) studied the language loyalty and language attitudes among Cuban Americans ranging from 14 to 18 years (N = 268) and representing the first generation of Cubans raised and educated in the United States. The majority of the respondents viewed Spanish as a positive cultural element (96% felt Spanish was important, 75% felt that the language should be encouraged, 72% saw no disadvantage in using the language, 55% were concerned about the "shift" taking place toward English usage). With respect to language use, 78 percent felt that their peers were using less Spanish than the older generation; 42 percent reported using both languages equally; and only 25 percent preferred English over Spanish.

In a study of intragroup differences and attitudes toward varieties of Spanish among bilingual pupils from California (N = 80) and Texas (N = 50), Ramírez, Milk, and Sapiens (1985) noted that Spanish was used primarily when talking with parents (74%); English was employed significantly during interactions with siblings (58%), teachers (68%), and other adults (54%). Attitudes toward four varieties of Spanish ("standard" Mexican Spanish, local Spanish, ungrammatical Spanish, and English/Spanish code alternation) were hierarchical, ranging from standard to codeswitching, with respect to acceptability, correctness, and the speaker's academic potential. Judgments about the four varieties were influenced by language use, location, birthplace, and sex.

In a similar study involving bilingual teachers attending a summer institute at a Texas university, Ramírez and Milk (1986) found that teachers (N = 61) used both languages to a similar extent when interacting with parents (32%), friends (44%), and neighbors (28%). Spanish was used significantly when speaking to brothers (mostly/only Spanish, 62%), friends (56%), fellow teachers (67%), and neighbors (69%). As with the study involving students from California and Texas, these teachers evaluated the four language varieties on a standard language continuum. Standard Spanish was rated higher than the two nonstandard varieties (local Spanish and ungrammatical Spanish) and code switching. The two nonstandard varieties were evaluated more favorably than Spanish/English code switching, and local Spanish was ranked higher than ungrammatical Spanish. While code switching did not contain nonstandard features of either English or Spanish, it did receive the lowest ratings. Teacher characteristics such as proficiency level in Spanish, ethnicity (Mexican-American, Anglo, or Latin American background), and birthplace (Texas, Latin America, or other parts of the United States) influenced some of the linguistic attitudes toward the four language varieties.

Attinasi (1985), in examining Hispanic language attitudes and use among groups from New York and northwest Indiana, found some differences between Mexican-Americans and Puerto Ricans living in Indiana with respect to the use of Spanish and shift to English. Changes in the use of the two languages can also be seen between these samples for New York and northwest Indiana. In New York, for example, there is the perception among over 75 percent in the two samples (identified by Attinasi as the New York teachers and New York Block samples) that many persons in the Hispanic community speak/use both ("mixed") languages. In the Indiana sample about 40 percent of the respondents report extensive bilingual (both English/Spanish) usage within the local community. Overall, the situation might be characterized as one of "bilingualism with greater fluency in English."

LANGUAGE RETENTION AND PUBLIC LIFE

The important question of Spanish language retention versus a shift to English has attracted considerable attention in recent years. The degree/level of language shift has been studied among college students in the lower Rio Grande Valley of southern Texas (Amastae, 1982), among university students from the Spanish-speaking community of Colorado (Floyd, 1982), families from a barrio in Albuquerque, New Mexico (Hudson-Edwards and Bills, 1982), and New York Puerto Ricans (Pedraza, 1985). The studies suggest generational differences in the use of Spanish. It may be the case that many third-generation Hispanics retain their Spanish no more than similar ethnolinguistic groups (Fishman, 1984). Fishman (1964) noted that most immigrant communities in the United States have tended to follow a four-stage pattern of language shift to English according to these steps:

Stage 1. Immigrants learn English through their mother tongue. English is utilized only in domains (such as work) where the mother tongue cannot be used. (This may be the case in the first generation.)

Stage 2. Immigrants learn more English and can use this language or their own in various domains (such as neighborhood or recreation). There is still a dependency on the mother tongue.

Stage 3. Speakers become bilingual, being able to use both languages with almost equal ease. Language separation does not occur by domain. (This is usually the case in the second generation.)

Stage 4. English displaces the mother tongue except in the most intimate domains (such as family affairs or religious services). (This may occur in the third generation.)

While a number of factors affect language retention and language loss, Gaarder (1977) has outlined nine variables that he feels will enhance Spanish language maintenance in the United States:

1. The length of time Spanish speakers, as indigenous groups, have been in this country prior to Anglos and other Euro-Americans

2. The large size of the Spanish-speaking population

3. The relative homogeneity of the Spanish speakers

4. Constant immigration of other Spanish speakers to reinforce the domestic population

5. Cultural access to a renewal from the hinterland (Mexico, Puerto Rico, Latin America)

6. Intergenerational stability of the extended family of Spanish speakers

7. Religiosocietal isolation among Spanish speakers

8. Present-day tolerance of cultural diversity in the United States

9. The relative isolation, and hence linguistic solidarity, of a Hispanic group

To this list Macias (1985) adds the development of an institutional language infrastructure, which includes bilingual schooling for Hispanic pupils, the availability of Spanish as a "foreign" language course in high schools and colleges, and Spanish-language mass media. According to a *New York Times* report (April 8, 1982), there was an extensive growth in mass media during the 1970-80 decade. The number of Spanish-language radio stations increased from 60 to 200, newspapers from 40 to 60, magazines from 25 to 65, and Spanish television stations from 12 to 167. A chain of Spanish-language television stations and cable companies with services to many cities in the United States receives daily satellite programming through SIN (Spanish International Network), which is associated with Televisa, the dominant television broadcaster in Mexico.

Veltman (1980) projects varying rates of linguistic assimilation for different ethnolinguistic groups in the Untied States. Using the *1976 National Survey of Income and Education*, which includes language data, he notes the following rate of anglicization (shift to English):

1. 80 percent shift to English monolingualism among United States citizens of German and Scandinavian origins.

2. 60 percent shift to English among persons from Native American, Filipino, Italian, and French-speaking groups.

3. 40 percent switch to English among persons from Portuguese, Chinese, and Greek American backgrounds.

4. 30 percent switch to English among Hispanic-American groups.

The rate of language shift to English is affected by the proportion of young adults and older persons in each language group. The number of French, German, and Italian speakers is expected to decline within a generation since a large proportion of persons are over forty years old. Speakers of Spanish, Native American languages, and Chinese are expected to increase during the next generation since these language groups have a significant number of young persons between the ages of twenty and thirty. . . . Within the Hispanic group, the anglicization rate varies depending on the geographic region (highest rates occurring in the Rocky Mountain states, lowest rates in Texas). (pp. 14-16)

A number of factors affect language maintenance or language shift among the various Hispanic communities in the United States. Some of the variables are related to the status of the group (economic standing, political power, social mobility, and occupations) and of its language (attitudes about the uses of the language, international or local language, standard written language or nonstandard variety); other factors are demographic (size of group, birthrate, immigration patterns—recent arrival and/or continuing immigration—geographic proximity to the homeland, geographic concentration, and isolation from other minority or majority groups) or institutional/governmental (use of native language and/or second language in the mass media, education, and government services; laws pertaining to languages and educational policies; and cultural support by a foreign state).

A specific example of the relative degree of language retention or language shift among persons of Spanish-language background can be seen in a study conducted by Laosa (1975). He compared the degree of bilingualism and the contextual use of language among three Hispanic groups in the United States: Mexican-Americans from central Texas, Cuban-Americans living in Miami, and Puerto Ricans residing in New York. He found the Puerto Rican group exhibited the greatest degree of maintenance of Spanish, while the Mexican-American group showed the highest degree of language shift from Spanish to code switching (alternation between English and Spanish) to English. The Puerto Ricans apparently had less contact with English-speaking institutions (the highest degree of unemployment and lowest occupational status) and maintained close contact with the island. The Mexican-American group evidenced the greatest length of stay in the United States. The children from the Mexican-American and Cuban-American samples tended to use less Spanish compared with adults in the familial context. Interestingly, Cuban children born in the United States used more Spanish than Cuban-born pupils in interactions with peers in school or recreational contexts.

Spanish in the United States has received considerable attention both as an academic discipline and as a social issue. Books such as *Bilingualism in the Barrio* (Fishman, Cooper, Ma, et al., 1971), *Studies in Southwest Spanish* (Bowen and Ornstein, 1976), *Latino Language and Communicative Behavior* (Durán, 1981), *Spanish in the United States: Sociolinguistic Aspects* (Amastae and Elías-Olivares, 1982), *Chicano Discourse: Sociohistoric Perspectives* (Sánchez, 1983), and *Spanish Language Use and Public Life in the USA* (Elías-Olivares et al., 1985) reflect various disciplinary perspectives, including sociolinguistics, psycholinguistics, communications, social psychology, and educational psychology. Many issues regarding Spanish language varieties, language attitudes and use, language retention and shift, language assessment, and the use of Spanish in health, law, education, and mass media remain to be addressed in order to capture the dynamic linguistic reality of Hispanic communities in the United States.

REFERENCES

Aguirre, A. 1982. "Language use patterns of adolescent Chicanos in a California border town." In F. Barkin, E. A. Brandt, and J. Ornstein-Galicia, eds., *Bilingualism and Language Contact: Spanish, English, and Native American Languages.* New York: Teachers College Press.

Amastae, J. 1982. "Language shift and maintenance in the Lower Rio Grande Valley of Southern Texas." In F. Barkin, E. A. Brandt, and J. Ornstein-Galicia, eds., *Bilingualism and Language Contact: Spanish, English, and Native American Languages.* New York: Teachers College Press.

Amastae, J., and L. Elías-Olivares, eds. 1982. *Spanish in the United States: Sociolinguistic Aspects.* New York: Cambridge University Press.

Attinasi, J. J. 1985. "Hispanic attitudes in Northwest Indiana and New York." In L. Elías-Olivares et al., eds., *Spanish Language Use and Public Life in the USA.* New York: Mouton.

Bowen, J. D., and J. Ornstein, eds. 1976. *Studies in Southwest Spanish.* Rowley, MA: Newbury House.

Cárdenas, D. 1970. "Dominant Spanish Dialects Spoken in the United States." ERIC Document Reproduction Service no. ED 042137. Washington, DC: ERIC Clearinghouse for Linguistics.

Conklin, M. F., and M. A. Lourie. 1983. *A Host of Tongues: Language Communities in the United States.* New York: The Free Press.

Craddock, J. R. 1981. "New World Spanish." In C. A. Ferguson and S. B. Heath, eds., *Language in the USA.* New York: Cambridge University Press.

Durán, R. P., ed. 1981. *Latino Language and Communicative Behavior.* Norwood, NJ: Ablex.

Elías-Olivares, L., and G. Valdés. 1982. "Language diversity in Chicano speech communities: Implications for language teaching." In J. A. Fishman and G. D. Keller, eds., *Bilingual Education for Hispanic Students in the United States.* New York: Teachers College Press.

Elías-Olivares, L., et al., eds., 1985. *Spanish Language Use and Public Life in the USA.* New York: Mouton.

Fishman, J. 1964. "Language maintenance and language shift as fields of inquiry." *Linguistics* 9:32-70.

Fishman, J. 1984. "Language, Ethnic Identity and Political Loyalty: Mexican Americans in Sociolinguistic Perspective." Paper prepared for the Urban Institute, Los Angeles.

Fishman, J. A., R. L. Cooper, R. Ma, et al. 1971. *Bilingualism in the Barrio.* Bloomington: Indiana University Press.

Floyd, M. B. 1982. "Spanish-language maintenance in Colorado." In F. Barkin, E. A. Brandt, and J. Ornstein-Galicia, eds., *Bilingualism and Language Contact: Spanish, English, and Native American Languages.* New York: Teachers College Press.

Gaarder, A. B. 1977. *Bilingual Schooling and the Survival of Spanish in the United States.* Rowley, MA: Newbury House.

Hudson-Edwards, A., and G. D. Bills. 1982. "Intergenerational language shift in an Albuquerque barrio." In J. Amastae and L. Elías-Olivares, eds., *Spanish in the United States: Sociolinguistic Aspects*. New York: Cambridge University Press.

Laosa, L. M. 1975. "Bilingualism in three United States Hispanic groups: Contextual use of language by children and adults in their families." *Journal of Educational Psychology* 67:617-627.

Macias, R. F. 1985. "National language profile of the Mexican-origin population in the United States." In W. Conner, ed., *Mexican-Americans in Comparative Perspective*. Washington, DC: Urban Institute Press.

Milán, W. G. 1982. "Spanish in the inner city: Puerto Rican speech in New York." In J. A. Fishman and G. D. Keller, eds., *Bilingual Education for Hispanic Students in the United States*. New York: Teachers College Press.

Pedraza, P. 1985. "Language maintenance among New York Puerto Ricans." In L. Elías-Olivares et al., eds., *Spanish Language Use and Public Life in the USA*. New York: Mouton.

Poplack, S. 1982. "Sometimes I'll start a sentence in English y termino en español: Toward a typology of code-switching." In J. Amastae and L. Elías-Olivares, eds., *Spanish in the United States: Sociolinguistic Aspects*. New York: Cambridge University Press.

Pousada, A., and S. Poplack. 1982. "No case for convergence: The Puerto Rican Spanish verb system in a language-contact situation." In J. A. Fishman and G. D. Keller, eds., *Bilingual Education for Hispanic Students in the United States*. New York: Teachers College Press.

Ramírez, A. G., et al. 1976. *CERAS Spanish/English Balance Tests*. Stanford, CA: Center for Educational Research, School of Education, Stanford University.

Ramírez, A. G., and R. D. Milk, 1986. "Notions of grammaticality among teachers of bilingual pupils." *TESOL Quarterly* 20: 495-513.

Ramírez, A. G., R. D. Milk, and A. Sapiens. 1985. "Intra-group differences and attitudes toward varieties of Spanish among bilingual pupils from California and Texas." *Hispanic Journal of Behavioral Sciences* 5:417-429.

Sánchez, R. 1983. *Chicano Discourse: Socio-historic Perspectives*. Rowley, MA: Newbury House.

Solé, C. A. 1982. "Language loyalty and language attitudes among Cuban Americans." In J. A. Fishman and G. D. Keller, eds., *Bilingual Education for Hispanic Students in the United States*. New York: Teachers College Press.

Valdés-Fallis, G. 1978. "Code switching and the classroom teacher." *Language in Education*, Theory and Practice, no. 4. Washington, DC: Center for Applied Linguistics.

Veltman, C. J. 1980. *The Retention of Minority Languages in the United States*. Washington, DC: National Center for Educational Statistics.

Waggoner, D. 1983. "Estimates from the 1980 Census on People in Homes in Which Spanish Is Spoken." Testimony presented before the Subcommittee on Census and Population, Committee on the Post Office and Civil Service, U.S. House of Representatives, September 13.

III

SOCIOECONOMIC
PROFILES

9

The Unrecognized: Mexican Immigrant Workers and America's Future

James D. Cockcroft

In this chapter we shall observe how, in the midst of a stubbornly persistent economic crisis, the talk of "regaining control of our borders"—inflamed by a decade of yellow journalism about a flood of Mexican immigrants— has moved the immigration issue to the center of American and Mexican politics. The anti-immigrant hysteria in the United States has served to scapegoat innocent victims of economic crisis for "causing" the crisis, as well as to divide workers along lines of race, ethnicity, or national background.

But it also has alerted more observant students of immigration policy and law to the fact that the United States faces a serious labor shortage, one projected to endure well into the twenty-first century. It is a labor shortage of a particular kind, the kind that employers insist on retaining in their push for recovered profit rates: low-paid "bad jobs." It is thus a labor shortage that the forces of capital and racism are unwilling to meet by placing the nation's nonwhite minorities to work. Consequently, for the forces of capital there exists an impelling need for more, not fewer, immigrant workers.

THE CRISIS IN THE UNITED STATES

However various the explanations for the U.S. economic crisis, few economists disagree in their descriptions of its broad contours. It started in the late 1960s, deepened in the 1970s, and became global by the 1980s,

This chapter is based on selections from James D. Cockcroft, *Outlaws in the Promised Land: Mexican Immigrant Workers and America's Future* (New York: Grove Press, 1986). Published with author's and publisher's permission.

experiencing three recession periods (1969, 1973-75, 1979-83), each deeper than the preceding one. The persistence of high employment rates, low productivity, and rising consumer prices and interest rates led to the description of it as "stagflation," stagnation with inflation.

Most big corporations, including those saved by federal bailouts, continued to make copious profits—even socially embarrassing ones, in the harsh light of an overall stickiness or decline in real wages from 1969 to 1984. Yet the corporations' expected *rates* of profit were not sufficient to cause them to plow these returns back into production or research and development for improved techniques of production. Instead, they played the international money markets; speculated in real estate or other activities; invested in the national debts of countries around the world; shifted more funds into gold-plated military and other nonproductive activities; and bought government bonds and one another's stock. Corporate mergers and buyouts became an everyday occurrence.

In the "recovery" year of 1983, net private nonresidential fixed investment (the common measure of productive investment) fell to 1.5 percent of the U.S. net national product, the lowest in nearly 40 years. This happened in spite of the Reagan administration's slashing of social programs, raising of depreciation and other allowances for industry, and near doubling of the defense budget. Preston Martin, a Reagan appointee to the Federal Reserve Board, spoke of a "growth recession"—a slow recovery in production growth accompanied by rising unemployment.[1]

Among industrialized countries, the United States had, by 1984, become the one with the most unequal distribution of income (except France). In 1980, it had slipped to the rank of eleventh in per-capita gross domestic product.

With hindsight it is possible to locate the roots of U.S. economic problems in the Vietnam War; the inflated rates of waste in war and/or nonproductive "defense" industry; the postponement of recessions; federal and corporate mismanagement; overproduction with inadequate markets at home and abroad; loss of U.S. domination in select foreign markets; declining real wages; shrinking future markets for expansion; slackened productivity. President Lyndon B. Johnson once told GIs stationed in South Korea that had it not been for the Vietnam War, the United States would have suffered unemployment rates on a par with those of the Great Depression. Some of that "delayed" unemployment remained in 1984. As *New York Times* economic commentator Leonard Silk pointed out (March 14, 1982):

Call it a repression—a chronic state of underemployment and industrial slack that has dogged the economy for the greater part of the past decade, a condition brought on by repressive actions by governments in the industrial world. . . . When did this Great Repression begin? Since history is a seamless web, it is hard to date it precisely. But the escalation of the Vietnam war in 1965 and 1966 seems the logical point.

If one assumes, as the federal government and most economists do, that a sustained high rate of profit for corporate investors is critical for economic growth, then one has to trace the economic crisis to the tailing off of the rate of profit after 1965. The two most common measures of corporate profitability are based on actual figures and potential figures. By either measure, the rate of profit, with only occasional short-lived upturns, showed an overall, dominant downward trend from the mid-1960s through the early 1980s.

Declining profit rates and profit expectations in turn lent momentum to the short-term shift of investments into speculative activities and to capital's long-term quest for low-wage labor. In that context, the commonly recognized rising rates of foreign labor immigration into the United States and "runaway shops" locating in low-wage foreign areas in the 1970s and early 1980s reflected capital's response to declining rates. Reduced employment caused by runaway shops rose from an estimated 1 million jobs lost by 1965 to 2.5 million by 1980.

USE OF IMMIGRANT WORKERS

Unlike earlier historical periods, when economic crisis in the United States led to relative drops in Mexican immigration, during the 1968-83 period, when U.S. unemployment rose so noticeably, the number of Mexican immigrant workers, by even the most conservative estimates, rose sharply. By 1984, low estimates placed the number of "illegal" immigrant workers in the United States at about 4 million, while high estimates approached 10 million. Another 5 to 7 million *legal* immigrants were expected to enter the country during the 1980s. During the 1970s, California alone admitted an estimated 782,000 legal immigrants and 1,086,000 "undocumented" immigrants, according to Dr. Thomas Muller's study, *The Fourth Wave: California's Newest Immigrants*, released by the Washington, D.C.-based Urban Institute.

Many people blamed the "fourth wave" of new immigrants for the economic crisis. Dr. Muller's study, however, like others before it, did not substantiate the charge. It found no decline in job availability for non-immigrants in southern California, where nearly 70 percent of the new immigrants located. Of these, 75 percent were Mexican, and the study found "no statistical relationship between the size of the Hispanic population and Black unemployment." On the contrary, the immigrants' presence served to open up additional jobs for both black and white English-speaking citizens in education, health, and other social services; the immigrants' spending of money in the local economy also contributed to job creation. In addition, from 1975 to 1981, some 325,000 new Spanish-speaking residents in Los Angeles County accepted wages that averaged only half those paid other workers, thereby helping to preserve the area's competitive advantage in manufacturing. While factories and workshops in the Midwest closed down, in the Southwest they either continued to open or closed more infrequently. The wage scale in the Southwest for some years, however, had been lower than in the Northeast, in part because of the depressant effect on wages of large-scale immigration.

Nor does the Muller study contradict the fact that unemployment continues to affect many U.S. citizens, especially blacks, in the Southwest and other locales of heavy Latino immigration, such as Miami. Because of employers' recognition that immigrant workers are more docile and inexpensive than blacks, and because of the deeply ingrained antiblack racism of most employers, it is highly unlikely that a black would be chosen for a job over an immigrant. This would be the case even if unemployed blacks were willing and anxious to accept the miserable wages and work conditions that Mexican immigrants accept. The same kind of antiblack racism among employers characterized the job market at the turn of the century and during other peaks of foreign immigration waves. If history is any guide, the bitter wisdom of an antiracist American folksong applies here: If you're white, you're right; if you're brown, stick aroun'; but if you're black, get back!

Employers correctly perceive that it is easier to tame a Mexican immigrant than an unemployed black. Of obvious advantage to employers is the fact that the immigrants are unable to speak English and unfamiliar with the local culture. The greatest advantage for employers, of course, is the fact that the immigrant workers are "illegal," making them subject to instant deportation should they fail to obey orders!

Dr. Muller's study, like so many others, confirms the picture given by earlier Labor Department statistics. These showed that in the eight Southwest and Midwest labor markets experiencing the greatest increase in Mexican "illegal" immigrant workers from 1968 to 1977, the unemployment rate was *lower* than the national average. Notwithstanding, it has remained consistent with the racism and self-interest of most employers to foment widespread black unemployment (or to tolerate growing white unemployment where necessary), and then put the blame on the shoulders of the Mexican immigrants they recruit for low-paying jobs most Americans will not touch.[2]

For now, as in the past, scapegoating Mexican immigrant workers as cause instead of solution for the economic crisis helps U.S. employers escape responsibility for their own failures to provide sufficient jobs at decent remuneration for the nation's work force. Scapegoating Mexicans also helps to derail criticism of the nation's politicians and the economic system as a whole for allowing or generating the crisis in the first place.

A belt-tightening economic policy to combat the crisis would, no doubt, have been implemented in any case. The increased numbers in the reserve army of labor made possible by the "fourth immigration wave" and the massive layoffs of workers in Mexico, however, has helped to assure the carrying out of such policies as wage "givebacks" and other concessions by labor undertaken in the 1980s in both the United States and Mexico. The role of millions of unemployed or poorly paid Mexican workers, immigrant or otherwise, as the backbone of an international reserve army of labor historically was—and today remains—that of disciplining all labor in both countries. As a reserve army of labor, they are fundamental to the corporations' attempts to combat falling profit rates.

In addition, the augmented migratory flow has been fueled by the rapidly deepening poverty in Mexico, particularly since 1981, when the difficulties of economic survival began spreading to even the best-paid employed workers' families and some of the better-off ranks of Mexico's intermediate classes. Thus, a rise in the number of Mexicans going to the United States in quest of employment not only helps U.S. employers but also provides, as it has always done—but now more so than ever—an "escape valve" for the pressures being built up inside Mexico by mass impoverishment. In this sense, too, migration serves as a weapon to combat economic crisis on both sides of the border.

The Mexican government's periodic verbal defense of migrant workers against abuses they experience in the United States obscures its role in supporting the economic system that drives Mexicans to emigrate in the first place. In practice, the Mexican government rarely lifts a finger to defend the migrants. This is no accident, since it knows that 70 years after the end of the Mexican Revolution, it has not been able to resolve the problems at home that obligate so many Mexicans to seek their survival abroad. From the government's viewpoint, it is better that the adventuresome, courageous, and economically desperate leave the country to seek their subsistence than that they stay in Mexico to undertake the fight for land, jobs, and decent wages—in sum, a more dignified life.

Affected both by a deeply insinuated history of racism and by a growing mass-media bombardment of stories critical of Mexican immigrant workers in the late 1970s and early 1980s,[3] most Americans have no reason to doubt the common allegation that Mexican immigrant workers are draining taxpayers' contributions to social welfare programs such as food stamps, unemployment insurance, hospital service, and Social Security. In actuality, the very opposite is the case. Bold and foolhardy would be the "illegal" worker who exposes himself to the network of authorities overseeing these social programs, only to have to show or prove his or her citizenship—a common demand among the bureaucracies administering programs in those states where the Immigration and Naturalization Service (INS) is most active in its patrol of migratory streams. A 1979 Labor Department study found over 75 percent of "undocumented" workers *paying* Social Security and income taxes, but only 0.5 percent receiving welfare benefits and 1 percent using food stamps—quite a subsidy to the U.S. economy![4]

Indeed, one of the more hidden and unrecognized reasons that the "illegal" migratory flow into the United States has increased during the recent economic crisis, and is likely to increase for the foreseeable future, is that Social Security checkoffs contributed by the migrant workers account for a significant chunk of the system's trust fund. In the absence of these contributions, the fund would be depleted even more quickly than the current financing schedule suggests.

The situation is similar in the case of union dues. Some 10 percent of all Mexican immigrant workers have joined unions in the United States, and the number may be rising as some mainline unions hard hit by falling membership and declining dues rush to sign up the unorganized. Immigrants' payment of union dues usually benefits the long-term American union members far more than the short-term, come-and-go Mexican migrants. The fact that most migrant workers are not unionized, on the other hand, benefits employers. Moreover, the migrants spend an average of 60 percent or more of their wages in the United States, further contributing to the economy. *In general, U.S. citizens benefit disproportionately not just from the migrants' labor and consumption but from all the tax and benefits program checkoffs paid by immigrant workers—the very opposite of what Americans have been told and still generally believe.*

While most of the discussion of Mexican immigrants focuses on the unskilled, a small but significant number of the migrants are trained professionals (an estimated 20,000 in 1981). The drain of income and skills caused by this out-migration contributes to Mexico's failure to develop more prosperously, thereby guaranteeing the ongoing presence of an international reserve army of labor. Mexico suffers extreme shortages in all areas of skilled labor, from engineers to skilled workers. Further, the composite educational level of all Mexicans migrating to the United States is above the Mexican national average of third grade—an often overlooked but not insignificant part of the "brain drain." About 14.4 percent of the migrants have 7 or more years of education, and almost all have been employed prior to their migration. The export of Mexican human capital, consisting of laborers whose education and training have been paid for in Mexico, subsidizes the U.S. economy. Little wonder that even in times of economic crisis their presence is sought.[5]

All of this does not mean that massive deportations during the 1970s and 1980s have not accompanied the ongoing demand for immigrant labor, even as happened during the 1953-55 "Operation Wetback" period. The border's "revolving door" has never stopped its efficient operation on behalf of employers.[6] But the level of immigration is now higher than it was a generation ago—and considerably higher than in the last period of long-term economic crisis, the 1930s. Increased immigration during prolonged economic hard times is, then, on the whole a new phenomenon for the United States—and one demanding an explanation.

Paradoxically, the crisis itself is the main explanation. In many economic sectors, such as agriculture, garments and textiles, other industrial manufacturing areas, and services and trade, the presence of immigrant labor has become crucial to a firm's survival. In the words of the *Wall Street Journal* (June 18, 1976): "Legal or not, the present wave of Western Hemisphere immigrants is already enriching and contributing to North American society . . . illegals may well be providing the margin of survival for entire sectors of the economy."

About half the Mexican migrants to the United States still go into agriculture. Of the other half, most are now employed in the services sector, while a rapidly growing portion is entering either industry proper or its subcontracted workshops, in garments, automotive parts, or electronics. This is because corporations, in order to combat the crisis, are attempting to deunionize and rotate the labor force in a concerted effort to improve profitability. In the course of rotating the work force, they are engaging in more mechanization, cost-cutting permanent layoffs, and hiring of more easily disciplined and low-wage immigrant workers.

By the deepest point of the economic crisis in 1982, when 12 million American workers were unemployed (more than 11 percent of the work force), the technological revolution in cybernetics, computers, telecommunications, and robotics already had eliminated the need for almost half of the U.S. mainline factory workers. Moreover, in part because of the high costs of production materials, it had increased the need for more inexpensive, easily disciplined, and rotatable workers. Mexican immigrant workers now are finding employment in highly technified and modernized production systems. In Los Angeles, some 200 undocumented, unskilled Mexicans run the machinery for Electrosound Company, which produces 25 percent of the phonograph records U.S. consumers enjoy in their homes; and 25 Mexican "illegals" at Tigard Industries in Alhambra operate its newly introduced sophisticated machinery. The employers' aim, in Manuel Castell's words, is to activate a "twenty-first-century technology with a nineteenth-century proletariat."[7]

Although high-tech industries have more than doubled the number of their employees since the early 1970s, this has not been the sector creating the most new jobs in the United States. By far that sector has been services, particularly the restaurant, health, sanitation, retail trade, and personal services, most of which depend heavily on immigrant labor.

Employers' demand for cheap, easily exploitable labor underlies not only their increased resort to immigrant workers but also the phenomenon of runaway shops. In both instances employers and the U.S. government maintain the legal fiction of the U.S.-Mexican border—long erased in the "silent integration" of the two economies—because the border serves to justify the deportation of "unwanted illegals" (such as those who attempt to unionize), that is, to discipline Mexican immigrant labor. Also, the idea of an international border serves as a barrier to U.S. and Mexican workers' integrating their common struggle against what are often the identical corporations.

It follows logically, of course, that if U.S. corporations use a fictitious border and Mexican immigrant laborers to divide the work force and drive wages down as a central element of their anticrisis strategy, then labor's response should be to unite workers on both sides of the border as an effective part of its own anticrisis strategy. Organizing instead of blaming the unrecognized moves to center stage. In the 1970s and early 1980s, small but growing numbers of labor unions in the United States began to undertake a strategy of "labor solidarity has no borders" and of organizing the unrecognized. Mexican immigrant workers have been in the forefront of this little-publicized but significant development.[8]

POPULATION AND JOB-MARKET CHANGES

Since 1980, the use of inexpensive, easily disciplined, nonunionized immigrant labor has grown in importance as a cornerstone of a multifaceted strategy by capital that also includes reindustrialization, hi-tech specialization, automation and mechanization, new educational curricula, and deunionization. As early as June 23, 1980, *Business Week* observed: "The U.S. will need immigrants to buttress the labor supply if the economy is to grow." Unlike Mexico, by all estimates the United States faces a labor shortage for generations to come.

According to the U.S. Census Bureau, declining numbers of workers will be entering the U.S. labor force—some 7.1 million fewer people between the ages of 15 and 24 in 1990 than in 1980; and the decline will continue into the next century. The Census Bureau's projections, based on a "middle" series of assumptions about birthrates, death rates, immigration, and other factors, show the percentage of people under 18 years of age residing in the United States steadily dropping, from 26.7 percent in 1983 to 22.9 percent in 2010. During the same time span, the median age of U.S. residents will rise from 30.9 to 38.4 years. Meanwhile, Mexico's population, facing massive unemployment and underemployment at miserable wages, is expected to double in size by 2010.

Diminishing U.S. labor force additions in the face of growing needs for job stimulation and economic growth do not spell upward pressures on wages and benefits. Recent experience indicates just the opposite. Average private-sector nonfarm wages and salaries dropped by more than 6 percent in the 1980-84 period, and nonunion wages edged ahead of union wages by more than a percentage point in early 1985. According to the Bureau of Labor Statistics (BLS), between March 1979 and March 1984, jobs shrank by 2.4 million in the relatively well-paying areas of manufacturing, construction, and mining, but they increased by more than 4 million in the generally lower-wage area of "services," including wholesale and retail trade and personal, business, and financial services. Real wages in all "services" area declined about 11 percent between 1970 and 1980 (a time when blue-collar manufacturing wages were rising 2 percent), dropping many employed people into the official "poverty" category. This trend accelerated during the first half of the 1980s. And for the rest of the century, the BLS projects most new job openings in such areas as clerical, fast-food outlets, janitorial, nurse's aides, and secretarial.[9]

It is almost certain that the second largest minority in the United States after women will no longer be blacks. It will be Latinos. Many Latin American workers, fearful of the INS and other authorities, go uncounted by census takers. Justifiable concern about racism and whether one can "prove" one's "legal" status keeps many Latinos "invisible." The Catholic Church's Ad Hoc Committee for Hispanic Affairs chose not to cooperate with the U.S. Census Bureau in the taking of the 1980 census, on the grounds that the confidentiality of the information could not be guaranteed. Thus, the 1980 census data are definitely incomplete when it comes to the number of "Hispanics." That census tabulated 6.4 percent of the population Spanish-speaking and 11.7 percent black, with the former group growing four times as fast as the latter between 1970 and 1980.

Subsequent Census Bureau estimates showed around 17 million Latinos in 1984, of whom 9 million were Mexican (double the number of Mexicans in 1970). Of the 17 million, about 14.6 million were U.S. citizens—suggesting a severe underestimate of the number of "illegals" in the country. If one takes the median of the most common estimates of "illegals"—7 million—and adds it to the number of "legal" Latinos, one gets 21.6 million. Subtracting a small portion of "illegals" who are not Latino, one still ends up with a number very close to the estimated number of black Americans in 1984.

This dramatic new demographic reality, a significant part of the "fourth wave" of Mexican immigrant workers and Latin American political refugees in the 1970s and 1980s, is not lost on the nation's most prominent racists. Former CIA director William Colby stated in 1978 that in future years Mexican immigration would represent a greater threat to the United States than would the Soviet Union. Conservative politicians like Senator Alan Simpson (R.-Wyo.), cosponsor of the Simpson-Mazzoli immigration reform bill, have repeatedly claimed that Mexican immigration threatens U.S. territorial and cultural integration with "Quebec-ization."[10]

As a result of the crisis and as a major part of capital's strategy to solve it, America's job market has in recent years become transformed from one of relative job permanence and steady pay raises to one of job rotation, moonlighting or extra hours of work on the side, part-time work at low wages, subminimum wages for youth, both parents entering the job market, and in wage increments that fail to keep up with the cost of living. The decline of smokestack industry has not been matched by a rise in hi-tech or other types of industry able to provide productive jobs for a majority of people. White-collar work has risen, blue-collar work has declined, and the fastest-growing area of the job market by far has been the increasingly low-skilled, low-paid services and maintenance area. The growth in white-collar and services work has been closely related to the growth of the public sector; from 1960 to 1975, one out of every three new jobs was in the public sector, mostly state and local government employment.

Total white-collar employment rose from 43.4 percent of the labor force in 1960 to 53.8 percent in 1982; employment of blue-collar factory workers fell from 18.1 percent to 12.7 percent. Moreover, clerical employment was the fastest-growing segment of the white collar job market, accounting for 18.5 percent of white-collar jobs in 1982, compared with 14.8 percent in 1960. Meanwhile, services employment nearly doubled to absorb 13.8 percent of the work force. Although the character of white-collar work varies according to profession, type of job, and other factors, it is widely recognized that, in the words of a 1972 federal study, "The office today, where work is segmented and authoritarian, is often a factory. For a growing number of jobs, there is little to distinguish them but the color of the worker's collar."[11] This has also become true among professionals and managers, who find themselves more and more in the role of employees.

The overall trend is one of "deskilling" jobs so that anyone can do them. This is true in both highly mechanized and labor-intensive areas of work. Making laborers easily replaceable adds to the pressures against workers' revolt or demands for decent wages. It serves to segment and divide workers from one another, to atomize them. It is the material basis for much of the alienation people feel. Rotating workers, laying some off here, hiring others there, adds a fluid quality to the reserve army of unemployed and irregularly employed labor, expanding the number of people passing through its ranks. Together with increased immigration, the deskilling, segmentation, and rotation of jobs are daily job-market trends encouraged by employers everywhere.

The use of new technologies should be viewed as part of this process of segmenting and controlling labor, and not merely as a possible means of increasing production. Indeed, as labor sociologist Martin Oppenheimer has pointed out, "Technological advances segment work and thereby control workers, and conversely the control of workers creates imperatives for the development of new technologies that will aid in such control."[12] The word-processing "pool," the computer operator "pool," the computerization of work supervision, standards, and paychecks—all these typify this new "high-tech" reality of controlling the ever more segmented and atomized work force. Not surprisingly, labor productivity continues to go down in the face of this alienating and dehumanizing process, even though total production may rise.

In addition, the new technologies make it possible to farm work out to individuals working at home. They accept lower wages and usually are not unionized. "Clerical homework," consisting of rote tasks anyone can learn quickly, has become more and more common. Blue Cross/Blue Shield, J. C. Penney, and American Express, for example, have all begun shipping out work in this fashion. The same is happening in light assembly work. Apple Computer, for example, "jobs out" to a subcontractor, who in turn distributes the work to women working at home.[13]

Immigrant workers increasingly find jobs in almost all sectors of the economy, so long as the skill levels are low or quickly learned. While in Los Angeles the majority of Mexican immigrants who find work are employed in manufacturing and services, in New York City immigrant labor is spread through a more diverse mix of activities. There the immigrant may be found establishing a family "business," usually a tiny vegetable stand or grocery store; driving a taxi; working in apparel or other manufacturing sweatshops (the number of which almost tripled in the 1970s and early 1980s); or working in the fast-growing "services and miscellaneous" sector, which grew by 148,500 jobs from 1977 to 1983. In California's "Silicon Valley," where the semiconductor industry employs some 200,000 workers, 85 percent of them women, about 40 percent of the assembly workers are Mexican, other Latino, or Asian. The wage hovers around $3.50 an hour, and only 5 percent of the work force is organized.[14]

The idea that high-tech industry will solve the economic crisis at the level of new job creation is now recognized as an unrealistic one. Depending on how high-tech jobs are defined, at best they account for only 3 percent of the U.S. economy. Many of them are in low-skilled, poorly paid assembly work. High-tech is the one area of production that, in its middle and lower echelons, most lends itself to the use of cheap immigrant labor. An October 14, 1984, special "National Employment Report" of the *New York Times* acknowledged that "high technology has not saved the American economy" and accounts "for only a tiny fraction of the nation's total employment." Even the most optimistic projections show that by 1995 only 1 new job in 25 will be "technology-oriented." The *Times* special report quotes Massachusetts Institute of Technology professor David L. Birch as saying that 12 to 14 million jobs must be created in the 1980s, but only "4 or 5 percent of those will come in the areas that most people define as 'high technology.' "

Companies that produce the high-tech goods used in industrial production are themselves highly automated. Robots do the welding at Cincinnati Milacron, a maker of robotics equipment. Computer-science college graduates no longer start as programmers; many now start as computer operators, a task requiring little professional training. The *Times* special report concludes: "In fact, high technology's biggest contribution to the job market may prove to be indirect, in the service sector." Evidence for this includes American Express and Federal Express as "highly computerized and rapidly expanding businesses that are also major employers."

It is becoming common knowledge that high-tech further profits the corporations while hurting labor. There are some 20 million office workers in the United States, 80 percent of them women and less than 10 percent organized. An estimated 7 million of them now work facing video display terminals, and by 1990 the number is expected to pass 40 million. How can these workers organize or strike in the face of such technology, when a flick of a switch can shift the work from one city to another? More and more jobs related to the introduction of high technology are now being transferred to areas of low labor cost—including Third World countries, where much of the publishing industry ships out some of its typesetting work. Even when large numbers of low-wage Chicanos and Mexican immigrants are hired by a high-tech firm, as in the case of the 1700 recently unionized employees of Atari in Los Angeles, there is no guarantee that the company will not shut down and "run away." Atari did this in 1982, moving to Hong Kong and Taiwan. It claimed declining profits, even though profits had risen from $80 million in 1980 to $287 million in 1981 and to $324 million in 1982. The real concern, of course, was labor unionism, wages, and the *rate* of profit. Thus, the economic crisis resulted in layoffs among high-tech workers as well as among citizen workers.[15]

The 1960s trend of growing income inequality among wage and salary earners sharpened in the 1970s and 1980s, giving rise to the recognizable contours of a future two-tiered American society, dividing a small number of well-off people from the rest of the population. A two-tiered society is already shaping up as one dominated by a handful of rich corporate magnates (monopoly capital), who command the loyalties of larger numbers of affluent managers and highly qualified professionals. This corporate/professional minority, if present trends continue, will eventually be able to lord it over a vast majority of poorly paid blue- and white-collar employees moving in and out of, or on the margins of, an ever larger and more international reserve army of labor, augmented by Mexican and other immigrants. Racial and sexual discrimination components of this two-tier trend are already placing more and more members of all minorities, especially blacks, Latinos, and women, into the lower tier.

In income terms, many "middle-class" people are already being driven into the lower tier. A Federal Reserve Board study released in 1984 showed the bottom 70 percent of all families getting 43 percent of total family income in 1969 but only 38 percent in 1982. Almost all their losses were gains for the top 10 percent, whose income share rose from 29 to 33 percent. Since 1979 the number of people living below the federal poverty line has grown by 20 percent.[16]

The much-heralded "rainbow coalition" promoted by Rev. Jesse Jackson and others may not yet be a powerful "coalition," but it is already shaping up as a powerless tier. In 1982, one in seven adults and one in five children were living below the *official* poverty line. By 1984, the number of people in this category had risen to 325.3 million! Many poverty watchers, recognizing that the government's poverty criteria border on starvation, put the number of poor at 50 million. The largest group among the poor, other than children, were female workers who provided the sole support of their families. With typical detached bad taste, some poverty buffs began referring to the "feminization of poverty." Even studies claiming to show an improvement in women's wages in the twentieth century, such as a Rand Corporation study publicized in late 1984, pointed out that the poverty-induced influx of women into the job market had dropped the average 1983 woman's wage to $.53 per male $1.[17]

Unemployment rates among black and Spanish-speaking youth have risen so high over such a long period of time that a sizable portion of one generation has stopped looking for regular employment. By 1984, some 78 percent of black youth in New York City were not finishing high school. An official 35.7 percent of the nation's black population was living below the poverty line—including 50 percent of all black children. For the nation's Spanish-speaking, the situation was little different. In New York City, their poverty rate was 10.1 points higher than that for blacks, while nationally it was only 5.7 points lower. In terms of median household per capita income, the Spanish-speaking earn less than half what a white family earns and about 3 percent less than what a black family earns. The nation's lowest-paying jobs, being filled more and more by immigrants willing and anxious to accept half or less the normal wage for unskilled labor, hold no economic attraction for black or Spanish-speaking youth—whom most employers refuse to hire in any case.[18]

Meanwhile, newly laid-off workers continue to find it difficult to get any employment other than in the lower-wage areas of services, retail trade, and high-tech—at half their former wages! The plummeting of growing numbers of whites into the ranks of the nonwhite underclasses has not produced rainbow unity so much as racial war. A 1980 *New York Times* survey indicated a rising negative attitude against nonwhites among those whites who most feared unemployment.[19]

This two-tier trend predates the Reagan presidency. The increase of 11 million jobs between 1973 and 1979 was largely in services and retail trade. The middle-income midriff of the population ("Middle America") was shrinking—not from dieting, but from economic hard times and basic structural faults in the economy. Markets that had boomed for this midriff section also began to contract, and so workers producing for "middle-class" consumers began losing their jobs as well. The downward spiral from the "affluent '50s" became a plummeting fall in the 1970s and 1980s, with weaker and weaker updrafts of economic "recovery." BLS income figures for 1978-83 showed nearly 10 percent of the nation's working population falling from "intermediate" to "low" income; the proportion receiving "intermediate" income dropped from 55 to 42 percent. Michael Harrington's *The New American Poverty* described a "reserve army of the future poor"—those with "good" jobs in the 1960s and 1970s that were most vulnerable to the economy's underlying structural faults.[20]

It is this falling away of the middle that has produced the contours of a future two-tiered America. Economists Gar Alperovitz and Jeff Faux have pointed out about middle-income workers whom they mistakenly call "the middle class":

There is growing evidence that the combined effect of slow growth, automation, and the shift to services is depleting the middle class itself. Between 1965 and 1975 the number of people earning incomes in the middle range—roughly 20 percent below average to 20 percent above—shrank by 23 percent. . . . The accelerated loss of manufacturing jobs since 1975 has aggravated the situation.[21]

Labor analyst Jeremy Brecher concurs about the overall trend in the job market:

The majority of workers will work in high-turnover occupations with no security, in which they are easily replaceable, frequently unemployed, or only employed part time. Middle-income workers will become increasingly the exception, as more and more workers come to receive a "common labor" wage rate at or slightly above the minimum wage. Despite mass unemployment, the labor force will continue to grow due to continuing population growth, immigration, and a rising rate of labor force participation due to the poverty-induced need of women and children to go to work.[22]

Federal Reserve head Paul Volcker, a banker, frankly stated the approach of the two-tiered era in 1979: "The standard of living of the average American has to decline. I don't think you can escape that."[23] The Reagan presidency has based its pro-business measures on the same premise, aggravating the economic evaporation of the middle-income group in America.

Even such pro-business organs of the mass media as *Business Week* suspected prior to Reagan's presidency that the government's giveaways to big business and crackdown on labor unionism (union deauthorization cases filed with the National Labor Relations Board tripled between 1966 and 1979) might not be enough to generate sustained economic recovery. In a special issue entitled "The Reindustrialization of America," *Business Week* acknowledged that the decline in real wages made labor so much cheaper than capital that the incentive for investment in more productive plant and equipment was undercut. Little wonder that as early as September 1981, Reagan's treasury secretary exclaimed: "Where are the expansion plans? It's like dropping a coin down a well—all I'm hearing is a hollow clink"; or that the president's now former budget director David Stockman confessed in the *Atlantic Monthly* that he had abandoned supply-side economics even before submitting the first Reagan budget, knowing that it was no more than a giveaway to big business.[24]

The two-tiered phenomenon is usually associated with the most impoverished Third World countries. Semi-industrialized giants like Mexico are typically viewed as on their way to becoming more "middle class." And industrialized nations like the United States supposedly show that "middle-class" bliss is the lot of the majority of people under conditions of modern capitalism. Never true in the first place, these myths are particularly insulting to human dignity in the late-twentieth-century era of mass starvation and spreading poverty.

"Inflation is still very high, growth is low, and the generation of employment is insufficient. . . . The government is seriously concerned about the drop in the standard of living of the lower and middle classes." These words could be those of a president of any nation. In fact, they were spoken by Mexico's President Miguel de la Madrid during his state-of-the-nation address on September 1, 1984. For all practical purposes, Mexico is already a two-tiered society—with the vanishing "middle" clinging to its presumably comfortable status in vain. A likely consequence for immigration will be a growing influx of better-educated Mexicans into the United States, a trend that immigration researchers say already has commenced.

Since 1982, because of repeated devaluations of the peso, the average Mexican worker's hourly wage has dropped from about 6 times lower to 12 times lower than that of an American worker doing the same job. The pressure on Mexican workers is so grave, their job security so fragile, that many who formerly wanted unions now hesitate to say they want them. For example, a survey carried out in the border city of Ciudad Juárez in 1978 showed 60 percent wanting unions, compared with a 1983 survey in the same city that showed not one of 5000 workers interviewed wanting a union.[25] These trends practically assure what employers in both nations have been seeking as a means to recover from the economic crisis: a growing international reserve army of labor, work forces experiencing declining real wages, and fading labor-union strength, the ideal circumstances for increased immigration, runaway shops, and recovered rates of profit.

GROWING NEED TO REGULATE THE FLOW OF IMMIGRANT WORKERS

As previously mentioned, growing numbers of Mexican immigrant workers have begun to protest their unfair treatment. Their efforts at unionization in the 1970s, in fact, led to an incipient internationalization of labor's struggle. This posed a serious threat to the interests of capital.

By the mid-1970s, therefore, employers were pressing in two ways to gain some kind of control over the quantity and quality of temporary Mexican workers. First, they were encouraging a yellow-journalism campaign against Mexicans, hoping thereby to make the immigrant labor force more tractable and the permanent domestic work force more likely to blame an outside source for labor's problems. This lent momentum to the second way in which employers sought to get a handle on the growing need for, and yet unrest among, Mexican immigrant workers. They quietly got behind policy changes and new legislative proposals on immigration that would bring the border under tighter control of a particular kind: one that could *regulate* the migratory flow in a predictable way.

Such regulation would not stop the flow; rather, it would assure it. It would do so in select and specific ways guaranteed to bring immigrant labor to heel completely, to break any chance for unionization or worker militancy, and to satisfy the Mexican government sufficiently so that it would cooperate in putting an end to any chance of cross-group international alliances. This type of regulation of the migratory flow, all in the name of "regaining control of our borders," was meant to avoid any chance of spontaneous worker eruptions, as well as the economic chaos threatened by the unpredictable character of the flow in the context of Mexico's collapsing economy. Above all, it was meant to prevent immigrant workers from further organizing and converting "bad jobs" into "good jobs" by means of unionization and strikes.

Thus, under President Jimmy Carter, the Border Patrol began receiving military training in counterinsurgency techniques. Work was begun on construction of what Mexican migrant workers dubbed the "tortilla curtain," a border fence, many feet high, made of spiked steel wire but easily cut through. President Carter's secretary of labor, Ray Marshall, unrealistically proposed closing the border, on the "liberal" premise that to avoid the exploitation of "undocumented" workers, their entry must be prevented, or they must be deported. These impractical and "tough" tactics drew the predictable rhetorical and hypocritical wrath of the Mexican government while serving notice on the migrants. A special commission was named to draw up proposals that would more adequately deal with the problem of border regulation. From the work of that commission came the seeds of legislation like the Simpson-Mazzoli bill, a labor bill to bring in at least 350,000 "legal" Mexican workers posing as an "immigration reform" bill![26]

Meanwhile, paramilitary units of the Ku Klux Klan began roaming the border, attacking Mexican immigrants. The INS in early 1981, and with greater intensity in subsequent years, stepped up the pace of factory roundups of alleged "illegals" for deportation. In May 1982 a major press fanfare was orchestrated from Washington around "Operation Jobs,"

when thousands of Mexicans were rounded up for deportation (most returning to work after a few days). Joaquín Ávila, president of the prestigious Mexican American Legal Defense and Educational Fund (MALDEF,
the U.S.-citizen Mexicans' equivalent of the NAACP), told the press,
"We're appalled at the raids. This will seriously affect the rights of Hispanics when they seek employment." By September 1982, deportations of
Mexicans were numbering about 1000 a day and generating tensions in
Mexican neighborhoods, whose older residents were comparing the deportation drive to 1954's "Operation Wetback." The historical comparison is
significant, for then, as now, mass deportations accompanied mass impor-
tations of Mexican workers—and, as we have seen, capital cannot prosper
without both.

The situation in the United States thus was gradually beginning to resemble more and more the one in Europe, where some of the most militant
protest activities in labor's ranks were coming from immigrant-worker
groups and a public racist outcry was being orchestrated by leading
politicians and the press. But unlike Europe, where deportations could
more easily be made permanent and where there was not an immediate need
for a fresh influx of cheap immigrant labor, the U.S. situation centered on a
group residing across a porous border whose labor was sorely needed and
whose destinies for almost 150 years had been inseparably linked to those of
their relatives and other working people in the "host" country (half of
which was originally Mexico). This made the international ramifications of
U.S. policy much more imminent and delicate than those affecting the
north European nations' handling of foreign immigrant labor.

Resorting to Mexican immigrant labor while increasing the tempo of
deportations—the sped-up spinning of the border's "revolving door"—
inevitably led to strains in U.S. relations with Mexico. Here, too, the
"unrecognized" become recognizable as a pivotal issue affecting not just
U.S.-Mexican relations but also the issues of war and peace rumbling from
Central America, the Caribbean, and all Latin America. This subject I
examine in detail elsewhere.[27]

NOTES

1. *New York Times*, July 9, 1984, and Oct. 21, 1984.
2. *The Hispanic Monitor*, May 1984; Gina Allen, "Across the River," *The Humanist*, November–December 1981.
3. Celestino Fernández, "The Border Patrol and News Media Coverage of Undocumented Mexican Immigration During the 1970s: A Quantitative Content Analysis in the Sociology of Knowledge," *California Sociologist*, 5 (1982).
4. Allen, "Across the River"; M. Vic Villalpando et al., *A Study of San Diego: Socioeconomic Impact of Illegal Aliens on the County of San Diego* (San Diego: Human Resources Agency, County of San Diego, 1977).

5. *San Diego Union*, Oct. 14, 1980; Allen, "Across the River"; Jorge A. Busta-mante and James D. Cockcroft, "Unequal Exchange in the Binational Relationship: The Case of Immigrant Labor," in Carlos Vásquez and Manuel García y Griego, eds., *Mexican-U.S. Relations: Conflict and Convergence* (Los Angeles: UCLA Chicano Studies Research Center, 1983).

6. The "revolving door" pattern of entry and deportation, as well as its speeding up during times of crisis (as in 1953-55), is examined in detail in James D. Cockcroft, *Outlaws in the Promised Land* (New York: Grove Press, 1986), Chs. 2, 3.

7. James D. Cockcroft, interviews with workers and employers at Electrosound and Tigart, 1981; Manuel Castells, *La teoría marxista de las crisis económicas y las transformaciones del capitalismo* (Mexico City: Siglo XXI, 1978), p. 16.

8. For a representative sampling of instances, see Cockcroft, *Outlaws in the Promised Land*, Ch. 7.

9. *New York Times*, June 19, 1984, Sept. 9, 1984, Jan. 20, 1985; Martin Oppen-heimer, *White Collar Politics* (New York: Monthly Review Press, 1985), Ch. 5.

10. Colby's statements were made in widely quoted interviews granted to *Playboy* and the *Los Angeles Times* in June 1978. Simpson has expressed his fears often in the Congress and to the press.

11. U.S. Department of Health, Education, and Welfare, *Work in America* (Cambridge, MA: MIT Press, 1973); Oppenheimer, *White Collar Politics*.

12. Oppenheimer, *White Collar Politics,* Ch. 5, p. 13.

13. Michael Moritz, *The Little Kingdom: The Private Story of Apple Computer* (New York: William Morrow & Co., 1984).

14. *The Hispanic Monitor*, July 1984; *International Report*, July 1983.

15. *New York Times*, May 22, 1984; *International Report*, July 1983; Gar Alperovitz and Jeff Faux, *Rebuilding America* (New York: Pantheon Books, 1984), p. 59; and for more examples of runaway "hi-tech" shops, Oppenheimer, *White Collar Politics*.

16. *In These Times*, Dec. 5-11, 1984; *New York Times*, Jan. 20, 1985.

17. *New York Times*, June 19, 1984 and Oct. 31, 1984.

18. *New York Times*, Oct. 9 and 31, 1984; New York City Urban League Report, CBS News, Nov. 1, 1984; *The Hispanic Monitor*, Jan. 1985; and U.S. Commission on Civil Rights, *Social Indicators of Equality for Minorities and Women* (Washington, D.C.: The Commission, 1978).

19. *New York Times*, June 27, 1980 (cited in Alperovitz and Faux, *Rebuilding America*, p. 63).

20. *The Nation*, Oct. 20, 1984; Jeremy Brecher, "Crisis Economy: Born-Again Labor Movement?" *Monthly Review*, March 1984.

21. Alperovitz and Faux, *Rebuilding America*, p. 62.

22. Brecher, "Crisis Economy," p. 24.

23. *New York Times*, Oct. 18, 1979 (cited in Alperovitz and Faux, p. 60).

24. *Business Week*, June 30, 1980; Alperovitz and Faux, *Rebuilding America*, pp. 46, 57-58.

25. *International Report*, July 1983.

26. See Cockcroft, *Outlaws in the Promised Land*.

27. Ibid.; James Cockcroft, *Neighbors in Turmoil* (New York: Harper & Row, 1988).

10

The Changing U.S.-Mexico Border Region: Implications for the Hispanic Labor Force

Gilbert Cárdenas

The southwest border region, part of the Sunbelt, is located along the 2000-mile U.S.-Mexican border. Over 4 million people reside in the region, which encompasses six metropolitan areas: San Diego, Tucson, El Paso, Laredo, McAllen-Mission-Edinburg, and Brownsville-Harlingen-San Benito. For many years, it has been characterized by its multitude of problems, not limited to high unemployment, poverty, and the lack of economic development. The southwest border region is also characterized by the large numbers of Mexican-Americans, and for many years Mexico has played a vital role in the development of the area. Today there is an economic interdependence between the United States and Mexico throughout their respective border labor markets.

Border labor markets are isolated geographically and economically from major metropolitan areas in both the United States and Mexico. U.S. border labor markets are different in geography, economics, and demographics from other metropolitan areas but similar to their Mexican counterparts. In Mexico, these markets are geographically, socially, and culturally remote from the trade centers of Mexico City, Monterrey, and Guadalajara. The economic interdependence between and among Mexican and U.S. border labor markets is an important characteristic of a region that is also bound by history, customs, and culture.

In the 1980s, the border region was among the fastest growing in the nation. Much of this was attributed to the Sunbelt migration, and legal and illegal immigration from Mexico. In spite of such growth, U.S. border labor markets continue to be among the poorest in the nation. The Hispanic population in this region still experiences severe problems in unemployment, poverty, and health. In 1982 alone, three Mexican peso devaluations significantly affected economic development along the border. In spite of these problems, the region shows promising potential for further economic development, particularly for Hispanics. The Hispanic labor force is helping in these efforts both politically and economically.

This chapter will examine the unique characteristics and state of the economy of the border region, and its impact on the Hispanic labor force. It provides an analysis of the human resource problems affecting the Hispanic population in the region, including immigration policy, economic development, water development, and the Mexican economy. It also provides an analysis of the potential and the growth industries in the region and of opportunities for the Hispanic community. Last, it considers some policy implications.

THE HISPANIC POPULATION

The U.S. border region has experienced tremendous population gains due to natural increases, Sunbelt migration and the flow of legal and illegal immigrants from Mexico. In terms of population, the urban labor markets of San Diego, Tucson, and El Paso are the largest (see Table 10.1). Nevertheless, the smaller labor markets along the border experienced the most significant growth between 1970 and 1980. Border communities in Texas were among the fastest growing in the state and nation during this period (see Table 10.2). In the case of El Paso, the population increased by 33.4 percent—from 359,300 in 1970 to 477,500 in 1980. However, the fastest growing were the metropolitan areas of McAllen and Brownsville. In McAllen-Edinburg-Mission, the population increased from 181,500 in 1970 to 279,900 in 1980, an increase of 54.2 percent. Similarly, the Brownsville-Harlingen-San Benito area increased by 48.3 percent, from 140,400 in 1970 to 208,200 in 1980.

The border region is characterized by a relatively young population. The median age for these labor markets varies from 30.0 years in Tucson and 28.3 in San Diego, to 22.9 in McAllen and 23.5 in Laredo. Because of the lack of economic development and the surplus of unskilled labor, the border region, with few exceptions, is characterized by high rates of unemployment and low income levels. Average annual unemployment rates in McAllen and Laredo are among the highest in the nation. In 1984, they were 21.2 percent in McAllen and 17.2 percent in Laredo (see Table 10.1). The economic base of the region, which is comprised of agriculture and wholesale and retail trade, has contributed to the low incomes. Border labor markets are ranked among the poorest in the nation in ter/.s of per capita personal income, which in 1982 was highest for San Diego ($11,638), and lowest for McAllen ($5,885) and Laredo ($6,174). The absence of a major manufacturing sector has also contributed to low wages. These areas are characterized by a high incidence of poverty, particularly among Mexican-Americans. In 1979, about 29.0 percent of the families in Laredo and McAllen had incomes below the poverty level. In San Diego and El Paso,

Table 10.1
Summary of Population Characteristics in Labor Markets along the U.S.-Mexico Border

	Population (in thousands) 1982	Percentage of Hispanics 1980	Median Age 1983	Average Annual Unemployment Rate 1984	Per capita Personal Income 1982
San Diego	1818.5	14.8	28.3	6.6	$11,638
Tucson	500.0	28.0	30.0	5.3	9,969
El Paso	507.5	61.9	24.3	9.7	7,832
Laredo	108.5	91.5	23.5	17.2	6,174
McAllen–Edinburg–Mission	310.2	81.3	22.9	21.2	5,885
Brownsville–Harlingen–San Benito	210.5	77.3	23.5	13.3	6,394

Source: U.S. Department of Commerce, U.S. Department of Labor, 1984.

Table 10.2
Population in Labor Markets along the U.S.-Mexico Border, 1970 and 1980 (in thousands)

MSA	1970	1980	% Change
San Diego	1,357.8	1,618.5	19.2
Tucson	351.7	485.0	38.0
El Paso	359.3	477.5	33.4
Laredo	72.9	99.1	35.9
McAllen-Edinburg Mission	181.5	279.9	54.2
Brownsville-Harlingen-San Benito	140.4	208.2	48.3

Source: U.S. Department of Commerce, 1982.

the incidence of poverty was much lower; 8.4 percent of the families in San Diego, and 18.0 percent of the families in El Paso, had incomes below the poverty level.

The region is also characterized by low investments in human capital, particularly among Mexican-Americans. The lack of educational attainment has contributed to the lack of adequate labor force skills needed for attracting new industry. In 1980, about 78.8 percent of the individuals 25 years and older in San Diego had completed high school, in contrast with 20.9 percent that completed college. A smaller percentage of this population completed high school in McAllen (41.1%) and in Brownsville (43.8%). About 48.3 percent of the Mexican-American population in Laredo had completed high school, compared with 10.8 percent who completed college.

The majority of the Hispanic population in the United States resides in the southwestern states, particularly along the border. In border labor markets like Texas, the majority of the population is Mexican-American. In 1980, over 91.5 percent of the population of Laredo was Mexican-American, and 81.3 percent of the population in McAllen. In relative terms, the Hispanic population is represented to a lesser extent in communities like San Diego (14.8 percent) and Tucson (28.0). The Hispanic population along the U.S.-Mexican border consists of Mexican-Americans, migrant farm workers, and Mexican illegal aliens. For many years, Mexican-Americans have played a vital role in the political, social, and economic development of the region. They are largely concentrated in blue-collar occupations, but are also represented in professional fields such as medicine, law, and education. Many of the border labor markets have among the highest per capita Hispanic professionals in the country.

THE BORDER ECONOMY

The border labor markets have not enjoyed the economic wealth and prosperity of major cities. In terms of national standards, they are generally poor in employment composition and wages. Agriculture and retail trade continue to be the major sectors of the economy. The Mexican economy plays a vital role in the economic development of the region, and the economic relationship between this area and Mexico encompasses much more than trade. Major developments in the Mexican economy often have their final repercussions on the border labor markets and the Southwest. Economic problems faced by Mexico—such as unemployment, inflation, and overpopulation—make their way to U.S. border communities. Three Mexican peso devaluations in 1982, and the current economic and financial crisis, have had severe consequences for the border region's retail trade, income, and unemployment.

Because of the border labor markets' dependence on trade with Mexico, the peso devaluations of 1982 affected them severely. Prior to the peso devaluations, the border region was slowly moving into a period of growth and prosperity in sales and employment. Through increased trade with Mexico, business activity had increased significantly. However, the economic boom that the region had been experiencing was dampened by the peso devaluations. As Mexican economic conditions deteriorated following the world economic recession and increases in the rate of inflation, the Mexican government was forced to make these devaluations in order to improve the country's economic position in the world. The Mexican peso devaluations have made it much more difficult for Mexican residents to buy U.S. foodstuffs. In 1982, the rate of exchange (pesos: dollar) was 50:1, compared with 220:1 in 1984 and 500:1 in 1985.

The peso devaluations contributed to decreases in sales and increases in unemployment, and affected major industries such as wholesale and retail trade, and real estate. Retail sales dropped by 90 percent between August and December 1982. Moreover, U.S. businessmen along the border experienced severe problems with inventories, payment of wages, and loss of hours. With the loss of international traffic, local governments along the border have experienced losses in revenues. In many instances, the cities have had to curtail employment through cutbacks in programs and services. Among the most affected have been the Mexican-American businessmen, since most of them are concentrated in these industries. Bankruptcies among them have continued to increase. In the employment sector, over 10,000 jobs were lost, and the unemployment rates in 1982 and 1983 were consistently higher than in earlier years (see Table 10.3). While the unemployment rates in San Diego decreased from 9.3 percent in 1982 to 5.0 in 1984, they increased in McAllen from 15.5 percent in 1982 to 21.1 in 1984.

In recent years, the border economy has been slowly but surely recovering, and appears most promising. It has been undergoing a transformation from agriculture to the manufacturing of goods and production of services, and thriving on U.S.-Mexico trade. For many years, the border labor markets have been largely dependent on agriculture and trade, and to a lesser extent on manufacturing. Nonagricultural employment patterns in border labor markets (see Table 10.4) seem to indicate that this economic transition and diversification will continue during the remainder of the decade. In labor markets like San Diego and Tucson, manufacturing is very well represented, and the extent of diversification is much more pronounced. In 1984, about 15.1 percent of the San Diego labor force was employed in manufacturing, compared with 24.2 percent in trade and 19.7 in government. In El Paso, about 23.2 percent of the labor force was in manufacturing, compared with 24.4 percent in trade and 19.7 percent in government. Manufacturing is prevalent to a lesser extent in McAllen, Laredo, and Brownsville (see Table 10.4).

Since the peso devaluations of 1982, the border labor markets have

Table 10.3
Average Annual Unemployment Rates in U.S., Texas, and Border Labor Markets, 1980-1984

Year	U.S.	Texas	San Diego	El Paso	Laredo	McAllen	Brownsville
1980	7.2	4.8	6.6	9.2	11.3	12.3	12.0
1981	7.6	4.2	6.9	9.2	10.1	13.2	9.6
1982	9.7	6.0	9.3	11.2	16.4	15.5	12.2
1983	9.7	5.3	8.4	12.3	25.5	19.5	15.3
1984	7.0	6.9	5.0	9.7	17.2	21.1	13.3

Source: U.S. Department of Labor, 1984.

Table 10.4
Nonagricultural Employment in Border Labor Markets,
by Industry, 1982, 1984 (in thousands)

MSA	Total Employment		Manufacturing %		Trade %		Government %	
	1982	1984	1982	1984	1982	1984	1982	1984
San Diego	663.6	719.2	15.9	15.1	23.7	24.2	21.3	19.7
El Paso	164.9	169.7	22.6	23.2	24.6	24.4	20.2	19.7
Laredo	31.3	30.7	5.8	5.9	32.6	30.9	21.7	23.1
McAllen	79.3	78.1	11.2	13.1	33.0	30.6	26.7	25.7
Brownsville	58.2	62.9	15.2	16.4	29.0	27.5	20.9	22.4

Source: U.S. Department of Labor, 1980, *Employment and Earnings*, December, 1984.

sought to reduce dependence on business activity related to U.S.-Mexico trade through the expansion and diversification of the other economic sectors. Data in Table 10.4 show that these markets are increasing manufacturing activity as trade has declined. Between 1982 and 1984, the relative representation of manufacturing employment in El Paso increased from 22.6 percent to 23.2 percent. During the same period, manufacturing activity increased in McAllen and Brownsville from 11.2 percent to 13.1 percent, and from 15.2 percent t 16.4 percent, respectively. Because of the devaluations, trade activity has declined in most of the labor markets except San Diego, where 23.7 percent of total employment in 1982 was in trade, compared with 24.2 percent in 1984. Federal cutbacks in domestic programs have contributed to decreases in employment in the governmental sector, with few exceptions (see Table 10.4).

In 1984, the unemployment rate in border labor markets subsided, but the average annual rates continued to be very high, particularly along the Texas border. As the national unemployment rate dropped from 9.7 percent in 1983 to 7.0 in 1984, average rates in border communities also dropped slightly. In San Diego, it dropped from 8.4 percent in 1983 to 5.5 in 1984. In El Paso, the unemployment rate declined from 12.3 percent in 1983 to 9.7 in 1984; similarly, in Laredo, it dropped from 25.5 percent in 1983 to 17.2 percent in 1984. In the last few years the McAllen area has continued to experience increases in population, and the economy has not been able to absorb these population gains. Thus unemployment continues to mount. In 1983, it averaged 19.5 percent in the McAllen Metropolitan Statistical Area (MSA); by 1984 it climbed to 21.1 percent.

Another economic indicator that shows the potential for economic development of the region is the growth in personal income, which has continued to increase in spite of the unfavorable consequences of the peso devaluation (see Tables 10.5 and 10.6). The vitality and potential of the region are shown by these increases. Total personal income for 1982 in San Diego was $22.8 billion, compared with $5.6 billion in Tucson, and $3.9 billion in El Paso (see Table 10.5). It reached $1.8 billion in McAllen and $1.4 billion in Brownsville, in contrast with $670 million in Laredo. The highest gains in total personal income between 1981 and 1982 were experienced in McAllen and San Diego, where it increased by 8.5 and 7.6 percent, respectively. The border communities also experienced significant gains in per capita personal income (see Table 10.6), which continued to be the highest in San Diego ($11,638) and the lowest in McAllen ($5885) in 1982. In El Paso, per capita personal income totaled $7832, and in Tucson, $9969. McAllen, El Paso, and San Diego experienced the highest gains between 1980 and 1982. In McAllen personal income increased by 19.8 percent between these years; in San Diego and El Paso, it increased by 17.0 percent and 17.9 percent, respectively.

Table 10.5
Total Personal Income in Border Labor Markets,
1980-1982 (in thousands)

	1980	1981	1982	1980-1982 % Change
San Diego	$18,629	$21,220	$22,832	7.6
Tucson	4,629	5,319	5,661	6.4
El Paso	3,203	3,704	3,958	6.9
Laredo	541	642	670	4.3
McAllen	1,401	1,682	1,826	8.5
Brownsville	1,169	1,370	1,444	5.5

Source: U.S. Department of Commerce, *Survey of Current Business*, April, 1984.

Table 10.6
Per Capita Personal Income in Border Labor Markets,
1980-1982

MSA	1980	1981	1982	1980-1982 % Change
San Diego	$9,948	$11,057	$11,638	17.0
Tucson	8,678	9,598	9,969	14.8
El Paso	6,642	7,474	7,832	17.9
Laredo	5,415	6,170	6,174	14.0
McAllen	4,910	5,677	5,885	19.8
Brownsville	5,541	6,279	6,394	15.3

Source: U.S. Department of Commerce, *Survey of Current Business*, April, 1984.

HUMAN RESOURCE DEVELOPMENT PROBLEMS

With the transition of the U.S.-Mexican border region into a more expansive economy, border labor markets are attempting to overcome barriers that have inhibited economic development. Numerous areas along the border are experiencing severe problems associated with the growing pains of economic development. Other markets have been unsuccessful in reducing the dependence on trade with Mexico, and the unfavorable and unpredictable economic conditions in that country have made it difficult for them. The Mexican economic recovery of 1984 brought some economic prosperity to the region in retail sales and employment, but the perennial economic problems of high inflation and further devaluations of the peso mounted again in 1986 and will probably continue to affect the U.S.-Mexican border region. Among the factors likely to shape the future development of the border region are (1) economic development (including water and energy development), and (2) illegal immigration from Mexico.

Economic Development

Although much of the region has experienced growth and expansion, economic development continues to be a major problem. The lack of it has been associated with the nature of the industry mix and the lack of an adequate labor force. Other barriers that have impeded economic growth have been low educational attainment, high unemployment, limited natural resources, and the absence of financial resources. Moreover, the role of the private and public sectors has been limited. Among the many barriers to industrial and economic development is the lack of viable transportation systems. Because of the large distances between the border and major markets, and the inaccessibility of viable transportation systems within the region, the transportation costs contribute to higher prices and costs of goods and materials coming into the region. Another problem that is likely to threaten economic development is the limited availability of water along the border. An adequate supply of water is essential to the growth of the area, and with population increases in both Mexican and U.S. border labor markets, there is a growing concern for the availability of water to meet future residential, industrial, and commercial needs.

The nature of the labor force is the impetus for enhancing economic development. Mexican-Americans and migrant farm workers are experiencing severe employment problems associated with the lack of appropriate labor force skills and education. The labor force in the border markets is characterized by a surplus of unskilled workers that includes Mexican illegal aliens and Mexican border commuters who reside in Mexico but work in the United States. The lack of diversity among the border economies has limited the growth of new industries and the creation of new jobs. Labor markets have been unable to absorb as many workers as are needed to reduce unemployment. Among Hispanics and migrant farm workers, the unemployment rate has increased partly because of the presence of Mexican undocumented workers and border commuters who compete for similar jobs. Much of the unemployment in the region is cyclical and associated with the lack of aggregate demand for goods and services. Nevertheless, structural unemployment is very prevalent, particularly among migrant farm workers who have been displaced by mechanization and automation. Teenage unemployment rates vary between 50 and 70 percent in the barrios of Laredo, El Paso, and San Diego. It is common to find Mexican-American teenagers competing for the limited number of jobs with women, adults, and illegal aliens. Mexican-American youths who are employed are usually found in agriculture, trade, or the service industries.

The prospects for the economic development of the border region are dependent on the further expansion of health, medical, military, and high-technology industries into the more depressed labor markets. With the decentralization of industry into the Sunbelt and the further development of high technology throughout the Southwest, it is plausible for new companies to come to the border. The boom of the Sunbelt and the Southwest since the late 1970s has not contributed to major gains along the border, with the exception of San Diego and El Paso. With further decentralization and industrialization of major markets like San Antonio, it is possible that economic development efforts may concentrate on the border region. Border communities have engaged in major efforts and campaigns to attract industry to the region through joint partnerships and the cooperative efforts of chambers of commerce, private industry, the government, and educational institutions.

The role of the Mexican-American in the political and economic development of the border region is changing throughout the Southwest. With increased emphasis on education and economic development, Mexican-Americans are making major strides in the political and economic development of the area. The number of Hispanics in key positions in state and local governments has increased significantly in the last decade. The Mexican-American businessmen are penetrating growth industries, and it is now common to find Mexican-American entrepreneurs engaging in joint ventures with Mexican businessmen. These entrepreneurs are slowly penetrating capital-intensive and growth industries in local, state, and national markets, and Mexican investments along the border have been significant. With the increased business activity in Mexico associated with the petrochemical industry, and the proximity of the border to major industrial centers in Mexico, Mexican-American entrepreneurs can benefit from these developments.

Mexican Illegal Immigration

Among the major issues that will continue to affect the social and economic development of the border region is the flow of illegal immigration from Mexico. Because of historical, cultural, and economic considerations, the flow of illegal aliens from Mexico and Central America has been very common. The proximity of Mexico and its unfavorable economic conditions have enhanced the flow of illegal immigration in recent years. The U.S.-Mexican border has also been the avenue for illegal immigrants from Central America to come to the United States and enter major markets like Dallas, Houston, and Los Angeles. Along the border, most of the Mexican illegal aliens are in the area temporarily, with a common pattern of working a few months there and then moving to other major markets. Illegal aliens from Mexican border towns like Reynosa (McAllen) or Juárez (El Paso) usually work in agriculture.

Although there has been a major concern as to whether Mexican illegal immigrants affect wage rates and working conditions in the United States, there is little alarm over the magnitude of the problem in border labor markets. The presence of Mexican border commuters or holders of green cards who reside in Mexico but work in U.S. border towns poses more of a threat to Mexican-Americans than do the Mexican illegal aliens. The "green carders" are often employed in the better-paying occupations in sales, clerical, or construction, or as managers in wholesale or retail trade. Mexican illegal aliens are usually employed in the lower-paying and casual labor markets, such as agriculture.

Illegal immigration is not posing a serious threat to economic development in the region. It is, however, affecting other labor markets, such as Chicago, Houston, and Los Angeles. The flow of illegals may increase as economic conditions in Mexico worsen, and the impact on Mexican-Americans in the border region may be more pronounced in the near future. Because of the interdependence of U.S. and Mexican border labor markets, especially with respect to trade, tourism, and agriculture, border communities are particularly concerned with any policies that may sever the relationship between the United States and Mexico. Future policy directions should be limited to the enforcement of federal laws governing immigration, employment, and working standards rather than overhauling the nation's immigration policies. Congress has considered numerous immigration reforms in the form of employer sanctions, amnesty, and guest worker programs that may have serious implications on the U.S.-Mexico border, particularly for the Hispanic population. The immigration reform measures may also affect future relations between Mexico and the United States, particularly along the border.

IMPLICATIONS FOR PUBLIC POLICY

The future development of the border region is likely to be influenced by many factors, including national economic development in both the United States and Mexico. Moreover, this development will be shaped by the nature of production and of the labor markets, and their impact on the

Mexican-American population in that region. Among the most promising efforts for increased economic activity for Mexican-Americans are two programs that have been implemented in some border labor markets: foreign trade zones and the *maquiladora* industry.

Since 1934, the United States has authorized free trade zones throughout the country that allow foreign and domestic merchandise to be brought into these zones and stored, repackaged, assembled, graded, manufactured, or reexported without payment of customs duties. The foreign trade zones are licensed by the U.S. Department of Commerce and are controlled by the U.S. Customs Service. These zones have been emerging since the late 1970s in communities like El Paso, Nogales, McAllen and Brownsville, and have contributed significantly to the border communities by increasing jobs and commercial activity.

Similarly, the border industrialization program and the expansion of the *maquiladora* industry have resulted in major corporations—Zenith, General Electric, and Sony—moving along the U.S.-Mexican border as in-bond plants. Under the in-bond industry program, U.S. companies can relocate in both Mexican and U.S. border towns; foreign companies can import into Mexico, free of duty, all necessary machinery, raw materials, and equipment for the production of goods that must then be exported from Mexico. The materials for these industries—mainly companies making electronic gadgets, car components, clothes, leather goods, and furniture—are imported tax-exempt and are then exported free of Mexican duties. In addition, in-bond plants are exempt from Mexico's 10 percent value-added tax, and excluded from Mexican immigration requirements that limit the number of foreign management and staff. The majority of the in-bond plants are concentrated in the border cities of Tijuana (San Diego), Juárez (El Paso) and Nuevo Laredo (Laredo). In 1983, there were over 629 in-bond plants located in Mexico, with the majority along the border, employing over 173,128 workers. These plants also hire many U.S. workers, and generate incomes and sales for consumption.

The future of the border area is likely to be shaped by political and economic developments in the labor markets. Without the assistance of the federal government and increased participation of the private sector, any further developmnent will be limited. In the past, federal government efforts in the areas of human resources and economic development have been scarce. In the last few years, the Reagan administration's cutbacks in social services and development programs have contributed to a decrease in business activity along the border. If the decentralization of business and labor continues into the Sunbelt, the focus of major business enterprises will probably switch to border labor markets rather than markets like Dallas and Houston. This will contribute to economic gains among the Hispanic labor force in their respective labor markets.

It is most important to develop a marketing program at the national, state, and local levels that promotes the potential of the border region. With the assistance of local chambers of commerce, economic development agencies, private industry councils, and community-based organizations, efforts should be increased to attract industry to the border communities and enhance economic diversification. Another potential for the region lies with major multinational corporations, especially electronic and apparel firms in Taiwan or Hong Kong moving their operations to U.S. border areas where they can enjoy the incentives for economic development: a viable semi-skilled labor force and lower wages. The transition of border labor markets to manufacturing and service industries is likely to attract new growth industries into the region with the aggressive support of the business community. The future development of the region will also depend on the role of Mexican-Americans in the area of human resource development. The Mexican economy will continue to play a vital role, and therefore there is a need for the United States to develop more favorable public policies toward Mexico on bilaterial issues of interest, such as trade, immigration, and energy.

REFERENCES

Banco de México. 1984. *Review of the Economic Situation of Mexico.* Mexico City: Banco de México.

Cárdenas, Gilbert, and Charles Ellard. 1979. *The Economics of the U.S.-Mexico Border Region.* Edinburg, TX: Pan American University.

Levitan, Sar A., Garth Mangum, and Ray Marshall, 1975. *Human Resources and Labor Markets.* New York: Harper & Row.

U.S. Department of Commerce. 1984. *Survey of Current Business.* December.

Selected Bibliography

Acosta-Belén, Edna. "Spanglish: A Case of Languages in Contact." In Marina K. Burt and Heidi Dulay, eds., *New Directions in Second Language Learning, Teaching and Bilingual Education*, pp. 151-158. Washington, DC: TESOL, 1975.

———, ed. *The Puerto Rican Woman: Perspectives on Culture, History and Society*. New York: Praeger, 1986. (First edition, 1979.)

Acuña, Rodolfo. *A Mexican American Struggle*. New York: American Books, 1971.

———. *Occupied America: The Chicanos' Struggle Toward Liberation*. San Francisco: Canfield Press, 1972.

———. *Occupied America: A History of Chicanos*. Second edition. New York: Harper & Row, 1981.

Aguirre, B. E. "The Marital Stability of Cubans in the United States." *Ethnicity* 8, no. 4 (1981): 387-405.

Alcalay, Rina. "Hispanic Women in the United States: Family and Work Relations." *Migration Today* 12, no. 3 (1984): 13-20.

Alvirez, D., and F. D. Bean. "The Mexican American Family." In Charles H. Mindel and Robert W. Habenstein, eds., *Ethnic Families in America: Patterns and Variations*, pp. 271-292. New York: Elsevier, 1976.

Andreu Iglesias, César, ed. *Memorias de Bernardo Vega*. Río Piedras, PR: Ediciones Huracán, 1977. Translated by Juan Flores as *Memoirs of Bernardo Vega*. New York: Monthly Review Press, 1984.

Arguelles, Lourdes. "Cuban Miami: The Roots, Development and Everyday Life of an Emigré Enclave in the U.S. National Security State." In Marlene Dixon and Suzanne Jonas, eds. *The New Nomads*, pp. 27-43. San Francisco: Synthesis Publications, 1982.

Babín, María T. *The Puerto Rican Spirit: Their History, Life, and Culture*. New York: Macmillan, 1971.

Baca-Zinn, M. "Political Familism: Toward Sex Role Equality in Chicano Families." *Aztlán* 6, no. 1 (1975): 13-26.

Bach, Robert L. "Mexican Immigration and the American State." *International Migration Review* 12 (Winter 1978): 536-558.

_____. "The New Cuban Immigrants: Their Background and Prospects." *Monthly Labor Review* 103, no. 10 (Oct. 1980): 39-46.

Bach, Robert L., Jennifer B. Bach, and Timothy Triplett. "The Flotilla Entrants: Latest and Most Controversial." *Cuban Studies* 11 (July 1981): 29-48.

Badillo-Veiga, Américo, Josh DeWind, and Julia Preston. "Undocumented Immigrant Workers in New York City." *NACLA Report on the Americas* 13 (Nov.-Dec. 1979): 2-46.

Baron, A., Jr. *Explorations in Chicano Psychology.* New York: Praeger, 1981.

Bean, F. D. "Components of Income and Expected Family Size Among Mexican Americans." *Social Science Quarterly* 54, no. 1 (1973): 103-116.

Becerra, Rocina, et al., eds. *Mental Health and Hispanic Americans: Clinical Perspectives.* New York: Grune and Stratton, 1982.

Belliaeff, A. *Understanding the Mexican American in Today's Culture.* San Diego: San Diego Project, 1966.

Bernard, H. R., and L. I. Duran, eds. *Introduction to Chicano Studies.* New York: Macmillan, 1973.

Bogardus, E. S. *The Mexican in the United States.* San Francisco: R & E Research, 1970.

Bonilla Santiago, Gloria. "Puerto Rican Migrant Farmworkers." *Migration World* 14, no. 4 (1985): 14-18.

Borjas, G. J. "The Labor Supply of Male Hispanic Immigrants in the United States." *International Migration Review* 17, no. 4 (1983): 653-671.

Boswell, Thomas. *The Cuban-American Experience: Culture, Images, and Perspectives.* Totowa, NJ: Rowman and Allanheld, 1984.

Briggs, V. M., Jr. *Chicanos and Rural Poverty.* Baltimore: Johns Hopkins University Press, 1973.

Brown, Lester B., John Oliver, and J. Jorge Klor de Alva, eds. *Sociocultural and Service Issues in Working with Hispanic American Clients: A Resource Guide for Human Service Professionals.* Albany, NY: Rockefeller College Press, 1985.

Bureau of the Census. "Persons of Spanish Origin in the United States: March 1980 (Advance Report)." *Current Population Reports*, Series P-20, no. 361. Washington, D.C.: U.S. Government Printing Office, 1981.

Buriel, R., and R. Vásquez. "Stereotypes of Mexican Descent Persons: Attitudes of Three Generations of Mexican Americans and Anglo-American Adolescents." *Journal of Cross-Cultural Psychology* 13, no. 1 (1982): 59-70.

Burma, John. *Mexican-Americans in the United States: A Reader.* Cambridge, MA: Schenkman, 1970.

Bustamante, Jorge A. "The Historical Context of Undocumented Mexican Immigration to the United States." *Aztlán* 3 (1973): 257-281.

_____. *Espaldas mojadas: Materia prima para la expansión del capital norteamericano.* México, DF: Centro de Estudios Sociológicos, Colegio de México, 1976.

Bustamante, Jorge A., and Gerónimo G. Martínez. "Undocumented Immigration from Mexico: Beyond Borders but Within Systems." *Journal of International Affairs* 33 (Fall/Winter 1979): 265-284.

Cabrera, A. *Emerging Faces: The Mexican-Americans.* Dubuque, IA: William C. Brown Co., 1971.

Cafferty, Pastora San Juan, and William C. McCready. *Hispanics in the United States: A New Social Agenda*. New Brunswick, NJ: Transaction Books, 1983.

Camarillo, Albert. *Chicanos in a Changing Society: From Mexican Pueblos to American Barrios in Santa Barbara and Southern California, 1848-1930*. Cambridge, MA: Harvard University Press, 1979.

Campos, Ricardo, and Juan Flores. "National Culture and Migration: Perspectives from the Puerto Rican Working Class." Centro Working Papers. New York: Centro de Estudios Puertorriqueños, CUNY, 1978.

Cardona, Luis A. *The Coming of the Puerto Ricans*. Washington, DC: Robert Press, 1974.

Cardoso, Lawrence. *Mexican Emigration to the United States, 1897-1931. Socioeconomic Patterns*. Tucson: University of Arizona Press, 1980.

Carreras-Carleton, A., and A. J. Jaffe. *Some Demographic and Economic Characteristics of the Puerto Rican Population Living on the Mainland U.S.A.* New York: Applied Research Center, Columbia University, 1974.

Carrillo-Beron, C. *A Comparison of Anglo and Chicano Women*. San Francisco: R & E Research, 1974.

Carter, Thomas. *Mexican Americans in School: A History of Educational Neglect*. Princeton, NJ: College Entrance Examination Board, 1970.

Casal, Lourdes, and Andrés R. Hernández. "Cubans in the United States: A Survey of the Literature." *Cuban Studies* 5 (July 1975): 25-51.

Casso, H., and G. Roman. *Chicanos in Higher Education*. Albuquerque: University of New Mexico Press, 1976.

Cayce, Morrison J. *The Puerto Rican Study, 1953-1957*. New York: New York City Board of Education, 1957.

Centro de Estudios Puertorriqueños. *Taller de migración. Conferencia de historiografía*. New York: Centro de Estudios Puertorriqueños, CUNY, 1974.

_____. *Documentos de la migración puertorriqueña, 1879-1901*. New York: Centro de Estudios Puertorriqueños, CUNY, 1977.

_____, Oral History Task Force. *Labor Migration Under Capitalism: The Puerto Rican Experience*. New York: Monthly Review Press, 1979.

_____. *From Hawaii to New York: Migraciones puertorriqueñas a los Estados Unidos*. New York: Centro de Estudios Puertorriqueños, CUNY, 1986.

Chenault, Lawrence. *The Puerto Rican Migrant in New York City*. New York: Russell and Russell, 1970. (First edition, 1938.)

Colón, Jesús. *A Puerto Rican in New York and Other Sketches*. New York: International Publishers, 1982. (First edition, 1961.)

Congressional Research Service. *The Hispanic Population of the United States: An Overview*. Washington, DC: U.S. Government Printing Office, 1983.

Cooper, P., ed. *Growing up Puerto Rican*. New York: New American Library, 1972.

Cordasco, Francisco, and Eugene Buccioni, eds. *Puerto Rican Children in Mainland Schools*. Metuchen, NJ: Scarecrow Press, 1968.

_____. *The Puerto Rican Experience*. Totowa, NJ: Littlefield and Adams, 1973.

Cornelius, Wayne. *Mexican Migration to the United States: Causes, Consequences, and U.S. Responses*. Cambridge, MA: Migration Study Group, Center for International Studies, 1977.

_____. *Building the Cactus Curtain: Mexico and U.S. Responses, from Wilson to Carter*. Berkeley: University of California Press, 1980.

_____. *Los Norteños: Mexican Migrants in Rural Mexico and the United States.* Berkeley: University of California Press, 1980.

Cortés, F., A. Falcón, and J. Flores. "The Cultural Expression of Puerto Ricans in New York: A Theoretical Perspective and Critical Review." *Latin American Perspectives* 3, no. 3 (1976): 117-152.

Corwin, Arthur F., ed. *Immigrants and Immigrants' Perspectives on Mexican Labor Migration to the United States.* Westport, CT: Greenwood Press, 1978.

Council on Foundations. *Hispanics and Grantmakers: A Special Report of Foundation News.* Washington, DC: Foundation News, 1981.

Cross, Harry E., and James A. Sandos. *Across the Border: Rural Development in Mexico and Recent Migration to the United States.* Berkeley: Institute of Governmental Studies, University of California, 1981.

Díaz-Briquets, Sergio, and Lisandro Pérez. "Cuba: The Demography of Revolution." *Population Bulletin* 36, no. 2 (April 1981): 2-41.

Domínguez, Virginia. *From Neighbor to Stranger: The Dilemma of Caribbean Migrations in the U.S.* New Haven, CT: Antilles Research Program, Yale University, 1975.

Edwards, M. *Mexican Americans.* Boston: Houghton Mifflin, 1973.

Ehrlich, Paul R., Loy Bilderback, and Anne H. Ehrlich. *The Golden Door: International Migration, Mexico and the United States.* New York: Wideview Books, 1981.

Elizondo, Virgilio P., Frank Ponce, Patrick L. Flores, and Robert F. Sánchez. *Los católicos hispanos en los Estados Unidos.* New York: Spanish American Printing Corp., 1980.

Fagen, Richard R., Richard A. Brody, and Thomas O'Leary. *Cubans in Exile: Disaffection and the Revolution.* Palo Alto, CA: Stanford University Press, 1968.

Fernández, M. R. "Three Basic Themes in Mexican and Puerto Rican Population Under the Influence of the Mainland." *Journal of Social Psychology* 48, no. 2 (1958): 167-181.

Fernández, Raúl. *The U.S.-Mexican Border: A Political-Economic Profile.* South Bend, IN: University of Notre Dame Press, 1977.

Fernández-Kelly, María Patricia. *For We Are Sold, I and My People: Women and Industry in Mexico's Frontier.* Albany, NY: SUNY Press, 1983.

Fishman, Joshua A. *Bilingualism in the Barrio.* Bloomington: Indiana University Press, 1971.

Fishman, Joshua, and Gary D. Keller. *Bilingual Education for Hispanic Students in the United States.* New York: Teachers College Press, 1982.

Fitzpatrick, Joseph P. *Puerto Rican-Americans: The Meaning of Migration to the Mainland.* Englewood Cliffs, NJ: Prentice-Hall, 1971.

_____. "The Puerto Rican Family." In *Ethnic Families in America: Patterns and Variations*, pp. 192-217. New York: Elsevier, 1976.

Fitzpatrick, Joseph P., and Douglas T. Gurak. *Hispanic Intermarriage in New York City.* New York: Hispanic Research Center, Fordham University, 1979.

Flores, Juan, John Attinasi, and Pedro Pedraza, Jr. "La Carreta Made a U-Turn: Puerto Rican Language and Culture in the United States." *Daedalus* 110, no. 2 (Spring 1981): 193-217.

Fogel, Walter. *Mexican-Americans in Southwest Labor Markets.* Advance Report no. 10. Los Angeles: Mexican-American Study Project, 1967.

Ford Foundation. *Hispanics: Challenges and Opportunities.* New York: Ford Foundation, 1984.

Fradd, Sandra. "From Cubans to Cuban Americans: Assimilation in the United States." *Migration Today* 11, nos. 4-5 (1983): 34-42.

Friedlander, Stanley L. *Labor Migration and Economic Growth: A Case Study of Puerto Rico.* Cambridge, MA: MIT Press, 1965.

Frías, G. *Barrio Warriors: Homeboys of Peace.* Los Angeles: Díaz Publications, 1982.

Frisbie, W. P., F. D. Bean, and J. M. Inman. "Household and Family Demography of Hispanics: A Comparative Analysis." *Population Index* 48, no. 3 (1982): 476.

Galarza, Ernesto. *Merchants of Labor: The Mexican Bracero Story. An Account of the Managed Migration of Mexican Farm Workers in California, 1942-1960.* Santa Barbara, CA: McNally and Loftin, 1966.

_____. *Spiders in the House and Workers in the Field.* Notre Dame, IN: University of Notre Dame Press, 1970.

Galarza, Ernesto, H. Gallegos, and J. Samora. *Mexican-Americans in the Southwest* Santa Barbara, CA: McNally and Loftin, 1970.

Gallager, P. *The Cuban Exile.* New York: Academic Press, 1980.

Gann, L. H., and Peter J. Duignan. *Hispanics in the United States: A History.* Boulder, CO: Westview Press, 1986.

García, F. C., ed. *La causa política: A Chicano Politics Reader.* Notre Dame, IN: University of Notre Dame Press, 1974.

García, Juan Ramón. *Operation Wetback: The Mass Deportation of Mexican Undocumented Workers in 1954.* Westport, CT: Greenwood Press, 1980.

García, Mario T. *Desert Immigrants: The Mexicans of El Paso, 1880-1920.* New Haven: Yale University Press, 1981.

García Cantú, Gastón. *Las invasiones norteamericanas en México.* México, DF: Ediciones Era, 1971.

García y Griego, Manuel. *The Importance of Mexican Contract Labor to the United States, 1942-1964: Antecedents, Operations, and Legacy.* San Diego: University of California at San Diego, 1981.

Garrison, Vivian, and Carol I. Weiss. "Dominican Family Networks and United States Immigration Policy: A Case Study." *International Migration Review* 13, no. 2 (Summer 1979): 264-283.

Garza, C., ed. *Puerto Ricans in the U.S.: The Struggle for Freedom.* New York: Pathfinder Press, 1977.

Glazer, Nathan, and Daniel Patrick Moynihan. *Beyond the Melting Pot: The Negroes, Puerto Ricans, Jews, Italians and Irish of New York City.* Cambridge, MA: MIT Press, 1963.

Golden, Marita. *Migrations of the Heart.* Garden City, NY: Anchor Press, 1983.

González, Nancie. *The Spanish-Americans of New Mexico: A Heritage of Pride.* Albuquerque: University of New Mexico Press, 1969.

_____. "Peasant Progress: Dominicans in New York." *Caribbean Studies* 10, no. 3 (1971): 154-171.

Gordon, M. W. "Race Patterns and Prejudice in Puerto Ricans." *American Sociological Review* 14, no. 4 (1949): 294-330.

Grebler, Leo, Joan M. Moore, and Ralph C. Guzmán. *The Mexican-American People: The Nation's Second Largest Minority.* New York: Free Press, 1970.

Gurak, Douglas T., and Joseph P. Fitzpatrick. "Intermarriage Among Hispanic Ethnic Groups in New York City." *American Journal of Sociology* 87, no. 4 (1982): 921-934.

Gurak, Douglas T., and Mary M. Kritz. "Dominican and Colombian Women in New York City: Household Structure and Employment Patterns." *Migration Today* 10, nos. 3-4 (1982): 15-21.

Haddox, J. G. *Los Chicanos: An Awakening People.* El Paso: University of Texas Press, 1970.

Halsell, Grace. *The Illegals.* New York: Stein and Day, 1978.

Handlin, Oscar. *The Uprooted.* Boston: Little, Brown, 1951.

————. *The Newcomers: Negroes and Puerto Ricans in a Changing Metropolis.* Cambridge, MA: Harvard University Press, 1959.

Hansen, Niles. *The Border Economy: Regional Development in the Southwest.* Austin: University of Texas Press, 1981.

Hauberg, Clifford A. *Puerto Rico and the Puerto Ricans: A Study of Puerto Rican History and Immigration to the United States.* New York: Hippocrene Books, 1974.

Heller, C. *Mexican American Youth: Forgotten Youth at the Crossroads.* New York: Random House, 1966.

Hendricks, Glenn. *The Dominican Diaspora: From the Dominican Republic to New York City—Villagers in Transition.* New York: Teachers College Press, 1974.

Hernández, José. *Puerto Rican Youth Employment.* Maplewood, NJ: Waterfront Press, 1983.

Hernández Alvarez, José. *Return Migration to Puerto Rico.* Berkeley: Institute of International Studies, University of California, 1967.

Hirsch, Herbert, and Armando Gutiérrez, *Learning to be Militant: Ethnic Identity and the Development of Political Militancy in a Chicano Community.* San Francisco: R & E Research Associates, 1977.

Hoffman, Abraham. *Unwanted Mexican Americans in the Great Depression.* Tucson: University of Arizona Press, 1974.

House, John W. *Frontier on the Río Grande: A Political Geography of Development and Social Deprivation.* New York: Oxford University Press, 1982.

Jaffe, A. *Puerto Rican Population of New York City.* New York: Arno Press, 1975.

Jaffe, A. J., Ruth M. Cullen, and Thomas D. Boswell. *The Changing Demography of Spanish Americans.* New York: Academic Press, 1980.

Jennings, James. *Puerto Ricans in Politics in New York City.* Washington, DC: University Press of America, 1977.

Jennings, James, and Monte Rivera. *Puerto Rican Politics in Urban America.* Westport, CT: Greenwood Press, 1984.

Johnson, Kenneth F., and Nina M. Ogle. *Illegal Mexican Aliens in the U.S.* Washington, DC: American University Press, 1978.

Johnson, Harry S., and William J. Hernández, eds. *Educating the Mexican Americans.* Valley Forge, PA: Judson Press, 1970.

Keeler, G. D., K. S. Van Hooft, and M. M. Keller, eds. *History, Culture, and Society: Chicano Studies in the 1980s.* Ann Arbor, MI: Bilingual Review Press, 1983.

Kirsten, P. N. *Anglo over Bracero: A History of the Mexican Worker in the U.S. from Roosevelt to Nixon.* San Francisco: R & E Associates, 1977.

Kiser, George C., and Martha Woody Kiser. *Mexican Workers in the United States: Historical and Political Perspectives.* Albuquerque: University of New Mexico Press, 1979.

Kramer, E. J., V. Green, and G. Valencia-Weber. "Acculturation and the Hispanic Woman: Attitudes Toward Women, Sex-Role Attribution, Sex-Role Behavior, and Demographics." *Hispanic Journal of Behavioral Sciences* 4, no. 1 (1982): 21-40.

Laosa, Luis M. "Maternal Teaching Strategies in Chicano Families of Varied Educational and Socioeconomic Levels." *Child Development* 49, no. 4 (1978): 1129-1135.

Lewis, Oscar. *La Vida: A Puerto Rican Family in the Culture of Poverty.* New York: Random House, 1965.

Long, Durward. "The Historical Beginnings of Ybor City and Modern Tampa." *Florida Historical Quarterly* (July 1966): 31-44.

López, Adalberto. *The Puerto Ricans: Their History, Culture, and Society.* Cambridge, MA: Schenkman, 1980.

López, Alfredo. *The Puerto Rican Papers: Notes on the Re-emergence of a Nation.* Indianapolis: Bobbs Merrill, 1973.

López y Rivas, Gilberto. *The Chicanos: Life and Struggles of the Mexican Minority in the United States.* New York: Monthly Review Press, 1973.

MacCorkle, L. *Cubans in the United States: A Bibliography for Research in the Social and Behavioral Sciences, 1960-1983.* Westport, CT: Greenwood Press, 1984.

Machado, Manuel A. *Listen Chicano: An Informal History of the Mexican American.* Chicago: Nelson Hall, 1981.

Maciel, David, and Patricia Bueno. *La historia del pueblo chicano, 1848-1910.* México, DF: Sepsetentas, 1974.

Madsen, William. *The Mexican-Americans of South Texas.* New York: Holt, Rinehart, and Winston, 1964.

Maldonado-Denis, Manuel. *Puerto Rico: A Socio-historic Interpretation.* New York: Random House, 1972.

_____. *Puerto Rico y Estados Unidos: Emigración y colonialismo.* México, DF: Siglo XXI, 1976.

_____. *the Emigration Dialectic: Puerto Rico and the U.S.A.* New York: International Publishers, 1980.

Mann, Evelyn S., and Joseph J. Salvo. "Characteristics of New Hispanic Immigrants to New York City: A Comparison of Puerto Rican and non-Puerto Rican Hispanics." *Hispanic Research Center Research Bulletin* 8, nos. 1-2 (Jan.-Apr. 1985): 1-7.

Mapp, Edward, ed. *Puerto Rican Perspectives.* Metuchen, NJ: Scarecrow Press, 1974.

Martínez, Robert A. "Dual Ethnicity: Puerto Rican College Students in New York." *Urban Education* 14, no. 2 (July 1979): 254-259.

Massey, Douglas S. "Hispanic Residential Segregation: A Comparison of Mexicans, Cubans, and Puerto Ricans." *Sociology and Social Research* 65, no. 3 (Apr. 1981): 311-322.

Matthiesen, Peter. *Sal si puedes—Escape if You Can: Cesar Chavez and the New American Revolution.* New York: Random House, 1970.

McWilliams, Carey. *Brothers Under the Skin*. Boston: Little, Brown, 1948.

————. *North from Mexico: The Spanish-Speaking People of the United States*. New York: Greenwood Press, 1968. (First edition, 1942.)

————. *Factories in the Field*. Third edition. Hamden, CT: Shoe String Press, 1969.

Meier, Matt S., and Feliciano Rivera. *The Chicanos: A History of Mexican Americans*. New York: Hill and Wang, 1972.

————. *Dictionary of Mexican American History*. Westport, CT: Greenwood Press, 1981.

Melville, M. B., ed. *Twice a Minority: Mexican American Women*. St. Louis: C. V. Mosby, 1980.

Méndez, M. Miguel. *Peregrinos de Aztlán: Literatura chicana*. Tucson, AZ: Editorial Peregrinos, 1974.

Miller, Tom. *On the Border: Portraits of America's Southwestern Frontier*. New York: Harper and Row, 1981.

Mills, C. Wright, Clarence Senior, and Rose K. Goldsen. *The Puerto Rican Journey: New York's Newest Migrants*. New York: Harper and Bros., 1950.

Miranda, Alfredo, and Evangelina Enríquez. *The Mexican American Woman*. Chicago: University of Chicago Press, 1981.

Moore, Joan W., and Alfred Cuéllar. *Mexican Americans*. Englewood Cliffs, NJ: Prentice-Hall, 1970.

Moore, Joan, and Robert García. *Homeboys: Gangs, Drugs, and Prisons in the Barrios of Los Angeles*. Philadelphia: Temple University Press, 1978.

Moore, Joan, and Harry Pachón. *Hispanics in the United States*. Englewood Cliffs, NJ: Prentice-Hall, 1985.

Moquin, Wayne, ed. *A Documentary History of the Mexican-American*. New York: Praeger, 1971.

Morales, Armando. *Ando Sangrando (I Am Bleeding): A Study of Mexican-American Police Conflict*. Fairlawn, NJ: R. E. Burdick, 1972.

Morin, Raul. *Among the Valiant: Mexican Americans in World War II and Korea*. Alhambra, CA: Borden Publishing Company, 1966.

Morrissey, M. "Ethnic Stratification and the Study of Chicanos." *Journal of Ethnic Studies* 10 (1983): 77-91.

Murguia, Edward. *Chicano Intermarriage: A Theoretical and Empirical Study*. San Antonio, TX: Trinity University Press, 1982.

National Commission for Employment Policy. *Hispanics and Jobs: Barriers to Progress*. Washington, DC: NCEP, 1982.

National Institute of Education. *Conference on the Educational and Occupational Needs of Hispanic Women*. Washington, DC: U.S. Department of Education, 1980.

National Puerto Rican Forum. *The Next Step toward Equality: A Comprehensive Study of Puerto Ricans in the United States Mainland*. New York: The Forum, 1980.

National Technical Information Service. *Hispanic Origin Workers in the U.S. Labor Market: Comparative Analysis of Employment and Earnings*. Springfield, VA: NTIS, 1981.

Nelson, Candace, and Marta Tienda. "Structuring of Hispanic Ethnicity: Historical and Contemporary Perspectives." *Ethnic and Racial Studies* 8, no. 1 (Jan. 1985): 49-74.

New York City Department of Planning. *The Puerto Rican New Yorkers: A Recent*

History of Their Distribution, Population, and Household Characteristics. New York: Department of Planning, 1982.

Nieves Falcón, Luis. *El emigrante puertorriqueño.* Rio Piedras, PR: Editorial Edil, 1975.

North, David S. *The Border Crossers: People Who Live in Mexico and Work in the United States.* Washington, DC: Trans-Century Corporation, 1970.

North, David S., and Marion F. Houston. *The Characteristics and Role of Illegal Aliens in the U.S. Labor Market: An Exploratory Study.* Washington, DC: Linton, 1970.

Ortiz, Roxanne Dunbar. *Roots of Resistance: Tenure in New Mexico 1680-1980.* Los Angeles: Chicano Studies Research Center and American Indian Studies Research Center, 1980.

Padilla, Elena. *Up from Puerto Rico.* New York: Columbia University Press, 1958.

Palmieri, Victor H. "Cuban-Haitian Fact Sheet." *Migration Today* 8, no. 3 (1980): 3.

Pedraza-Bailey, Silvia. "Cubans and Mexicans in the United States: The Functions of Political and Economic Migration." *Cuban Studies* 11 (July 1981): 79-97.

_____. "Cuba's Exiles: Portrait of a Refugee Migration." *International Migration Review* 19, no. 1 (1985): 4-33.

Pérez, Louis A., Jr. "Reminiscences of a Lector: Cuban Cigar Workers in Tampa." *Florida Historical Quarterly* (April 1975): 443-449.

Philipson, Lorrin, and Rafael Llerena. *Freedom Flights: Cuban Refugees Talk About Life Under Castro.* New York: Random House, 1981.

Pino, F. *Mexican-Americans: A Research Bibliography*, 2 vols. Lansing: Michigan State University, 1974.

Pitt, Leonard Marvin. *The Decline of the Californios: A Social History of the Spanish-Speaking Californians, 1846-1890.* Berkeley and Los Angeles: University of California Press, 1966.

Portes, Alejandro. "Towards a Structural Analysis of Illegal (Undocumented) Immigration." *International Migration Review* 12 (Winter 1978): 469-484.

Portes, Alejandro, and Robert L. Bach. "Immigrant Earnings: Cuban and Mexican Immigrants in the United States." *International Migration Review* 14 (Fall 1980): 315-341.

_____, and Robert L. Bach. *Latin Journey: Cuban and Mexican Immigrants in the United States.* Berkeley: University of California Press, 1985.

Portes, Alejandro, Juan M. Clark, and Robert L. Bach. "The New Wave: A Statistical Profile of Recent Cuban Exiles in the United States." *Cuban Studies* 7 (Jan. 1977): 1-32.

Portes, Alejandro, Juan M. Clark, and Manuel M. López. "Six Years Later: A Profile of the Process of Incorporation of Cuban Exiles in the United States: 1973-1979." *Cuban Studies* 11 (July 1981): 1-24.

Portes, Alejandro, and Rafael Mozo. "The Political Adaptation Process of Cubans and Other Ethnic Minorities in the United States." *International Migration Review* 19, no. 1 (1985): 35-63.

Portes, Alejandro, et al. "Assimilation or Consciousness: Perceptions of U.S. Society Among Recent Latin American Immigrants to the United States." *Social Forces* 59, no. 1 (Sept. 1980): 200-224.

Prago, A. *Strangers in Their Own Land: A History of Mexican-Americans.* New York: Four Winds, 1973.

Price, John A. *Tijuana: Urbanization in a Border Culture.* South Bend, IN: University of Notre Dame Press, 1973.

Queralt, Magaly. "Understanding Cuban Immigrants: A Cultural Perspective." *Social Work* 29, no. 2 (Mar.–Apr. 1984): 115-121.

Rand, Christopher. *The Puerto Ricans.* New York: Oxford University Press, 1958.

Reimers, C. W. "Sources of the Family Income Differentials Among Hispanics, Blacks, and White non-Hispanics." *American Journal of Sociology* 89, no. 4 (1984): 889-903.

Reisler, Mark. *By the Sweat of Their Brow: Mexican Immigrant Labor in the United States, 1900-1940.* Westport, CT: Greenwood Press, 1976.

Rendon, Armando B. *Chicano Manifesto: The History and Aspirations of the Second Largest Minority in America.* New York: Collier Books, 1972.

Rivero Muñiz, José. "Tampa at the Close of the Nineteenth Century." *Florida Historical Quarterly* (Apr. 1963): 332-342.

Rodríguez, Clara E. *The Ethnic Queue in the United States: The Case of Puerto Ricans.* San Francisco: R & E Research Associates, 1973.

Rodríguez, Clara E., Virginia Sánchez-Korrol, and José O. Alers, eds. *The Puerto Rican Struggle: Essays on Survival in the U.S.* Maplewood, NJ: Waterfront Press, 1985. (First edition, 1980.)

Rogg, Eleanor. *The Assimilation of Cuban Exiles: The Role of Community and Class.* New York: Aberdeen Press, 1974.

Rogler, Lloyd H. *Migrant in the City: The Life of a Puerto Rican Action Group.* New York: Basic Books, 1972.

Rogler, Lloyd H., et al. "Intergenerational Change in Ethnic Identity in the Puerto Rican Family." *International Migration Review* 14, no. 2 (Summer 1980): 193-214.

Romo, Ricardo. *East Los Angeles: History of a Barrio.* Austin: University of Texas Press, 1983.

Rosenbaum, R. J. *Mexicano Resistance in the Southwest.* Austin: University of Texas Press, 1981.

Ross, Stanley R. *Views Across the Border: The United States and Mexico.* Albuquerque: University of New Mexico Press, 1978.

Samora, Julian, et al. *Los Mojados: The Wetback Story.* Notre Dame, IN: University of Notre Dame Press, 1971.

Samora, Julian, and Patricia Vanotel Simon. *A History of the Mexican-American People.* Notre Dame, IN: University of Notre Dame Press, 1976.

Sánchez Korrol, Virginia E. *From Colonia to Community: The History of Puerto Ricans in New York City, 1917-1948.* Westport, CT: Greenwood Press, 1983.

Santana Cooney, Rosemary. "Nativity, National Origin and Hispanic Female Participation in the Labor Force." *Social Science Quarterly* 64 (1983): 510-523.

Santana Cooney, Rosemary, Lloyd H. Rogler, R. M. Hurrell, and Vilma Ortiz. "Decision Making in Intergenerational Puerto Rican Families." *Journal of Marriage and the Family* 44, no. 3 (1982): 621-631.

Santana Cooney, Rosemary, and Alice Colón Warren. "Work and Family: The Recent Struggle of Puerto Rican Females." In Clara E. Rodríguez, Virginia Sánchez Korrol, and José O. Alers, eds. *The Puerto Rican Struggle: Essays on Survival in the U.S.* Maplewood, NJ: Waterfront Press, 1980.

Santiago, Carlos. *Hispanics in the Labor Force: A Survey of Recent Empirical Research and Recommendations for Economic Policy Issues in the Detroit*

Metropolitan Area. Detroit, MI: Center for Urban Studies, Wayne State University, January 1987.

Seavin, M. P. *The Mexican Americans: An Awakening Minority.* Encino, CA: Glencoe, 1970.

Senior, Clarence. *Puerto Rican Emigration.* Río Piedras: Social Science Research Center, University of Puerto Rico, 1947.

_____. *The Puerto Ricans: Strangers-Then Neighbors.* Chicago: Quadrangle Books, 1965.

Sexton, Patricia Cayo. *Spanish Harlem: An Anatomy of Poverty.* New York: Harper and Row, 1965.

Shafer, Robert Jones, and Donald Mabry. *Neighbors—Mexico and the United States: Wetbacks and Oil.* Chicago: Nelson Hall, 1981.

Sjostrom, Barbara. "An Analysis of Value Orientations of Mainland and Island Puerto Ricans, and non-Puerto Rican College Students." Ph.D. diss., SUNY at Albany, 1983.

Snipp, Matthew, and Marta Tienda. "New Perspectives on Chicano Intergenerational Occupational Mobility." *The Social Science Journal* 19 (1982): 37-50.

Sosnick, Stephen H. *Hired Hands: Seasonal Farm Workers in the United States.* New York: McNally and Loften West, 1979.

Spicer, Edward. *Cycles of Conquest: The Impact of Spain, Mexico, and the United States on the Indians of the Southwest.* Tucson: University of Arizona Press, 1962.

Steiner, Stan. *La Raza: The Mexican Americans.* New York: Harper and Row, 1970.

_____. *The Islands: The Worlds of the Puerto Ricans.* New York: Harper and Row, 1974.

Stevens Arroyo, Anthony. *Prophets Denied Honor: An Anthology on the Hispanic Church in the United States.* Maryknoll, NY: Orbis, 1980.

Stoddard, Ellwyn R. *Mexican Americans.* New York: Random House, 1973.

Sullivan, Teresa A. "The Occupational Prestige of Women Immigrants: A Comparison of Cubans and Mexicans." *International Migration Review* 18, no. 4 (1984): 1045-1062.

Szapocznik, José, ed. *Mental Health, Drug and Alcohol Abuse: An Hispanic Assessment of Present and Future Challenges.* Washington, DC: COSSMHO Publications, 1979.

Taylor, P. A., and S. W. Shields. "Mexican Americans and Employment Inequality in the Federal Civil Service." *Social Science Quarterly* 65, no. 2 (1984): 381-391.

Teske, R. H., and B. H. Nelson. "An Analysis of Differential Assimilation Rates Among Middle Class Mexican Americans." *The Sociological Quarterly* 17 (1976): 218-235.

Thernstrom, Stephen, ed. *Harvard Encyclopedia of American Ethnic Groups.* Cambridge, MA: Harvard University Press, 1980.

Tienda, Marta. "Familism and Structural Assimilation of Mexican Immigrants in the United States." *International Migration Review* 14, no. 3 (1980): 383-408.

Trejo, Arnulfo D., ed. *The Chicanos: As We See Ourselves.* Tucson: University of Arizona Press, 1980.

Tyler, G. *Mexican-Americans Tomorrow.* Albuquerque: University of New Mexico Press, 1975.

Ugalde, Antonio. "International Migration from the Dominican Republic: Findings from a National Survey." *International Migration Review* 13, no. 2 (Summer 1979): 235-254.

U.S. Commission on Civil Rights. *Mexican Americans and the Administration of Justice in the Southwest*. Washington, DC: U.S. Government Printing Office, 1970.

———. *El Boricua: The Puerto Rican Community in Bridgeport and New Haven*. Washington, DC: U.S. Government Printing Office, 1973.

———. *Puerto Ricans in the Continental United States: An Uncertain Future*. Washington, DC: U.S. Government Printing Office, 1976.

———. *Unemployment and Underemployment Among Blacks, Hispanics, and Women*. Washington, DC: U.S. Government Printing Office, 1982.

U.S. Department of Labor, Bureau of Labor Statistics. *A Socio-economic Profile of Puerto Rican New Yorkers*. Regional Report no. 46. New York: Middle Atlantic Regional Office, July 1975.

Vásquez, Carlos, and Manuel García y Griego, eds. *Mexican-U.S. Relations: Conflict and Convergence*. Berkeley and Los Angeles: University of California Press, 1983.

Vásquez, Richard. *Chicano*. Garden City, NY: Doubleday, 1970.

Vidal, Mirta. *Chicanas Speak Out: New Voice of La Raza*. New York: Pathfinder Press, 1971.

Vivó, Paquita, ed. *The Puerto Ricans: An Annotated Bibliography*. New York: R. R. Bowker, 1973.

Wagenheim, Kal. *A Survey of Puerto Ricans on the U.S. Mainland in the 1970s*. New York: Praeger, 1975.

Wagner, Nathaniel, Marsha J. Haugh, and Carrol A. Hernández, eds. *Chicanos: Social and Psychological Perspectives*. 2nd edition. Saint Louis: C. V. Mosby, 1976.

Wakefield, Daniel. *Island in the City: The World of Spanish Harlem*. Boston: Houghton Mifflin, 1959.

Washburn, David E. *Ethnic Studies, Bilingual/Bicultural Education and Multicultural Teacher Education in the United States*. Miami: Inquiry International, 1979.

Weber, David J. *The Mexican Frontier, 1821-1846: The American Southwest Under Mexico*. Albuquerque: University of New Mexico Press, 1982.

Weber, David, ed. *Foreigners in Their Native Land: Historical Roots of the Mexican Americans*. Albuquerque: University of New Mexico Press, 1973.

Weintraub, Sydney, and Stanley R. Ross. *The Illegal Alien from Mexico: Policy Choices for an Intractable Issue*. Austin: Mexico-United States Border Research Program, University of Texas, 1980.

Wenk, M. G. "Adjustment and Assimilation: The Cuban Refugee Experience." *International Migration Review* 3 (1968): 38-49.

Woods, R. *Reference Materials on Mexican Americans: An Annotated Bibliography*. Metuchen, NJ: Scarecrow Press, 1976.

Zambrana, Ruth E., ed. *Work, Family and Health: Latina Women in Transition*. New York: Hispanic Research Center, Fordham University, 1982.

Index

About the Editors
and Contributors

EDNA ACOSTA-BELÉN is an associate professor in the Department of Latin American and Caribbean Studies, and the Department of Hispanic and Italian Studies, at SUNY-Albany. She received her Ph.D. from Columbia University and has been a postdoctoral fellow at Princeton, Yale, and the University of Massachusetts at Amherst. She has edited *The Puerto Rican Woman: Perspectives on Culture, History, and Society* (New York: Praeger, 1986; first edition, 1979), and *La mujer en la sociedad puerto-rriqueña* (Río Piedras, PR: Ediciones Huracán, 1981). She has also published extensively in the areas of Latin American, Caribbean, and U.S. Hispanic literature and cultural history, and women's studies.

BARBARA R. SJOSTROM is an associate professor in the Teacher Education Program at SUNY-Old Westbury, and an adjunct faculty member in the Bilingual Education Program at Hunter College. She received her Ph.D. from SUNY-Albany and has published in the areas of ethnicity, gender and education, and bilingual/multicultural education. Her publications include "Guidelines for the Analysis of Classism, Racism, and Sexism" and "The Educational and Professional Status of Puerto Rican Women" (with Edna Acosta-Belén). She is also an evaluator of bilingual and English-as-a-second-language instructional programs for the New York City Board of Education, the Multicultural Resource Center at Hunter College, and Teachers College, Columbia University.

GILBERT CÁRDENAS is an associate professor of economics at Pan American University. He was formerly an economic policy fellow at the Brookings Institution in Washington, D.C., and has done extensive work on human resource development along the U.S.-Mexican border. His research interests include economic development, Mexican illegal immigration, employment and training policy, employment problems of Hispanic workers, and the Mexican economy.

JAMES D. COCKCROFT is a widely published political scientist and social historian, and a recognized expert on international affairs. He received his Ph.D. from Stanford University, and has been a Fulbright scholar on three separate occasions. He is the author of a dozen books, including *Neighbors in Turmoil* (1988). Among his other books are *Outlaws in the Promised Land, Dependence and Underdevelopment, Latin America: The Struggle with Dependency and Beyond,* and *Mexico.*

CARY DAVIS is director of administration at the Population Reference Bureau. He holds an M.A. in demography from the Center for Population Research at Georgetown University. He has specialized in population projections, United States ethnic and racial populations, and international population policy development.

DOUGLAS T. GURAK is an associate professor of sociology with a joint appointment in Puerto Rican/Latin American studies at Fordham University. He is also a senior research associate at the Hispanic Research Center. He has coauthored *A Conceptual Framework for Mental Health Research on Hispanic Populations, Hispanic Intermarriage in New York City,* and *International Migration in Latin America.*

CARL HAUB is director of demographic analysis and public information at the Population Reference Bureau. He holds an M.A. in demography from the Center for Population Research at Georgetown University.

J. JORGE KLOR DE ALVA is an associate professor in the Department of Latin American and Caribbean Studies, and the Department of Anthropology, and is director of the Institute for Mesoamerican Studies at SUNY-Albany. He received his Ph.D. from the University of California at Santa Cruz, and is a 1987 Guggenheim fellow. He is coeditor of *Sociocultural and Service Issues in Working with Hispanic American Clients* (with L. Brown and J. Oliver) and *The Work of Bernardino de Sahagún: Pioneer Ethnographer of Sixteenth-Century Mexico* (with H. B. Nicholson and E. Quiñones Keber).

ARNULFO G. RAMÍREZ is professor of language education, linguistics, and Hispanic studies at SUNY-Albany. He received his Ph.D. from Stanford University and has published extensively in the areas of sociolinguistics, bilingualism, language learning/teaching, and language testing. He is the author of *Bilingualism Through Schooling* and is presently conducting a nationwide study of Spanish in the United States.

HELEN I. SAFA is a professor of anthropology at the University of Florida, Gainesville. She is a former president of the Latin American Studies Association. She received her Ph.D. from Columbia University. Some of her major publications are *The Urban Poor in Puerto Rico, Sex and Class in Latin America* (ed. with J. Nash), *Women and Change in Latin America* (ed. with J. Nash), *Women's Work: Development and the Division of Labor by Sex* (ed. with E. Leacock), *Migration and Development* (ed. with B. DuToit), and *Toward a Political Economy of Urbanization in Third World Countries.*

VIRGINIA SÁNCHEZ KORROL is an associate professor in the Department of Puerto Rican Studies, and codirector of the Center for Latino Studies, at Brooklyn College. She received her Ph.D. in history from SUNY-Stony Brook. Some of her major publications are *From Colonia to Community: The History of Puerto Ricans in New York City, 1917-1948* and *The Puerto Rican Struggle: Essays on Survival in the U.S. (*ed. with C. Rodríguez and J. O. Alers).

JOANNE L. WILLETTE is a research sociologist with Development Associates, Inc., of Arlington, Va. She holds a Ph.D. in sociology from the University of Maryland. She has been doing research on minorities for a number of years with a special interest in Hispanics. She has done comparative research on the Hispanic, Asian, Black and American Indian populations in areas such as role-modeling, career aspirations, education, business development, economic assimilation, and the effects of limited English proficiency.